KT-233-953

Effective Practice in Youth Justice

WITHDRAWN FROM
THE LIBRARY
UNIVERSITY OF
WINCHESTER

KA 0355142 3

Effective Practice in Youth Justice

Martin Stephenson, Henri Giller and Sally Brown

WILLAN
PUBLISHING

UNIVERSITY OF WINCHESTER
LIBRARY

Published by

Willan Publishing
Culmcott House
Mill Street, Uffculme
Cullompton, Devon
EX15 3AT, UK
Tel: +44(0)1884 840337
Fax: +44(0)1884 840251
e-mail: info@willanpublishing.co.uk
website: www.willanpublishing.co.uk

Published simultaneously in the USA and Canada by

Willan Publishing
c/o ISBS, 920 NE 58th Ave, Suite 300,
Portland, Oregon 97213-3786, USA
Tel: +001(0)503 287 3093
Fax: +001(0)503 208 8832
e-mail:info@isbs.com
website: www.isbs.com

UNIVERSITY OF WINCHESTER

0355423   364.36
            STE

© Youth Justice Board 2007

The rights of Martin Stephenson, Henri Giller and Sally Brown to be identified as the authors of this book have been asserted by them in accordance with the Copyright, Designs and Patents Act of 1988.

Reprinted 2007, 2008 (twice), 2009

All rights reserved; no part of this publication may be reproduced, stored in a retrieval system, or transmitted in any form or any means, electronic, mechanical, photocopying, recording or otherwise without the prior written permission of the Publishers or a licence permitting copying in the UK issued by the Copyright Licensing Agency Ltd, Saffron House, 6–10 Kirby Street, London EC1N 8TS.

Paperback
ISBN 978-1-84392-286-5

British Library Cataloguing-in-Publication Data

A catalogue record for this book is available from the British Library

Project managed by Deer Park Productions, Tavistock, Devon
Typeset by Pantek Arts Ltd, Maidstone, Kent
Printed and bound by TJI Digital, Trecerus Industrial Estate, Padstow, Cornwall

Contents

Part III

Figures and tables

Figures

Tables

List of acronyms

Asset	Youth Justice Board assessment tool
ABU	Anti-social Behaviour Unit
APIR	Connexions Service's assessment, planning interventions and review system
CAMHS	Child and Adolescent Mental Health Services
CRISS	Crime Reduction Initiative in Secondary Schools
CRO	Community Rehabilitation Order
DARE	Drug Abuse Resistance Education
DfES	Department for Education and Skills
DTO	Detention and Training Order
DTTR	Drug Treatment and Testing Requirements
EBD	Emotional and Behavioural Difficulties
EMA	Education Maintenance Allowance
ETE	Education, Training and Employment
ICD-10	International Statistical Classification of Disease and Related Health Problems, 10th Revision
ISP	Integrated Support Plan
ISSP	Intensive Supervision and Surveillance Programme
ISO	Individual Support Order scheme
JYIP	Junior Youth Inclusion Programme
KYPE	Keeping Young People Engaged
LASCH	Local Authority Secure Children's Home
LEA	Local Education Authority
LSU	Learning Support Unit
MAPPA	Multi-Agency Public Protection Plan Arrangements
MST	Multi-systemic therapy
OCJS	Offending, Crime and Justice Survey
ONS	Office for National Statistics
Onset	Youth Justice Board assessment tool for prevention
PAYP	Positive Activities for Young People
PNC record	Police National Computer record
PRU	Pupil Referral Unit
PSHE	personal, social and health education
RBI	Reducing Burglary Initiative
RCT	Randomised controlled trial
ROSH	Risk of Serious Harm form
RoTL	Release on Temporary Licence
SEN	special educational needs
SIfA	Screening Interview for Adolescents
SMS	Scientific Methods Scale
SNASA	Salford Needs Assessment Schedule for Adolescents

SQIFA	Screening Questionnaire Interview for Adolescents
SSP	Safer Schools Partnerships
WHO	World Health Organisation
YAP	Youth Advocate Programme
YIP	Youth Inclusion Programme
YISP	Youth Inclusion and Support Panel
YJB	Youth Justice Board
YOI	Young Offender Institution
Yot	Youth Offending Team

Acknowledgements

This publication is based on a series of Readers commissioned by the Youth Justice Board. Some have been substantially changed with elements of guidance removed. They have also been amended to take account of the latest evidence in the areas covered in light of Henri Giller's review of the most up-to-date-research. Acknowledgements are due therefore to the original authors of the Readers, in particular to: Kerry Baker and Sarah Jones (Assessment, Planning Interventions and Supervision); Alison Clare and Janet Maitland (Mental Health); Fiona Hackland and Bob Baker (Substance Misuse); Claire Green and Maggie Kelly (MBE) (Targeted Neighbourhood Prevention Programmes); Sarah Lindfield, Anna Elliott, Janice Kusick and Josie Melia (Parenting); Guy Masters, Paul Crosland, Roger Cullen and Liz Nelson (Restorative Justice); Dee Keane (Mentoring); Tim Bateman (Offending Behaviour Programmes); and Kerry Baker, Emily Gray, Sarah Jones, Robin Moore and Alex Sutherland (Intensive Supervision and Surveillance Programmes).

Particular thanks are due to David Monk of the Youth Justice Board for his commitment to making the book possible in the first place.

The authors would also like to thank Renie Shaw (Inclusive Learning Solutions) and Kate Bielby (Pen Creative Communication) for their painstaking work in editing, proof reading and checking the referencing. And of course we would like to acknowledge the patience and support of Brian Willan and colleagues from Willan Publishing and Deer Park Productions in getting this book into print.

Preface

Youth justice has perhaps never been so much in the news or so politicised. The political vocabulary of the day both reflects and shapes this – 'tough on crime, tough on the causes of crime', 'respect', 'no more excuses', 'anti-social behaviour' litter the political landscape and dominate media headlines. Many critics view the quest for more effectiveness in public services and the 'what matters is what works' approach as disingenuous at best. At worst it is regarded as a camouflage for attempts to demonise young people and adopt increasingly punitive measures and extended social control in pursuit of electoral gains.

To enter such a battleground with a text on the putative effectiveness of youth justice is therefore to risk being caught in the crossfire between those who view the remodelled youth justice system as a prime example of modernising government and their opponents who portray it as one of the most dismal policy failures. While there is no safe middle ground here or such a thing as a value-free text on youth justice, we have attempted to balance the apparent certainties of 'What Works' with the more cogent criticisms of this approach. Debate and intellectual contest are prerequisites for the further development of reflective and knowledgeable practitioners. Equally, enjoyable though firework polemics may be, they do not help equip managers and practitioners who cannot change the system within which they work.

New Labour stands accused of several key policy failures: a high number of young people in custody; insufficient access to mainstream services, particularly education but also health and housing for socially excluded young people; extending the remit of the criminal justice system; overemphasising control and surveillance at the expense of care and children's rights and focusing on the responsibility of individuals and parents rather than structural deficits.

Within these broad criticisms of New Labour's approach there are specific accusations levelled at the Youth Justice Board (YJB) that it has:

- adopted a 'ground zero' approach denying the previous achievements in youth justice;

- over claimed on its policy initiatives;

- 'zombified' youth justice practitioners through its attempts to micromanage the system.

It is not the remit of this book to engage in detail with such criticisms, valid or not, but it is essential that they are at least acknowledged. While the Youth

Justice Board commissioned the original Readers upon which this text is based, this is not a collection of policy edicts and prescriptive guidance. The book is rather an attempt to synthesise and make sense of the available evidence base in some core areas of youth justice. Where research is equivocal or limited or shortcomings are revealed then this has been pointed out.

The wider debate upon evidence-based practice is discussed and reading is encouraged of the more provocative polemical works even though the attacks on New Labour and the Youth Justice Board often have a resonance of 'what have the Romans ever done for us?' and are occasionally suffused with a nostalgia not shared by everyone who was working in this area in the 1980s. Our contention is that the Youth Justice Board's approach to effective practice is qualitatively different from that of the Prison and Probation Services. A far less dogmatic line has been taken with far greater scope for the development of a workforce that reflects critically upon the research evidence and uses its creativity to come up with solutions to demanding policy initiatives within the constantly challenging, uncertain, and often frustrating world of youth justice.

A further contested area is that of evidence-based policy and evidence-based practice and its application to criminal justice. The role of evidence in policy formation is often questioned if not derided given that a wide range of criminal justice policy initiatives appear to either ignore some of the messages from research and evaluation or rest on the flimsiest of findings.

Evidence-based practice has been attacked from several directions. Fundamental criticisms include its alleged inapplicability to explaining the complexities of human behaviours, its prescriptive reliance on certain limited but expensive research methodologies, and a simplistic attraction to policy makers. A relatively pragmatic approach is taken here which is explicit about the shortcomings of the 'What Works' approach and open about the lack of hard evidence to underpin many interventions. However there is an attempt to translate the principles underlying evidence-based practice into a practical framework for practitioners to make sense of the research evidence. While the robustness of the evidence is assessed it has not been filed into the neat hierarchical categories currently espoused by the Home Office, partly because the evidence judged by such criteria is so limited.

The audiences for this text include students on the OU youth justice courses, particularly the Certificate in Effective Practice (K208), although hopefully it will be useful to a wider range of people. The learning outcomes for this course have influenced the purpose, content and structure of the book such as the relationship between research evidence and practice and key skills such as critical reflection and acquiring and using the information needed for effective practice in youth justice. Accordingly each chapter reviews the evidence base for effectiveness in each topic, places interventions in the context of evidence-based practice principles and highlights some of the challenges to practice.

There are three sections: the first dealing with broad areas such as assessment and planning and access to key mainstream services such as education; the second looks at areas of intervention that tend to be used mainly for preventative activity such as parenting programmes and restorative justice while the final section examines the most intensive interventions culminating in custody. Each chapter is relatively self-contained so readers interested in, for example, offending behaviour programmes would hopefully find that chapter useful in itself. While each of these chapters is in effect an updated version of the Youth Justice Board's Readers on Effective Practice they do not include the Board's guidance documents (Key Elements of Effective Practice). Similarly each chapter should not be interpreted as a DIY guide to a particular intervention but rather as a summary of relevant research evidence to be filtered through the professional judgement of those working in youth justice.

1

Evidence-based practice and effective practice

Introduction

One of the success stories of the 1990s in the development of healthcare and policy was the emergence of evidence-based practice. This approach rapidly developed into an international movement. Evidence-based practice has spread across most areas of healthcare such as mental health, dentistry, nursing and physiotherapy. This has now become a theme across social policy with education, criminal justice and social care all being encouraged to be evidence based. These disciplines and professions have adopted this approach but to varying degrees. In criminal justice the new emphasis on evidence-based practice has converged with the 'What Works' movement. But although some of its more enthusiastic adherents see this as bringing a clearer, more consistent and effective way of working it has been criticised heavily by opponents in various disciplines such as education, youth justice and social care.

This chapter examines critically the underlying assumptions about the nature of evidence and the methodology in this model. As well as looking at the shortcomings of a simplistic 'What Works' approach, it also assesses how far the principles underpinning evidence-based practice in youth justice provide a useful framework for designing and applying interventions by practitioners. This sets the scene for the following chapters which place each topic within the framework of these principles. The role of the practitioner is appraised in the 'What Works' context as is the influence of guidance and reflective practice.

The headline message from government is that 'what matters is what works' and that practice should be derived from the latest and most reliable research findings. This has an instant, rational appeal. While the small print conceals conceptual difficulties and significant challenges for implementation, the evidence-based practice approach has been promoted vigorously across criminal justice.

The youth justice context

Significant though the structural changes have been since 1998, the present youth justice system did not simply fall out of clear skies with the Crime and Disorder Act. Some of the Youth Justice Board's early rhetoric led to complaints of a 'Year Zero' style (Pitts 2001a) and an 'apparent expurgation of all youth justice knowledge and practice prior to 1998' (Jones 2002: 15). The antecedents of the current system go back at least until the early nineteenth century and many, perhaps most, current practitioners were working in this field before 1998. Equally its development is perhaps characterised by certain recurrent themes rather than a simple linear, progressive development of increasingly effective solutions to youth crime. Neither are the size and character of youth justice services a simple reflection of the scale and nature of offending by young people. It has been argued that in effect each society gets the youth justice system it deserves, as how a society defines and reacts to the behaviour of young people 'ultimately tells us more about social order, the state and political decision-making than it does about the nature of young offending and the most effective ways to respond to it' (Muncie 2004: 303). This wider socio-political context is often considered crucial to understanding youth crime and youth justice (Hendrick 2006) and this also applies to the current emphasis on evidence-based practice.

For much of its history youth justice has seen lurches between welfare and justice approaches. Welfarism is derived from the notion that a child should be treated differently to an adult where offending is concerned, with an emphasis placed on meeting the child's needs. In contrast to this, the justice approach focuses on matching the levels of formal intervention to the gravity of the offence rather than to putative needs. There has always been a complex and often confused blend of justice and welfare although the balance between the two has shifted considerably at times. Both have had unintended consequences, with welfare tending to increase formal interventions and control unnecessarily, and justice ignoring individual needs and sometimes human rights.

The current preoccupation with the behaviour of young people is nothing new and what is striking is the recurrent discovery of the degeneracy of youth and how much worse their behaviour is than in some golden age in the past (Pearson 1983). What may be new is the rise of what might be termed 'the politics of behaviour' whereby there is a convergence of the New Labour and Conservative positions on law and order (Downes and Morgan 2002) and across other social policy areas such as education. Linked to this has been the rise of managerialism, central to which has been an emphasis on evidence-based practice.

Why has evidence-based practice emerged?

Like all such movements evidence-based practice is a product of its time. It is derived partly from wider social influences, developments in public services, changing notions of professionalism and practitioner concerns with their effectiveness. Much of the attraction of an evidence-based approach to practice lies in the fact that it is an ostensibly neat and coherent approach to the messy and ill-defined complexities of practice. Politically it is the epitome of managerialism and purports to be value-free as the application of proven methods to treat the particular social ill. After all, who could possibly argue in favour of what does not work? Perhaps, too, the language of 'dosage' and 'treatment' has been borrowed so readily from medicine because it conveniently supports the idea of offending as a symptom of individual pathology. Despite the confidence of government agencies in this approach many academic commentators have contested it.

> A considerable body of research has been identified demonstrating clearly that a firmly evidence-based approach to the prevention of youth crime is both a realistic proposition and a strategy that can be confidently expected to be successful. (Communities that Care 2001: 121)

> The doctrinaire tyranny of the 'what works' movement is wasting the creativity of the youth justice professionals as it places at risk much of the genuinely good practice undertaken by them (Bateman and Pitts 2005: 258.)

Such is the popularity of evidence-based practice that it runs the risk of being perceived as either simply a fashionable accessory to current practice or a panacea. Before engaging with the notion and detailed implementation of effective practice, it is essential to become familiar with the origins of evidence-based practice in order to understand its strengths and limitations.

The risk society

Commentators agree that one of the defining characteristics of twenty-first-century society is accelerating and often dramatic social change. Societies are increasingly moulded by global rather than national or regional influences. Many fixed and locally based traditions are being replaced by rapid endings and transitions in life and social norms, and with these changes comes a heightened concern with risk.

In a much more unsettled social and economic environment where lifelong careers and traditional family structures are no longer the norm, coping with uncertainty has become much more important. Dealing with this uncertainty is increasingly defined as an individual rather than an organisational or state responsibility. The interpretation and management of risk is an increasingly

3

important feature of our personal and professional lives. Arguably, evidence-based practice has won so many adherents so quickly because it promises a consistent risk management methodology resting on a platform of knowledge. In some ways, it is essentially a cautious and defensive response to the challenges of modern society.

The evolution of youth justice mirrors these wider trends. Social policy increasingly focuses on children who are 'at risk'. Management of risk is starting to permeate nearly every sphere of activity within youth justice. The start of intervention is itself regulated through a detailed assessment of risk through the *Asset* (Youth Justice Board assessment tool) profile. Interventions that focus on the management of this risk represent a significant contrast to previous approaches such as system management and diversion in the late 1980s and early 1990s, or earlier approaches such as intermediate treatment. The recent emphasis on the swifter administration of justice reflects not only concerns with more effective management of risk in terms of further offences, but also the impact of uncertainty and more challenging transitions in young people's lives.

The Crime and Disorder Act 1998 and subsequent youth justice reforms reflect the emphasis on the individual in terms of people's responsibility for their actions and the ability to modify their behaviour. Offending Behaviour Programmes, for instance, could be seen as being partly about equipping young people with risk-management skills. Coping strategies and decision-making skills, particularly in relation to planning, are prerequisites for participation in modern society.

Arguably, young people who offend are in even greater need of acquiring such skills. Most of the young people in custody or on high-level interventions such as Intensive Supervision and Surveillance Programmes (ISSPs) will face more complex, significant challenges (e.g. limited access to education, substance misuse) in their lives than will their peers, including much earlier transitions (e.g. leaving home, becoming a parent).

More critical interpretations see this as a manifestation of the tendency of current social policy to focus on the deficits of an individual young person and their responsibility whilst ignoring the social and economic circumstances of the young people (Goldson and Muncie 2006). Similarly it is argued that the preoccupation with 'risk' has displaced consideration of 'need', and that actuarial justice as exemplified by the use of *Asset* provides a spurious sense of certainty and reliability over something as troubling and uncertain as the delinquent behaviour of young people (Smith 2006).

Managerialism and the audit society

In parallel to the increased awareness of risk has been the growth of managerialism in public services. Over the past 20 years, issues such as value for money, effectiveness, accountability and transparency have come to dominate public services. As trust in the traditional authority of professionals has diminished, it has been replaced with reliance on audit and inspection systems.

Evidence-based practice draws much of its strength from an audit culture. For instance, both processes share an overwhelming emphasis on effectiveness and the need to demonstrate accountability and transparency. Both approaches are also characterised by an attempt to reduce complexity to manageable proportions through the introduction of batteries of guidelines, checklists and procedures. Within youth justice, both processes are combined in the Youth Justice Board's Effective Practice Quality Assurance Framework, whereby practitioners audit their own performance within a framework of evidence-based practice.

The perceived challenge to professionalism by the new managerialism as it has been dubbed has evoked a fierce response claiming that 'these developments suggest a wholesale dehumanisation of the youth crime issue, such that the sole purpose of youth justice becomes one of simply delivering a cost-effective and economic "product"' (Muncie 2004: 275). Other commentators have claimed the 'zombification of youth justice professionals' (Pitts 2001a) and that 'the professional skills of youth justice practitioners were neutered, and the principled "systems management" of the 1980s was replaced by a technocratic managerialism with no principles or independent rationale' (Smith 2003: 3).

An uncritical defence of professional autonomy however may ignore vested interests and the negative effects of many welfare interventions. There is no necessary conflict between an approach that focuses on children's rights and a managerialist and audit culture. Arguably there is a paucity of information about the lives of many young people who become drawn into the youth justice system. Useful management information is signally lacking for example on those young people who are detached from mainstream education. Information flows into and out of custody are a trickle despite the considerable financial and human costs associated with incarceration (ECOTEC 2001a). Neither is bemoaning the lack of resources devoted to remedying the underlying structural factors behind crime always compatible with railing against managerialist approaches that emphasise effectiveness, value for money and the opportunity costs of interventions. It could just as easily be argued that there is not enough of a managerialist or audit culture within youth justice which would more readily expose under-resourcing or poor performance locally and the low priority given to many of these young people by mainstream services (Stephenson 2007).

Research and practitioners

Although members of the public might reasonably assume that the actions of professionals are determined largely by the most up-to-date and reliable research findings, in reality this is often not the case. Studies across most disciplines indicate that for a variety of reasons many professionals only make relatively limited use of research findings in their day-to-day decision-making.

5

More significant influences on practice are:

- knowledge gained during primary training;
- prejudice and opinion;
- outcomes of previous cases;
- fads and fashions;
- advice of senior and not so senior colleagues (Trinder and Reynolds 2000).

One contributing factor to this situation is that much of the research available to practitioners lacks methodologies which are robust enough or appropriately consistent to be applied confidently. In addition, the volume of available research (irrespective of its methodological merits) can often overwhelm busy practitioners. Also, many do not possess the appraisal skills to assess the validity of the research methodologies employed and the overall quality of the research.

In this context evidence-based practice provides a framework which attempts to:

- narrow the research–practice gap;
- enhance the take-up rate of research by practitioners;
- provide a consistent methodology for researchers.

Some studies suggest that in disciplines such as social work the application of theory or research to practice tends to be at best *ad hoc*. Although judgement, values and intuition are always extremely important, it makes it more difficult for practitioners to make decisions regarding choices where there is a lack of empirical evidence as to the effectiveness of the options. Despite this, it has been argued that the ethos within social work and to some extent probation does not always support an empirical approach.

'What Works' in youth justice

The expression 'What Works?' provides a further historical dimension to this discussion. It derives from the title of an article by Robert Martinson (1974: 49), which concluded, on the basis of research existing at that time, that there was 'no clear pattern to indicate the efficacy of any particular method of treatment'. This conclusion was not universally accepted at the time, and Martinson himself acknowledged that the poor design quality of many research programmes might preclude the detection of any positive outcome. Nonetheless, it is only in more recent years that a certain consensus has developed among researchers that some approaches to working with young people who offend seem capable of having an impact on reducing their offending.

Meta-analysis (a statistical tool which facilitates the aggregation of results from different studies) has been used since the mid-1980s to review a large number of research studies which, in combination, confirm a positive overall effect. Clear trends have been detected concerning the ingredients of programmes with higher or lower levels of effectiveness in reducing offending. The term 'What Works' is often used to refer to that body of research knowledge and to the principles deriving from it, although it has now become associated with a much narrower definition with a strictly defined methodology, a concentration on programmes and a specific type of guidance.

Determining effectiveness

Practitioners are beset by a confusing array of ill-defined labels to describe particular interventions or programmes. Just how are 'good', 'best', 'innovative' or 'excellent' practices to be differentiated? Without clear criteria to define and thereby judge the impact of particular practices, how can replicable and sustainable programmes be identified, let alone transplanted to different environments?

The definition and application of effective practice are rooted in the wider concept of evidence-based practice. The term 'effective practice' is not used here as a synonym for evidence-based practice. Rather, it refers to those programmes, processes or ways of working which have the highest level of validation from research and evaluation. Evidence-based practice refers to the wider, cross-disciplinary approach to delivering those products and services that has been validated according to the accepted criteria.

Based on a widely used definition of evidence-based medicine (Sackett *et al.* 1997: 71) the equivalent for youth justice could be:

> the conscientious, explicit and judicious use of current best evidence in making decisions regarding the prevention of offending by individual young people based on skills which allow the evaluation of both personal experience and external evidence in a systematic and objective manner.

This has the advantage of not being constrained by too slavish an adherence to purist 'What Works' methodologies and definitions of evidence and places due emphasis on the role of the practitioner.

The criteria for judging the validity of any intervention can be generic, but effectiveness is determined in the context of the required outcome. This varies considerably and can be contradictory even among allied professions. While meeting the needs of the child is of paramount importance in social work, the primary aim of all interventions in youth justice (as laid down in the Crime And Disorder Act 1998) is to prevent offending. Similarly, interventions which have been shown to increase self-esteem, for example, but not to reduce offending may be deemed ineffective in youth justice terms (although some interventions are effective in reducing offending and as a by-product increase self-esteem).

7

Evidence-based practice represents a new cultural approach for youth justice services to adopt, but strictly speaking most approaches to preventing offending in the UK must be deemed 'promising' or 'unknown' rather than truly effective.

Evidence

The fierceness of the 'What Works' debate is generated by problems over what constitutes sufficient evidence, the extent to which the scientific rigour of the natural sciences can be applied to youth justice policy and practice and assumptions about the relationship with research evidence and practice. The issue is not whether evidence is significant but the kind of evidence and how different kinds of evidence are valued. Practitioners are continually drawing on a wide range of evidence – from listening to others, observing young people, reading reports, reasoning or reflecting in addition to research evidence in its different forms. The 'What Works' movement is about establishing particular ways of generating or marshalling evidence.

Relatively little account has been taken about how this and other evidence is transmuted into practice. Arguably there needs to be more emphasis on the fact that evidence can only indicate a balance of probabilities and that there is a significant challenge in reconciling research evidence with knowledge acquired from other sources.

The allegedly selective use of evidence by policy makers has led to a gap between research findings and policy formation and practice development (Goldson and Muncie 2006). This can be compounded by a lack of methodological rigour of some evaluations (Bottoms 2005). Accordingly it may also be that many practitioners may resist 'What Works' research evidence if it is perceived as a tool to enforce government policy. The dialogue between practitioners and researchers is important and may be better serviced by a more flexible approach about what should be valued as evidence. This may be enhanced by more concentration on the application of research methods to practice rather than simply research findings.

The hierarchy of evidence

There are several frameworks for classifying crime prevention interventions according to the extent and nature of the supporting research evidence. For example, Utting and Vennard (2000) use the following four categories.

● **What works** – where a programme has been positively evidenced by at least two evaluations which show statistically significantly different outcomes for participants against a comparable group of non-participants.

- **What doesn't work** – where a programme has at least two evaluations (comparing participants against a group of non-participants) which demonstrate ineffectiveness.

- **What's promising** – where a programme has been positively evidenced by at least one evaluation which shows statistically significantly different outcomes for participants against a comparable group of non-participants.

- **What's unknown** – any programme not classified in the three previous categories.

Such a framework can provide a means of assessing the weight of the evidence base in respect of particular interventions. It is worth emphasising that although the framework specifically mentions crime prevention, it is a hierarchy of validation which constitutes a means by which to judge any aspect of the functioning of the Youth Justice System.

It is also worth remembering that just because a particular intervention or programme lacks a thorough evaluation it does not necessarily mean that it is any the less effective. What is more challenging however is when a team or individual continues with an intervention or programme that the research evidence indicates is likely to be ineffective.

What is unlikely to be effective

According to the evidence compiled on behalf of the Youth Justice Board (Communities that Care 2001: 124) the characteristics of interventions that may be less likely to be effective include those that:

- are given to those at lower risk of offending and reoffending;

- use vague, unstructured counselling;

- are unable to address multiple problems presented by young people whose offending behaviour is persistent and/or serious, including poor mental health and drug and alcohol abuse;

- are too brief or diluted to establish the conditions in which young people can make sustainable changes in their lives;

- focus on restraint, without significant effort in the direction of rehabilitation.

Risk and protective factors

Despite the very different theoretical backgrounds, most studies adopt a risk and resiliency approach in trying to disentangle the causes of delinquency. While risk factors are associated with an increasing likelihood of the commencement, frequency and duration of offending, protective factors reduce

UNIVERSITY OF WINCHESTER
LIBRARY

the probability of such outcomes despite these risks. Not only do risk factors tend to be interrelated and occur at the same time but they may also be symptoms rather than potential causes. For example failure at school has often been linked with offending and in this context non-attendance may be highly associated with poor academic attainment, and both may be correlated with delinquency. There are several possible directions of influence. Not being in school could equally be either a cause or an effect of low attainment. Similarly, both risk factors could be the cause or effect of delinquency. Alternatively an independent variable, such as learning difficulties or high impulsivity, may be creating these intervening variables.

Although there are weaknesses in the evidence relating to the causes of youth crime the body of research particularly that derived from longitudinal studies provides significant insight into the risk and protective factors that lead to some young people developing offending behaviour whilst others do not. While no single factor can be specified as the 'cause' of offending behaviour it is possible to elicit relatively short series of the main risk factors that, particularly when clustered together in the absence of the most important protective factors, are implicated in the onset and continuation of offending behaviour. A significant criticism of this approach is that it may give too great a weight to individual risk factors at the expense of ignoring socio-economic influences (Goldson and Muncie 2006).

Risk and protective factors model

In order both to take account of the research findings and to provide practitioners with a straightforward approach to implementation it may be helpful to adopt a simple risk and protection model. Within this model the twin objectives are to reduce the exposure to risk and to enhance protective factors identified by the research for children and young people.

These risk and protective factors could be grouped in the following way:

Risk factors	Protective factors
Family factors	Social bonding
School factors	Healthy beliefs and clear standards
Community factors	Opportunities, skills and recognition
Personal, individual or peer factors	

(Adapted from Communities that Care 2001)

Risk factors

Exposure to the risks listed below appears to increase significantly the chances of young people becoming involved in crime.

Family	School
Deprivation, particularly low income, poor housing and large family size	Organisational weaknesses in the school
Conflict within the family	Low achievement from primary onwards
Ineffective supervision	Lack of attachment to formal schooling
Passive or condoning attitudes in relation to anti-social and criminal behaviour	Aggressive behaviour, particularly bullying
A history of criminal activity from parents or siblings	
Community	**Individual/peer**
A disadvantaged and neglected neighbourhood	Delinquent peer groups
A lack of attachment to the neighbourhood	Hyperactivity and impulsivity
Ready availability of drugs	Attitudes sympathetic to offending
High turnover of local population	Substance misuse

Protective factors

The absence of all or any of the risk factors may afford protection against involvement in offending. A range of protective factors that will safeguard against involvement in crime and mitigate the influence of the risk factors listed above has been identified. These protective factors include:

- being female;

- possessing a resilient temperament;

- being attached to community and school;

- opportunities for developing social and reasoning skills;

- recognition and due praise.
  (Rutter *et al.* 1998)

Salience, prevalence and modifiability

There are three important dimensions to risk and protective factors. Evidence is accumulating that indicates how widespread is a particular risk factor such as low attainment in school, i.e. the prevalence. In contrast salience measures how influential is a particular risk factor, such as low achievement beginning in primary school, in predicting the likelihood of offending. The degree to which a particular risk factor can be modified is very important from a practitioner's perspective in deciding which to tackle. Obviously being a male is a widespread and significant risk factor but is not susceptible to change.

Matching programmes/interventions to risk factors

It is possible to map particular interventions and programmes that have been validated to a greater or lesser extent for their effectiveness against those risks which have been identified as being the most widespread or important for youth crime.

Table 1.1 Effective interventions by youth crime risk factor reduced

Risk factor	Programme strategy
Poor parental supervision and discipline	**Pre-natal services; family support using home visiting; parenting information and support; pre-school education:** *after-school clubs*
Family conflict	**Family support using home visiting; parenting information and support**
Family history of problem behaviour	**Pre-natal services; parenting information and support; family support using home visiting; family literacy**
Parental involvement in/ attitudes condoning problem behaviour	**Pre-natal services; parenting information and support; family support using home visiting; family literacy**
Low family income/ poor housing	**Pre-natal services; family support using home visiting;** *after-school clubs*; housing management initiatives
Low achievement beginning in primary school	**Pre-natal services; parenting information and support; pre-school education; family literacy; reading schemes; reasoning and social skills education; organisational change in schools;** *after-school clubs; mentoring; youth employment with education;* preventing truancy and exclusion; further education for disaffected youth
Aggressive behaviour, including bullying	**Parenting information and support; pre-school education; reasoning and social skills education; organisational change in schools;** *mentoring;* preventing truancy and exclusion; youth work
Lack of commitment, including truancy	**Pre-school education; family literacy; reading schemes; reasoning and social skills education; organisational change in schools;** *mentoring; youth employment with education;* preventing truancy and exclusion; further education for disaffected youth; youth work
School disorganisation	**Reading schemes; reasoning and social skills education; organisational change in schools;** preventing truancy and exclusion
Alienation and lack of social commitment	**Parenting information and support; reasoning and social skills education; organisational change in schools;** *after-school clubs; mentoring; youth employment with education;* preventing truancy and

	exclusion; further education for disaffected youth; youth work; peer-led community programmes
Individual attitudes that condone problem behaviour	**Parenting information and support; organisational change in schools; *after-school clubs; mentoring;* preventing truancy and exclusion; youth work; peer-led community programmes**
Early involvement in problem behaviour	**Parenting information and support; reasoning and social skills education; organisational change in schools; *after-school clubs; mentoring;* preventing truancy and exclusion; youth work; peer-led community programmes**
Friends involved in problem behaviour	**Parenting information and support; reasoning and social skills education; organisational change in schools; *after-school clubs; mentoring;* preventing truancy and exclusion; youth work; peer-led community programmes**
Disadvantaged neighbourhood	*Community mobilisation; community policing; youth employment with education;* housing management initiatives
Community disorganisation and neglect	*Community mobilisation; community policing; youth employment with education;* youth work; housing management initiatives
Availability of drugs	**Organisational change in schools; *community policing;* youth work; peer-led community programmes**
High turnover and lack of neighbourhood attachment	**Organisational change in schools; *after-school clubs; mentoring; youth employment with education; community mobilisation; community policing;* further education for disaffected youth; peer-led community programmes; housing management initiatives**

Strategies in bold are those for which programmes have been evaluated in the UK and shown to reduce the relevant risk factors.
Strategies in bold italics are those for which programmes have been evaluated outside the UK and shown to reduce the relevant risk factors.
Strategies in normal type are those which have not undergone either form of evaluation.
Source: derived from Communities that Care (2001: 64)

The limitations of the 'What Works' approach

Despite its rational appeal the 'What Works' approach has attracted significant criticisms. Although purportedly value free, being the objective application of rigorous research findings to interventions to prevent offending or reoffending, it can be seen as being quite the opposite. 'What Works' is the manifestation of the current political emphasis on competence in delivering hard outcomes to key parts of the electorate (Bateman and Pitts 2005). Under the guise of its apparent simplicity and rigour which enables its

13

messages to be neatly packaged to both the public and practitioner, 'What Works' stands accused of distorting research findings, deskilling and wasting the creativity of practitioners and justifying interventions that increase offending. While the condemnation of the Youth Justice Board sometimes veers into polemics rather than objective analysis these are cogent criticisms that require discussion.

The 1997 New Labour government through the Crime and Disorder Act 1998 attempted to modernise youth justice and to legitimise its changes. In doing so it not only made some decisive breaks with the past but inevitably through the Youth Justice Board emphasised the failures of both past governments and interventions by practitioners. Evidence-based policy is only the servant and not the master of political priorities. Accordingly where evidence supported the value of diversion, the ineffectiveness of custody and indicated caution over the effectiveness of ISSPs which were at odds with political imperatives it tended to be ignored. This was at times perhaps accompanied by an unwarranted degree of confidence in the success of the post-1998 policy initiatives such as the Detention and Training Order (DTO).

Philosophical issues

One fundamental issue is that 'What Works' is predicated upon the assumption that a straightforward natural science approach is achievable. This positivist approach can lead unwary policy makers into a belief that universal truths can be produced for the social sciences, in this case criminal justice, with the same uniformity and reliability as for physics or chemistry. Certainly this approach has fitted readily into certain aspects of medicine and healthcare. Acute medicine and other areas such as primary care and mental health have been relatively enthusiastic supporters. Yet even within health there are concerns about the displacement by randomised controlled trials (RCTs) of qualitative research looking, for example, at patient preferences and values (Reynolds 2000).

But it has been argued that disciplines such as social work and probation are inherently different from medicine. Here the effect of a 'dose' of intervention is not readily predictable from person to person and where a great diversity of external elements can influence the outcome. This complexity and unpredictability does not always sit comfortably within the rigid methodologies of 'What Works'. As Trinder (2000: 149) concluded:

> ... social work encounters are not straightforward or linear relationships, but multiple, multilayered, relational and complex, and located in a social and political context. Within this framework of the inherently messy and complex nature of social work and probation relationships, classic formulations of evidence are impoverished and potentially constraining.

Randomised controlled trials

In evaluating treatment or intervention measures the most widely recognised research methodology in the evidence-based practice movement is that of the randomised controlled trial (RCT). This is often dubbed the 'gold standard' method of assessing the effectiveness of an intervention. The principal characteristic of an RCT is that the participants are randomly allocated to either the group receiving the intervention or the control group. This is designed to limit bias, particularly where neither the participants, the practitioners or those gathering the data know the difference between groups. A comparison of the changes in outcomes or behaviours between the participants of the two groups reveals the existence and size of any effect of the intervention. If several such studies are carried out with similar findings then there can be considerable confidence in replicating the intervention more widely.

In tandem with the use of RCTs has been the application of meta-analysis, a statistical approach whereby results are aggregated from different studies that use experimental and control groups. This enables a large number of evaluations of different interventions to be combined to assess whether there has been any effect (positive or negative) and to gauge the size of this effect. The advantage of this aggregation is that it highlights the overall effects of interventions whilst minimising or statistically controlling for small differences between studies. Its strength therefore is in identifying broad patterns of findings in an arguably clearer and more consistent way than more traditional reviewing techniques of research.

Reviewing the findings of meta-analysis it was claimed 'that the net effect of "treatment" in the many studies surveyed is, on average, a reduction in recidivism rates between 10 per cent and 12 per cent' (McGuire and Priestley 1995: 9). Given the considerable volume of research involved, these results may appear modest but for example similar meta-analysis of many medical interventions such as heart bypass surgery or some cancer treatments reveal effects of this scale.

Criticisms of RCTs

There are significant criticisms of the 'What Works' approach being so heavily dependent on RCTs. This may seem a rather esoteric debate, of little relevance to practitioners, but it does pose important questions about the nature of evidence and its translation into effective practice. Taken together the criticisms undermine an oversimplified approach to devising and implementing a 'What Works' approach but also indicate productive ways forward.

It has been argued that the RCT is much more effective where singular treatments are applied to a well-defined set of subjects with specific outcome targets. This could be deemed simplistic when applied to the complexity of many of the circumstances and interactions within youth justice. To take a practical example: the education and training of young people in custody which is supposed to be much the most important intervention (judged by numbers of hours at least). In the context of evaluating the education of prisoners Pawson (2000: 66) emphasised a series of complexities that undermines an RCT approach:

(a) education is not a 'treatment' applied in dosages but a multi-faceted and prolonged social encounter involving a range of ideas, curricula, and personnel;
(b) the 'subjects', namely inmates, are hardly uniform and whilst they do not represent an exact cross-section of society, they do present a mighty range of social backgrounds, a positive jumble of prior educational experience and, indeed, an unfortunate array of offences;
(c) the rehabilitative 'outcome' of prisoner education is rarely perceived in simple, therapeutic terms but is considered to work *indirectly* via building character, raising self-confidence, acquiring competence, gaining credentials, promoting self-reflection, creating moral standards, improving social skills, enlarging cultural aspirations and so on.

While Pawson dismisses such an approach to answering the question 'Does prisoner education work?' as a 'dangerous over-simplification' he does not abandon attempts to answer it. Faced with the multi-faceted nature of education acting on individuals in such chaotic circumstances as is often the case in a Young Offender Institution (YOI) it is arguably much more sensible to be asking questions such as 'why' the education of young people who offend might work, and going on to inquire 'for whom' and 'in what circumstances' and 'in what respects' it appears to work (Pawson 2000).

RCTs are often perceived to be weak at establishing causal connections and there is little attention given to the mechanisms by which change in an individual occurs. Similarly the context is often ignored. As Pring has highlighted, 'such large-scale explanations cannot be sensitive to the complexity and variability of social rules and expectations through which decisions and actions are made intelligible' (2004: 207). The social rules and the institutional framework within which young people and practitioners operate can vary enough to mean that an intervention that might be apparently effective in one context might not be in another. For instance a similar intervention in a custodial environment might have a very different outcome to one in the community.

A related assumption underlying the quasi-experimental method of RCTs is that the administration of the appropriate intervention dosage to the individual will result in the desired cognitive behavioural change with little consideration of the motivation and predisposition of the individual. Rather than programmes simply working on individuals it has been argued that they must work *through* individuals.

Potential subjects will consider a programme (or not), volunteer for it (or not), become interested (or not), cooperate closely (or not), stay the course (or not), learn lessons (or not), retain the lessons (or not). Programmes are thus learning processes and, as with any learning process, certain groups and individuals are much more likely to have the appropriate characteristics which will allow them to stay the course. (Pawson 1997: 155)

The blunt nature of the quasi-experimental approach that masks the differences in context and the interactions with individuals perhaps explains why the results of RCTs with matched cohorts of young people can be inconsistent.

Clearly, too, when aggregating many studies through meta-analysis only average measures of changes in recidivism are used. Even on the most effective programmes where recidivism has decreased on average by about 40 per cent this disguises a performance range both above and below this central score. The inference that practitioners can therefore draw is that even when they apply interventions which are rated the most 'effective', the outcomes could range from a complete cessation of offending through to a significant increase. Equally there may well be individuals who participate in interventions that in aggregate appear to be ineffective, such as custody, who nevertheless find it a life-changing experience.

It is important though in recognising the limitations of the quasi-experimental approach that this is not exaggerated to the extent of committing the 'uniqueness fallacy' as Pring has warned (2004: 208). A false dualism can be created whereby the kind of evidence which relates to the explanation of physical events such as the effectiveness or not of medical interventions is portrayed as inapplicable to the uniqueness of the human condition. While these methodologies cannot at present provide universal truths it is undeniable that much of human behaviour is predictable. Certain types of intervention can be identified that, other things being equal, can have particular consequences.

There are other difficulties with quasi-experimental methods. There are ethical problems in denying potentially helpful interventions, no guarantee that random selection will produce the essential comparison groups, imperfect data gathering and transmissions systems, and perhaps importantly, strong vested interests. Few managers would go to all the extra work involved in such research and risk exposing their existing interventions as ineffective if they were compared with a comparison group.

RCTs tend to produce guidance for practitioners that relates to interventions with individuals rather than for initiatives that focus on neighbourhoods or cities. In practical terms it is obviously much simpler and less expensive to allocate individuals randomly to different intervention groups than to do so with cities or neighbourhoods. In addition it is far harder to conduct large-scale trials without the design being compromised by the treatment group's knowledge of the intervention and this being transmitted to and affecting the control group (Tilley 2006).

The quasi-experimental approach is not necessarily useful in assisting practitioners to decide what does not work, partly due to its inherent methodological limitations. Commenting on the largely consistently negative findings for Scared Straight and similar programmes (where a young person is exposed to confrontational insights into prison life) Tilley (2006) points out that as there is no understanding of why failures occur then the conclusions must be necessarily limited. He goes on to list the possible explanations – were the young people not scared? Or did they enjoy being scared and so the experience acted as an inducement? There could have been significant variations within the group with certain subsets being deterred whilst others were encouraged. Then again the dosage may simply have been too low to make an impact. Perhaps for those already committing offences or inclined to do so the visits removed the mystique of custody, rendering it less scary?

In any event public and political opinion is not necessarily amenable to certain research messages that conflict with common sense or more punitive approaches. One well-known American project highlights this problem – Drug Abuse Resistance Education (DARE). Strong empirical evidence including studies using a random assignment design has indicated that DARE is not effective (Howell 2003). Yet it remains a very large programme employing more than 50,000 police officers lecturing in nearly half of America's elementary schools. One explanation for its continuing popularity despite being apparently a failed intervention is because it is founded on a mistaken belief in the effectiveness of deterrence. It appears that fundamental beliefs in the efficacy of repressive deterrence are irresistible, particularly when combined with an apparent common sense approach. The zero tolerance approach applied to schools has also been found to be ineffective but this has not restricted its popularity in the United States and its potential spread to the UK (Howell 2003; Smith 2005).

More benign motives can lie behind projects where the evidence does not suggest that they are effective. Flexible provision linked to schools, with the ostensible aim of reintegrating young people, can often counter-intuitively lead to a greater detachment. The youth inclusion programme developed by the Youth Justice Board is a structured youth work programme combining elements of education and personal development targeted on the 50 most at risk young people in a neighbourhood. Referral criteria include poor attendance or exclusion from school. Its targets included reducing recorded crime by 30 per cent and reducing non-attendance and school exclusion each by 30 per cent. The outcomes have however included a 6 per cent increase in offending and a significant deterioration in attendance. While this approach might have made common sense from a youth justice perspective, from an educational perspective it ran the risk of providing young people with an easy option educationally and enabled schools to divert young people who may have been challenging in school settings towards more 'appropriate' education provision without resort to exclusion (Youth Justice Board 2003b).

Implementation

From a policy making perspective rigorous, consistent evaluation of pilot projects followed by the refinement of the model and then the faithful implementation of this model subsequently maintained by data returns and inspection appears straightforward. From a political standpoint it is axiomatic that communities and young people should have access to the same quantity and quality of public services. Yet significant and perennial problems with implementation consistently undermine this process.

The inconsistent and limited findings of 'What Works' studies have been attributed to the weaknesses of implementation: 'the results reported in this volume say a great deal about implementation, its problems and its effects on outcomes rather than the true effect of interventions' (Chitty 2005: 79). This is disputed on two counts. Given that an intervention can only have effects if it is implemented this appears an artificial distinction (Smith 2006). Others feel that researchers and policy makers have accused practice and thereby practitioners of poor performance. In this line of argument 'the problem appears to have been more fundamental than this, having its origin in the researchers' understanding of the nature of the human sciences and their beliefs about human nature' (Bateman and Pitts 2005: 250).

This may be overstating the case and certainly ignores the effects of for example poor recording and weak exchange of key information between professionals but, equally, over-reliance on a methodology that does not explain how particular outcomes are achieved in detail constrains replicability.

The past decade has seen very substantial increases in expenditure on public services and there have been consistent problems in implementation of initiatives to time, cost and volumes of services. This has a significant impact on evaluating, particularly using more sophisticated approaches such as RCTs which require sufficient numbers of young people who have similar characteristics and antecedents. In youth justice projects that have been set up later than planned, data collection has been limited and referrals lower than expected. These problems would have beset any evaluation strategy but can have damaging consequences within a 'What Works' approach. Where the implementation of new initiatives or interventions has drifted and invalidated the research design, potentially erroneous inferences may be drawn by policy makers. The enormous attrition of participants involved in the Basic Skills Pathfinders programme for example meant that the original research intention to judge the impact of improvements in basic skills on offending had to be abandoned and this has led some civil servants to query whether there is any effect rather than to challenge the model of implementation used (McMahon et al. 2004).

The disparity between the certainty with which research findings can be hailed by policy makers and the cautious, limited and often ambiguous nature of those findings can be considerable. This is underlined by much of the evaluation commissioned by the Youth Justice Board. The first notable attempt to gather evidence systematically was through the evaluation of initiatives supported through its development fund. These initiatives included cognitive behaviour; restorative justice; substance misuse; education training and employment; parenting; final warning interventions; and generic preventative services. Each had a separate evaluation and all the national evaluators questioned the extent to which there was evidence of effectiveness (Fullwood and Powell 2004). All suffered from poor data collection, late starts and fewer referrals than the Youth Offending Teams (Yots) had predicted.

So widespread and apparently endemic are the problems with implementation that what is needed according to Smith (2006) is a theory of implementation. This would assist in disentangling the effects of programme and implementation weaknesses. There may be all sorts of constraints inherent in the circumstances that affect for example engagement in groupwork programmes or education, training and employment.

It may be that implementation and project management skills in both central and local government are in relatively short supply compared to the demands of the many initiatives that have been launched. There may also be diminishing returns as an initiative moves from its early stages which tend to attract the most motivated managers and practitioners only to find effects diluted later when the less enthusiastic or downright hostile teams become involved.

While it may be unfair to blame practitioners for the shortcomings of researchers' theories and the over-reliance on methodologies that are important but not sufficient there is abundant evidence that many practitioners do not always put a premium on recording and data collection. This goes beyond a failure to comply with the managerialist demands of a perceived technocratic government and perhaps partly reflects the lack of a practice culture that is routinely evidence-informed.

Many research studies have been stymied by the lack of the most basic information on key aspects of a young person's life. Studies incorporating large samples of *Assets* for example can find problems with the quality of its completion, its transfer when necessary and keeping it up to date, for example ECOTEC 2001a. These problems persist both within the youth justice system, particularly between custody and community, and between youth justice and key agencies such as education and health (Stephenson 2007). The systemic weaknesses over data exchange continue through time as the recording practices and management information systems are unable to keep pace with the often turbulent lives of young people who appear and disappear within the purview of a range of agencies. Very few studies are able to follow large enough groups of young people who have been in the youth justice system over a significant period of time to judge the longer term impact of an intervention and to gain insight into why it appeared to have had the effect it did. The use of reconviction data has its limitations and longitudinal studies tend to suffer attrition amongst the group who have detached from mainstream services.

A major concern about placing too much emphasis on RCTs and meta-analysis is that they tend overwhelmingly to be North American in origin whereas the British equivalents are much more limited both in scope and positive findings (Chitty 2005). Not only does there appear to have been a longer-standing evaluation culture with significant resources devoted to the more costly research methods such as longitudinal studies or RCTs but of course the context and mechanisms for change may be radically different from those of the UK. Despite the government's espousal of evidence-led policy making (Cabinet Office 1999) evaluation often appears to be relatively *ad hoc* and small scale.

The Crime Reduction Initiative in Secondary Schools (CRISS) programme in the UK comprised a series of school-focused development projects from which it was hoped to identify measures to reduce actual and potential offending by young people. There is a marked contrast in the nature of this initiative compared to some of the American examples. The CRISS programme was relatively short term (two years), contained a very wide range of rather disparate initiatives (38 projects involving over a hundred schools with each school implementing between five and 10 separate interventions) and there was a much less rigorous evaluation methodology with a considerable emphasis on qualitative research. Not surprisingly, although a central objective of this programme was the collection of robust evidence the best that could be achieved were recommendations for promising approaches (Home Office 2004b). None of these programmes could be validated using the hierarchy of evidence outlined above.

Given all these difficulties it has to be seriously questioned whether the widespread use of RCTs is actually practicable in the youth justice field, at least at present. Paradoxically the Home Office reaction has been to call for greater methodological rigour in its pursuit of policy certainties (Harper and Chitty 2005). Apparently RCTs are robust enough to ensure 'that our knowledge of "What Works" is truly improved and the existing equivocal evidence is replaced with greater certainty' (Chitty 2005: 82). The Youth Justice Board although rejecting the strict 'What Works' approach adopted by the probation and prison services has nevertheless been drawn more closely into the Home Office approach to research.

Guidelines for more effective practice

While the use of RCTs and meta-analysis clearly has limitations, it has enabled a series of principles to be identified regarding the design of effective programmes and interventions. These principles do not provide a prescription of what to do, let alone how to do it, in terms of reducing or stopping a young person's offending. What they offer though is a framework within which projects can be developed and evaluated, or guidelines when constructing a package of interventions. The following seven principles are drawn from

McGuire and Priestley (1995) supplemented with that of 'dosage' (Lipsey 1995). Each chapter places the topic such as mentoring or restorative justice within this framework to illustrate their application in practice.

Principles of effective practice

- **Risk classification**: matching the level and intensity of intervention to an assessment of the seriousness of offending and the risk of reoffending.

- **Criminogenic need**: programmes should focus on those factors that directly contribute to offending, as opposed to more distantly related causes.

- **Dosage**: programmes must be of sufficient intensity and duration to achieve their aims.

- **Responsivity**: matching the learning styles and strategies of young people to the staff working with them.

- **Community based**: learning takes place in a context that is meaningful to the young person – i.e. close to the young person's experiences and life contexts.

- **Intervention modality**: programme content and methods are skills-based, focused on problem-solving with a cognitive behavioural approach. Programme interventions mirror the multiple needs (criminogenic) of the young person.

- **Programme integrity**: effective programmes have a clear rationale. They link aims to methods, are adequately resourced, staff are trained and supported, and there is appropriate monitoring and evaluation.

Risk classification

The evidence suggests that levels of intervention should be commensurate with the likelihood of offending. Therefore those young people deemed to be at greater risk of offending should be placed on more intensive programmes. Equally those of lower risk should receive lower or minimal intervention. This is not simply a matter of the efficient allocation of resources but also because intensive interventions with those at low risk can have counter-productive results and be associated with increases in offending (Nacro 2006). The reasons for this are unclear but may lie in similar explanations as to net-widening whereby labelling and the effects of mixing with more delinquent peers tend to draw a young person further into the youth justice system.

Risk is defined here on an actuarial basis whereby *Asset* uses prior history of offending and a range of other dimensions such as education, family and health to predict the likelihood of subsequent offending. The designers of *Asset* advocate that a banding is used to establish risks of reoffending.

Asset *score*	Risk of reoffending
0 – 4	Low
5 – 9	Low – medium
10 – 16	Medium
17 – 24	Medium – high
25 – 48	High

Source: Baker *et al.* (2005)

Asset scores can therefore be helpful in assigning those most at risk of reoffending to more intensive interventions. Of course *Asset* has limitations. Its predictive accuracy, although similar to actuarial systems for adults who offend, is only about two-thirds. There is much less emphasis in *Asset* on the role of protective factors which may ameliorate risk though this reflects a wider lack of knowledge. The negative aspects of young people's lives tend therefore to be overemphasised. There will often tend to be gaps in the evidence needed for scoring. In matching young people to particular intensities of intervention, *Asset* is a helpful tool but should be used in the context of a practitioner's skills and experience (Annison 2005).

There are dangers, particularly for young children, if an actuarial approach does not take account of existing needs and problems rather than focusing simply on some future risk of criminality. Assessment (of which *Asset* is but one component) underpins effective planning by practitioners who have to make judgements often on the basis of unreliable information.

Criminogenic need

Where young people have particularly chaotic lives, which is a characteristic of many of those in the youth justice system, a practitioner is often faced with such a welter of problems, for example homelessness, substance misuse, family discord, detachment from education, that it is often difficult to set priorities for interventions. This principle stresses the need to distinguish between those problems or features that appear to contribute to or underlie offending rather than those that may be only distantly related, if at all. The criminogenic needs will of course in practice often be difficult to distinguish for a particular individual. Practitioners have to become adept at deciding which are the priority issues to focus on in their work with a young person. This would not mean that those factors apparently more distantly related to offending should be ignored but might mean that a caseworker would broker access to other services rather than dealing directly.

The assessment process is clearly crucial in constructing a plan with interventions that are targeted effectively at those factors considered most likely to be direct contributors to offending behaviour. The *Asset* assessment revolves around 12 dimensions of dynamic risk factors, each of which is scored according to the extent to which it is considered to be linked to the young person's offending. So both the principle and the *Asset* process are designed through the exercise of professional judgement to lead to planned interventions with clear priorities.

Sentencing of young people who offend is, in effect, based on the principle of proportionality: any punishment imposed by the court should be commensurate with the seriousness of the offence (and previous offending, where this is relevant) (Nacro 2000). In addition, as Yots become more conversant with *Asset* and the requirement to assess 'risk' factors, the possibility of future risk posed to a community by a young person will become a relevant factor. The view taken by the court of the seriousness of the offending determines the type of order available to the court. Thus, in most circumstances, a custodial sentence can only be made where the offending is so serious that only a custodial sentence can be justified. Similarly, a community sentence can only be made where the offending is serious enough to justify a community sentence. In both cases, the restriction of liberty involved in any court order, as determined by the length of the order and the intensity of intervention, must be proportionate to the young person's behaviour.

While the statutory framework technically applies to sentencing, there are good reasons for adopting a similar approach at the pre-court stage in relation to Final Warning interventions, and when determining the content of a youth offender contract. Article 40 (4) of the United Nations Convention on the Rights of a Child (UNCRC), to which the UK is a signatory, requires that young people who offend should be dealt with in a manner 'proportionate to their circumstances and the offence'.

The situation is further complicated by what is commonly referred to as 'the welfare principle'. Section 44 of the Children and Young Persons Act 1933 requires that:

> every court in dealing with a child or young person who is brought before it, either as being in need of care and protection or as an offender or otherwise, shall have regard to the welfare of the child or young person.

The welfare principle is reiterated in Article 3 (1) of the United Nations Convention on the Rights of the Child:

> In all actions concerning children, whether undertaken by public or private social welfare institutes, courts of law, administration authorities or legislative bodies, the best interests of the child shall be a primary consideration.

The effect of the Human Rights Act 1998 is to make it unlawful for any public authority to act in any way that is incompatible with the European Convention on Human Rights. Yots and establishments within the juvenile secure estate clearly fall within the definition of a public authority, and in those circumstances at least two articles of the Convention have potential relevance to planning and delivering interventions to young people who offend.

The right to a fair trial (Article 6) has a broad application. It includes all actions taken, from the arrest of an individual through to sentence. The delivery of an offending behaviour programme at any stage should therefore be a 'fair' response to the young person's behaviour. At one level, this is simply to reiterate the earlier point about interventions being proportionate to the level of offending. In addition, however, it might be argued that Article 6 obliges practitioners to ensure that:

- any programme is appropriate to the young person's circumstances;

- any programme is delivered in a way that maximises the chances of compliance;

- in the case of a Final Warning, where participation in the programme is technically voluntary, the young person's consent is sought (*R v. Metropolitan Police Commisioner* and *R v. Durham Constabulary* (2002)).

Article 8, on the other hand, deals with the right to respect for private and public life. To comply with this Article, an intervention which involves disclosure of personal information, or intervention with the young person's family, must be justifiable on the basis that it is a reasonable response to the offending.

The human rights framework is broader than that provided for in domestic legislation. The UNCRC and the United Nations Standard Minimum Rules for the Administration of Juvenile Justice (commonly known as the Beijing Rules) provide more detailed guidance for the delivery of programmes to young people who offend. In general, the overall effect is to suggest that any programme designed to address offending behaviour should be tailored to meet the particular circumstances of the young person, and should form part of an integrated approach aimed at promoting healthy development.

Dosage

Despite its medical overtones this is a straightforward principle, i.e. the amount of contact received by a young person in relation to reducing their offending. This comprises both duration and intensity. In Lipsey's (1995) meta-analysis of the effectiveness of interventions he defined low dosage as interventions that were of 26 or fewer weeks, with less than two contacts per week and a total contact time of 100 or fewer hours. High dosage was more than 100 hours' total contact time over more than 26 weeks with two or more contacts per week. Given the entrenched nature of the disadvantages that many young people in the youth justice system have suffered from, or their chronic involvement in harmful behaviours such as substance misuse, it is fanciful to suppose that limited sporadic interventions will have much impact on their circumstances or behaviours. Equally, where the risk classification principle is not observed and young people are targeted who have not offended or are at low risk of reoffending, then a high dosage may increase the chances of offending.

It might be supposed that the volume of interventions would be well established given how relatively straightforward it is to measure compared to other aspects of intervention. This is not the case. The great majority of evaluations lack this important evidence and this is mirrored by similar deficiencies in monitoring returns. Consequently, evaluations often focus on completion rates and their association with outcomes such as reductions in offending. Useful though this is it leaves open the question of just how much intervention is necessary and for how long interventions should last for optimum outcomes.

Even in controlled institutional settings very little is known about the levels of participation and consequent outcomes. In custody the most intensive intervention is supposed to be education or training yet this appears to be extremely difficult to ascertain (Stephenson 2007). Apparently, 'it is clearly still the case that in many establishments reporting systems are not sophisticated enough to provide information on the actual take-up of learning and skills as opposed to what is on offer' (Youth Justice Board 2004e). This confusion between what is planned and what is actually delivered extends more widely within the prison service. The Chief Inspector of Prisons' recent report produced a series of examples illustrating how the hours of 'purposeful activity' were greatly exaggerated in half of the local prisons inspected. With Soviet-style creativity, the prison ship *Weare* even had pre-printed forms containing hours out of cell prepared in advance (HM Inspectorate of Prisons 2006).

These problems may also be commonplace in the community. The evaluation of the ISSP noted that the monitoring software was used for constructing timetables rather than recording actual delivery and recording non-compliance (Moore *et al.* 2004). Government targets can also exert a powerful influence on returns, perhaps leading to an emphasis on what is planned rather than actually achieved for a young person. For example the Youth Justice Board's target of 90 per cent of Yot supervised young people being in suitable full-time education, training or employment averages about 75 per cent nationally yet a national census revealed a figure of less than 50 per cent (Youth Justice Board 2006c). A lack of detailed registration systems, generous interpretation of counting rules, including counting arranged destinations, may have been behind this.

Despite the importance of programmes it is the individual supervision of a young person that is the spine for interventions. Yet the amount of such supervision appears both poorly recorded and relatively limited (Audit Commission 2004). This is an important but underevaluated area. The inadequacy of available resources, or more often the difficulty of accessing for example mainstream services such as education, also tends to undermine adherence to this principle. Often managers and practitioners may take refuge in the notion that a young person is so 'disaffected' that they are not yet ready for full-time interventions. Ostensibly reasonable though such assumptions are they ignore the impact of the pervasive low expectations of these young people which tend to be self-fulfilling. These rather convenient assumptions which implicitly attribute responsibility to the young people rather than lack of resources, appropriate provision or engagement skills do not take account of studies such as Hurry's (2003) evaluation of ETE projects which demonstrated that relatively high levels of engagement were possible. The one project which achieved this also had recording systems that enabled an analysis of dosage in relation to outcomes and shed light on the possible relationship between literacy and numeracy gains and subsequent reductions in offending (Hurry *et al.* 2006).

Responsivity

Apart from the issue of special educational needs very different learning outcomes can result for individual young people. This is despite the nature of the topic, the knowledge and skills of the learner, their motivation, their previous experience of learning and the knowledge and skills of the person facilitating this learning. The gap between the theoretical understanding of such individual differences and a practical application in particular learning circumstances has been bridged by a wide range of style constructs.

Differential learning outcomes despite common contexts has been tackled by several criminologists. Bonta (1996: 31) for instance asserts 'offenders differ in motivation, personality, and emotional and cognitive abilities, and these characteristics can influence the offenders' responsiveness to various therapists and treatment modalities'.

Out of the extensive literature that has resulted over many years, academics in both education and criminal justice have adopted learning styles as being useful in understanding and supporting learning. Within education the concept of learning styles appears to be widely accepted and various instruments are employed to assign learners to particular categories.

In youth justice, while managers and practitioners may view formal learning as being largely the province of education professionals there is to some extent a recognition that for example interventions that aim to change behaviour depend upon learning. Certainly those academics concerned with the identification of the effectiveness of interventions in preventing offending and reoffending have often embraced the validity of learning styles constructs: 'Programmes work best when there is a systematic matching between the styles of workers and the styles of client. But on balance the learning styles of most offenders require active, participatory methods of working, rather than either a didactic mode on the one hand or a loose, unstructured, "experiential" mode on the other'. (McGuire 1995: 15)

There are three key assumptions that can be questioned within this principle: that learning styles can be clearly defined and measured and are relatively unchanging for individuals; that matching this learning style with the respective teaching/instructional styles makes a significant difference; and that young people who offend tend to have an active and participatory learning style.

Even bolder claims have been made for the negative impact of a lack of responsivity in education. It has been argued for example (Hodges 1982) that the urban poor (in America) and young people who offend are more likely to possess a right-brain dominance and be spatial/holistic, visual learners. This is contrasted with the assertion that most learners in society possess a left-brain dominance and are verbal/analytic learners. This chain of reasoning has linked disruptive behaviour, detachment from school, low attainment and associated offending by so many of the urban poor to their inability to learn effectively due to the verbally based instructional methods that allegedly characterise most American schools.

Although learning styles are meant to be stable psychological constructs, they have been remarkably difficult to assess reliably for any learners, let alone young people who offend. A recent comprehensive literature review commented that despite the weight of material this area was 'opaque, contradictory and controversial' with 'very few robust studies which offer ... reliable and valid evidence and clear implications for practice based on empirical findings' (Coffield *et al.* 2004: 2,1).

This report concluded that not only were most of the psychometric instruments unreliable and lacking in validity but they were unsuitable for learners with relatively low levels of literacy, which is a common characteristic of many young people who offend.

A more fruitful approach probably needs to take account of the relationship between learners' use of effective learning strategies and their academic attainment (Adey *et al.* 1999: 21). It is possible that children and young people with low academic attainment did not absorb some of the basic learning strategies required for school learning during their primary education.

A recent report into learning styles and young people who offend (Youth Justice Board 2005a) concluded: '... the evidence does not have sufficient weight to justify claims of the existence of a discrete, stable learning styles construct. Indeed it could be constrictive and unhelpful to rely heavily on such a simplistic approach.'

Accordingly each of the chapters interprets the responsivity principle in terms of understanding and responding to a young person's learning strategies and learning skills. One of the key differences is that unlike putative learning styles, strategies and skills are under conscious control and can be learned and improved upon. The challenge for practitioners here then is, firstly, assessment of a young person's repertoire of learning strategies and skills, and then taking account of it in a subsequent intervention and working as far as is possible to enhance it.

One important element in enhancing a young person's repertoire is the process known as meta-cognition – the awareness of one's own thinking and the control of that knowledge as one engages in a cognitive event. While this approach may seem directly relevant to skill acquisition such as literacy and numeracy it is equally applicable to certain interventions that focus on thinking skills.

It is important under this principle that other factors that may be relevant to the relationship between the practitioner and the young person in facilitating learning are taken into account, such as maturity, gender and ethnicity. Similarly the young person's readiness to change is a crucial component depending on what stage of change they may be at (see p. 54).

Community based

On balance interventions delivered in the community appear to be more effective than those in custodial or institutional settings. This can be developed further in that interventions carried out closer to a young person's home environment may be more likely to achieve transferable learning. It appears very difficult to enable learning that can transfer between very different environments. This may partly explain the ineffectiveness of custody and also of interventions such as Outward Bound programmes, particularly if delivered in isolation.

Within the community this principle could be taken to include enabling young people to gain access to and participate effectively in mainstream provision, particularly education but also health, leisure and cultural activities such as libraries and museums. The majority of young people in the youth justice system who have any education provided experience it through on- or off-site units (Learning Support Units (LSUs) or Pupil Referral Units (PRUs)), or post-16 through specialist training providers who cater largely for those who offend. Such settings may share fundamental weaknesses such as the formation of negative or delinquent peer groups, trying to change behaviour out of the original context and marginalisation of staff.

Given that young people will ultimately have to return to mainstream environments such as further education colleges or employment then arguably segregated education or training could create more problems than it solves. Similarly small group or one-to-one contacts may be more effective in enabling the transfer of learning if conducted in ordinary community settings, libraries, youth clubs, etc.

Intervention modality

There were consistent findings from Lipsey's meta-analysis (1995) regarding the nature of effective interventions. Those programmes that appeared to be more effective tended to recognise the breadth of challenges facing many people who had offended and to devise a range of interventions to match them – multi-modal. These interventions also had a focus on the acquisition of skills intended to enhance problem-solving, social interaction or other kinds of coping skills. The methods were often drawn from the two traditions within psychology of behaviourism and cognitive theory or a synthesis of the two – cognitive-behavioural.

One important potential application of this principle is that interventions that in isolation have not been demonstrated to be effective can if combined into a broader, structured approach focused on criminogenic needs have better outcomes. For example outward bound activities or sports or arts interventions can be integrated into a wider programme (Chapman and Hough 1998).

This principle has often tended to be dominated by cognitive-behavioural approaches, particularly with adults. The prison and probation services have invested heavily in such approaches through formally accrediting pro-grammes. Many commentators see a disproportionate emphasis on such programmes with Rod Morgan when Chief Inspector of Probation warning of 'programme fetishism' (HM Inspectorate of Probation 2002). This is partly because the evidence regarding the effectiveness of these programmes can be questioned: 'while the studies indicate that programmes of this kind have an influence on some offenders, for the majority the programmes *by themselves* are unlikely to deliver the outcomes in reducing offending that have been expected of them' (Roberts 2004: 156). Other factors were seen to play an important part in encouraging desistance, some of which – such as access to employment, training and education, and appropriate accommodation – could be influenced by practitioner intervention (Roberts 2004).

The results of evaluations of the effectiveness of Youth Justice Board spon-sored cognitive-behavioural programmes had similar messages although some methodological weaknesses and low completion rates limited the find-ings (Feilzer *et al.* 2004). There are other flaws in the accredited cognitive-behavioural programmes that require other interventions such as the fact that the literacy skills of many of the young people in custody are not of a suffi-cient level to succeed in these programmes (ECOTEC 2001b; Davies *et al.* 2004). In contrast to the prison and probation services the Youth Justice Board has not adopted an accredited programmes approach, thereby giving more scope for a range of intervention modalities.

Programme integrity

This principle espouses that there should be an explicit theoretical base to an intervention and that it should be faithfully implemented. One of the explanations given for inconsistent findings of effectiveness of particular interventions is implementation failure. This is seen as potentially masking what might otherwise have been effective interventions (Harper and Chitty 2005). Threats to the integrity of an intervention have been identified as due to drift, reversal and non-compliance (Hollin 1995). Drift refers to the gradual slippage of the aims of the intervention whereby perhaps a lack of clarity over initial longer term objectives means they are eclipsed by more immediate concerns, or simply the inertia of existing ways of working prevents change. Reversal is where some staff actively work to undermine or reverse a new approach, perhaps because they are operating from a different theoretical perspective or value base (Hollin 1995). Non-compliance is where elements of a new initiative are ignored or replaced by staff so that a customised version emerges that can have little resemblance to the original intended objectives and methodologies.

These threats to faithful implementation are largely separate from the exercise of creativity to adopt and improve a particular approach or to fit it more closely to the local context but rather, deliberately or unconsciously, prevent a new initiative from being tested for the first time.

The barriers to faithful implementation can be presented by the organisation, the practitioner or the young person. The culture of particular Yots or custodial establishments may be inimical to change or have elements of disorganisation that prevent a staff group from effectively implementing a new initiative or intervention as originally intended. This can often include a lack of training although training by itself will not necessarily turn an ineffective organisation culture around.

Practitioner resistance can spring from several sources. It may be that a particular programme appears so prescriptive as to erode professional autonomy or that evaluation is intrusive and time consuming.

The engagement of young people in evaluation processes could be considered as part of the wider issues concerning participation and completion of interventions. Knowledge of the nature of engagement is increasing, albeit often from a standpoint of education (Fredericks et al. 2004). If particular practitioners are half-hearted in their support of evaluation then it might be expected that some young people would mirror this.

It has been suggested that close researcher involvement in the design and implementation of an intervention leads to a higher level of programme integrity. Lipsey (1995) highlighted that researcher involvement was second only to the type of intervention in being associated with positive effects on reducing offending.

The role of the practitioner

The implicit role of the practitioner in some examples of guidance can appear somewhat mechanical with little scope for the exercise of their expert judgement or discretion. Whilst the methodology of meta-analysis appears insensitive to the influence of practitioners the approach to the implementation of accredited programmes or simplistic 'What Works' guidance has also been criticised for neglecting the importance of effective relationships (McNeill and Batchelor 2002; Tilley 2006).

While research has tended to concentrate on the characteristics of effective programmes or interventions there is no reason why the particular elements of a practitioner's craft cannot be subject to an evidence-based approach. Unfortunately most of the research has been on adults who have offended and applying these findings to young people has to be done with great care. The effects of maturation, the very different contexts and opportunities such as access to the labour market could alter the effectiveness of particular practitioner styles and approaches.

In contrast the centrality of relationships is often emphasised in discussions regarding the role of parents. If ineffective parenting, characterised by such features as harsh and inconsistent disciplining, weak supervision and monitoring, and limited positive involvement, has been found to be related to the development of anti-social behaviour then it is a reasonable supposition that equivalent practices by practitioners within schools, custody or Yots could have similar negative outcomes.

Using the findings from studies of desistance and resilience to explore the effectiveness of the relationship between young people and practitioners Batchelor and McNeill (2005) highlighted the potential of motivational interviewing and pro-social modelling. While motivational interviewing is not yet supported by convincing evidence as to its effectiveness with young people who offend, it has been found to have positive effects with those who have substance misuse problems, albeit they are older than those in the youth justice system (Harper and Hardy 2000). Within this approach key factors in more effective styles of practice have been identified such as the abilities to express empathy, develop discrepancy (between current and desired behaviour), avoid arguments and confrontation, support self-efficacy and deal flexibly with resistance (Batchelor and McNeill 2005).

Certain principles for effective supervision can also be drawn from pro-social modelling. These principles include: role clarification – being clear about the purpose of supervision (or any intervention), mutual expectations, the tension between control and welfare, the constraints on confidentiality and any scope for negotiating.

There is some evidence with those older young people supervised by probation officers who had been trained in and made use of a range of relationship skills that more positive outcomes including lower reoffending rates were achieved compared to a control group (Trotter 1996).

What must always be borne in mind is that the particular context of the opportunities available to a young person can exert powerful negative influences that can overcome the effects of accredited programmes or defy the exercise of considerable skills and energy by practitioners.

Does guidance work?

Managers and practitioners in youth justice can sometimes feel besieged by guidance from central and local government and there is an abundant supply from various voluntary organisations. But does it work? In medicine it is claimed that there is strong evidence that guidance and guidelines have little effect on changing the behaviour of doctors to become more evidence based (Peile 2004). The two major weaknesses with regard to guidance in criminal justice are first that it is widely ignored, and second that when it is not ignored it is poorly followed (Tilley 2006).

The reasons for this appear to be a combination of inherent deficiencies in guidance and barriers to its adoption. Most guidance is very limited in describing exactly how a practitioner can encourage desistance and why it will work with some young people in some circumstances but not with others. Where accredited programmes are concerned the level of prescription has been accused of crowding out the exercise of practitioners' discretion and limiting effective case management, which is reflected in high rates of attrition with very few people completing an intervention (Raynor 2004a).

More fundamentally perhaps is that detailed prescriptive guidance does not tend to reflect that much practice knowledge is not necessarily acquired or used consciously. The classic example of learning how to ride a bike emphasises the tacit nature of some knowledge:

> We cannot learn to keep and balance on a bicycle by taking to heart that in order to compensate for a given angle of imbalance (a), we must take a curve on the side of the imbalance, of which the radius (r) should be proportionate to the square of a 5th of the velocity (v) over the imbalance: $r \sim v^2/a$. Such knowledge is ineffectual, unless known tacitly. (Polanyi 1969: 144)

Much of the craft of a practitioner in youth justice when interacting with a young person may be known tacitly. Such knowledge is usually acquired through personal contact and some variation of apprenticeship. The professional training of for example medics or teachers is not just about acquiring the theoretical knowledge but finding personal understanding through supervised practice training. Written guidance is therefore intrinsically insufficient to transmit this personal understanding.

In addition to these problems a range of other barriers prevents the ready absorption of research evidence disseminated through guidance. Much guidance flounders on inertia as the perpetuation of routine practices can be a formidable obstacle to change. Equally there can be a tendency simply to reframe traditional practice so that it fits with the latest policy guideline (Burnett and Appleton 2004). Similarly it has been argued that professionals such as teachers bring to teaching a set of beliefs and understandings that are resistant to particular kinds of research evidence (Thomas 2004).

Guidance based on research evidence often has to compete with information and advice from familiar local sources which may be more trusted or perceived as more authoritative. Adopting an analytical, reflective approach that takes into account the latest research evidence with its qualified and possibly ambiguous messages becomes very constrained in these circumstances.

While a considerable amount of energy has gone into amassing evidence of what might be effective in criminal justice, there has been very little research into the most effective processes by which this evidence can be transmitted into the knowledge and skills deployed by practitioners.

The stance adopted here is to encourage a more systematic incorporation of social science evidence into the tacit or craft knowledge of practitioners rather than claiming that practice is little more than the application of formulaic guidance or recipes. If a particular kind of evidence is seen to be imposed on practitioners through official guidance as the only means of achieving effectiveness it is unlikely to be accepted. Rather the research evidence set in the framework of the same principles of effectiveness is being made available to add to the evidential storehouse of the youth justice practitioner. Some of the more vitriolic attacks on the perceived approach of the New Labour government's initiatives in youth justice see an imposition of a crude and ultimately ineffective 'What Works' approach.

Some critics of the 'What Works' movement come dangerously close to indulging in what Raynor (2004: 171–2) has dubbed the 'myth of nostalgia, the belief that *everything was better in the old days*, when practitioners' autonomy and "established methods" (NAPO 2002) provided all the guarantees of effectiveness that were needed'.

Reflective practice

Just as it is vital that all work with young people who offend should be subject to formal review processes, arguably so too must practitioners and managers evaluate their decision-making in a less formal and more introspective way. Reflective practice then is an essential part of developing an evidence-based approach.

Reflection is required in situations where the subject matter or material is unstructured or uncertain, and where there is no obvious solution or course of action. (Moon 1999)

Practitioners must learn how to frame the complex, ambiguous problems they are facing and interpret and modify their practice as a result. (Schon 1983)

Applying this in the context of evidence-based public health and the need to adopt very new approaches to medical education produced a different model of learning:

Paradigms in learning

Old	New
Knowing what you *should* know	Knowing what you *don't* know
Much learning 'complete' at the end of formal training	Able to question received wisdom
	Able to generate and refine a question and find, appraise, store and act on evidence to solve it
Apprenticeship, learning from accepted wisdom	
Finite amount of knowledge to be absorbed	Lifelong learner
	Complementing experience with knowledge from research
Intuition – very powerful	Problem-based learning
Dominated by knowledge from experience	
Knowledge-based learning	

Source: Gray, J., 2000: 94)

Evidence-based practice can therefore be understood in terms of a different approach to learning for practitioners and managers within youth justice with more emphasis on a process of continuous self-directed learning in working to prevent offending. This generates the need for significant information to inform the key processes of assessment, planning and intervention.

Figure 1.1 shows the cycle of activity that is required for a systematic approach to reflective practice to be adopted:

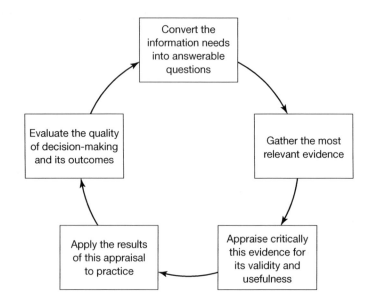

Figure 1.1 A systematic approach to reflective practice

Tilley has posed a series of relevant questions for policy makers, managers and practitioners to consider.

Some questions relating to evidence-based effective practice guidance:

1 **How is effective practice to be construed?**
● Is it to be defined by method?
● Is it to be defined by theory?
● Is it to be defined by specific measures or tactics?
● Is it to be consistent with specific values?

2 **What counts as research findings?**
● Must they be 'experimental'?
● Must they have internal and/or external validity?
● Must the research be independent?
● Must there have been peer review?

3 **What should be done where research findings appear to contradict one another?**
● Should only the best or most plausible findings be drawn on?
● Should the findings be aggregated in a meta-analysis to find net effects?

- Should the conclusion be that patterns really vary by place, time and subgroup?
- Should the conclusion be that the intervention differed in more or less subtle ways?

4 What should be done where there is a shortage of research findings to draw on?

- Should guidance remain silent?
- Should lack of evidence just be noted?
- Should evidence for the underlying theory behind the practice be described?

5 At what threshold of quality, consistency or volume of relevant research findings can policies or practices be described as good practice?

- Must research consistently indicate no unintended harm?
- Must research show consistent benefits, at least for a subset of intended subjects?
- How many studies or how many subjects are needed as a basis for establishing good practice?

6 How are research findings to be applied in effective practice?

- How is successful work replicated?
- How is successful work rolled out?
- Which areas of what was done in a successful project are to be represented as effective practice?

7 What should be included in effective practice?

- Should it include evidence used to identify the problem?
- Should it include methods used to analyse the problem?
- Should it include means by which the decisions were taken to put the measure in place?
- Should it include results?

8 How are research-based good practice guidance messages to be communicated?

- Should there be clear and specific injunctions about what to do?
- Should there be clear injunctions about what not to do?
- Should advice be given about what is promising?

- Should there be discursive advice on methods of approaching crime prevention, evidence about their track record to date, and factors to be taken into account in choosing among them?
- Should advice be pitched at specific problems or general issues?

9 **Are there aspects of good practice which lie beyond research findings?**

- Are there ideological issues that need to be mentioned?
- Are there tacit features of successful measures that need to be acknowledged?

(derived from Tilley 2006: 219, 220)

Conclusions

'What Works?' is a seductively simple approach to both policy making and practice. Its appeal lies in its promise to cut through value-laden arguments, to bind different professionals and agencies together and provide *the* treatment. While it has been argued that this is a simplistic approach, neither is it as apolitical as it purports to be.

It must be emphasised that the research findings are rather cautious and incremental in nature, and build on the evolving knowledge base. This is not always echoed in the language of policy makers. Application of these findings may result in modest but significant reductions in recidivism. The systematic implementation of evidence-based practice is designed to minimise risks of offending. It offers no guarantees of success, but aims to minimise the chances of failure.

It is salutary to remember that despite all the expenditure in recent years relatively little is known about *what* works, let alone *how* it works with young people who get drawn into the youth justice system.

It can be argued convincingly that work in youth justice is not always directly comparable to medicine in that a drug cannot simply be prescribed to achieve results when working with young people who offend. Despite this, it cannot be used as an excuse for not striving to develop practitioners who are qualified, research literate and evidence based.

If the foundations of empirical evidence are to be strengthened and built upon it will be essential that not only is a reflective, evidence-based approach to practice in youth justice developed but that crucially there is an evaluation culture within teams.

Summary

- 'What Works?' is a deceptively simple and apparently apolitical concept, but it is not value-free, and its applicability to youth justice has been contested. Very few interventions have been subject to the most rigorous of evaluations, and the evidence is better suited to indicating promising approaches rather than definitive prescriptions about exactly what works.

- There are inherent limitations in a simplistic 'What Works' approach, and complete reliance on RCTs and meta-analyses explains little about the mechanisms by which change occurs in an individual.

- Using a strict 'What Works' approach based on UK evidence alone means that most interventions with young people can at best be deemed promising rather than effective. Wider studies have indicated that modest but significant reductions in offending can be achieved through certain interventions.

- 'What Works' guidance of itself appears to be a relatively weak way of transmitting research messages in order to inform practitioners and has to compete with other influences.

- The exercise of professional judgement and discretion by practitioners through casework and supervision may be undervalued by an overemphasis on accredited programmes. The effect of individual practitioner discretion and skills on outcomes has had little research attention.

- The main findings of meta-analyses may provide a useful set of guidelines for managers and practitioners to design, develop and evaluate their interventions.

Further reading

Raynor, P. (2004b) 'Seven Ways to Misunderstand Evidence-Based Probation', in D. Smith (ed.) *Social Work and Evidence-Based Practice*. London: Jessica Kingsley Publishers.

Rutter, M., Giller, H. and Hagell, A. (1998) *Antisocial Behaviour by Young People*. Cambridge: Cambridge University Press.

Smith, D. (2006) 'Youth Crime and Justice: Research, Evaluation and "Evidence"', in B. Goldson and J. Muncie (eds) *Youth Crime and Justice*. London: Sage.

Part 1

2

Assessment, planning interventions and supervision

Systematic assessment is central to work in youth justice. The underpinning model for its main assessment tools – *Asset* and *Onset* – is actuarial in that it focuses largely on risk. That is not to say that Yot practitioners are not strongly advised to take protective factors into account when planning an intervention, although how far this always happens is debatable. Opinions vary about the reliability and validity of *Asset*. This chapter explores some of those issues. It also considers where *Asset* fits within the plethora of other assessment and planning systems that young people may be subject to. There are some critics who would question the whole actuarial approach to assessment on the basis that it focuses too heavily on the risks posed by a young person to society, i.e. it does little to help practitioners in supporting young people to overcome barriers to social inclusion they may be experiencing. The onus is on short-term planning of structured programmes that focus on the young person rather than on more fundamental change at a social level.

The evidence base for assessment, planning interventions and supervision

There is consistent evidence (Chapman and Hough 1998; McGuire 1995; Andrews 1995; Utting and Vennard 2000) to show that interventions are more likely to be effective in preventing offending if they are characterised by:

- appropriate targeting of services to meet assessed levels of risk and need;
- work that addresses a range of offending-related problems;
- agreed objectives that are identified and adhered to.

At the heart of this process is high-quality assessment. Systematic assessment is central to the design, delivery and evaluation of both structured rehabilitative programmes and other types of intervention (for example one-to-one work with a young person that is closely tailored to his/her particular needs and capacity

40

to respond). Assessment tools are designed to provide a common approach to the process of assessment. They can assist practitioners in planning their work, gathering appropriate and relevant information and analysing that information. This is intended to provide the basis for arriving at informed judgements and making decisions which are clearly rooted in assessment outcomes and transparent to young people, their parents/carers and professionals alike.

In the context of recent youth justice policy, assessment has been defined to focus upon the principles of effective practice in crime prevention and rehabilitation interventions. As Utting and Vennard (2000) explain, 'prevention and rehabilitation based on the "What Works" principles requires the adoption of dependable methods for analysing the risks that individuals will continue to commit crime, and for recognising the criminogenic needs that interventions should address'.

Three types of possible risks are given priority in youth justice:

- **Reoffending**: the likelihood that the young person will commit further offences.

- **Vulnerability**: the risk that the young person might be harmed in some way by his/her own acts or omissions, or the acts or omissions of others.

- **Serious harm to others**: the risk that the young person might inflict death or injury (either physical or psychological) which is life threatening and/or traumatic and from which recovery will be difficult, incomplete or impossible.

These risk categories are not mutually exclusive; young people may experience two or more of the priority risk areas when engaging in certain risky activity. For example, a young person engaged in a high-speed chase while taking and driving away a car may be putting themselves at risk of injury as well as others who may be out on the road.

Assessment of risk

Assessment of risk will usually be by way of the *Onset* or *Asset* core profile, supplemented by specialist assessments relating to mental health needs, substance misuse or sexual offending.

Onset is a referral and assessment framework that identifies if a young person would benefit from early intervention and determines the risk factors that should be reduced and the protective factors that should be enhanced in order to prevent him or her from offending. It is intended for use in all Youth Justice Board prevention programmes including:

- youth inclusion programmes (YIPs) and junior YIPs;

- youth inclusion and support panels (YISPs);

- safer schools partnerships (SSPs);

- individual support order (ISO) schemes.

Asset is the structured assessment tool used by Yots and the juvenile secure estate in England and Wales with all young people who have offended and come into contact with the criminal justice system. It examines a young person's offending and identifies the risk factors which may have contributed to it. It also highlights the young person's other needs and difficulties along with positive factors that need to be bolstered and supported. The information gathered from *Asset* informs decisions on interventions so that risks and needs may be addressed. *Asset* may be used when considering:

- bail;

- final warning;

- sentence;

- the content of programmes and interventions;

- identifying the risks of reoffending, vulnerability and serious harm to others;

- evaluating changes in needs and risk over time.

The *Onset* and *Asset* assessment tools have a theoretical underpinning based on examining the pattern of a young person's offending behaviour in the context of their 'life course' or 'developmental pathway' (Loeber and Le Blanc 1990; Sampson and Laub 1993). They facilitate the identification of significant life events – personal, social, situational – and ask practitioners to evaluate how they may interact to produce behaviours over time (Thornberry 1996). Such an analysis enables an evaluation of the different developmental pathways of young people who offend and those young people who do not, the differences between young people who offend and differences in the pattern of offending of an individual young person over time. *Asset*, particularly when applied over time, may provide practitioners with an insight into a young person's 'criminal career' (Farrington 1997). Practitioners may be able to gain an understanding of what are the critical features that contribute to the different stages of offending – onset, escalation, persistence, specialisation and desistance. Although offending may be widespread among young people (Graham and Bowling 1995), there are different patterns of criminal career. A distinction is made between 'adolescence-limited' and 'life-course persistent' anti social behaviour (Rutter *et al.* 1998; Moffitt 1993). Understanding and identifying these varying patterns is an important part of assessment and intervention.

With respect to serious harm to others, the *Onset* and *Asset* 'Risk of Serious Harm' (ROSH) form is intended to support practitioners in making professional judgements on the level of risk and the nature and intensity of interventions needed to meet it. With respect to vulnerability, the 'indicators of vulnerability' section of the assessment documentation allows the bringing together of relevant risk factors.

Arguably the primary purpose of assessing is to prepare a plan for intervention if found necessary. This plan could include:

- the risk factors to be targeted;

- the protective factors to be bolstered;

- the role of designated staff in the risk management plan;

- the role of staff in allied organisations in managing the risk; and

- the review arrangements for the plan.

Where risks posed by young people in the community are deemed to be high or very high, local inter-agency risk management may be required either through an individually negotiated plan or through the Multi-Agency Public Protection Plan Arrangements (MAPPA) structures. A vulnerability plan may be needed to focus on key issues such as risk of suicide, self-harm or physical/sexual abuse.

Risk factors

An assessment is likely to cover a wide range of issues, but within the context of youth justice, its primary focus is on risk factors relevant to offending behaviour. These are 'factors that increase the risk of occurrence of events such as the onset, frequency, persistence or duration of offending' (Farrington 1997). A greater number of risk factors appears to increase the likelihood of offending behaviour (Farrington 2002). Broadly speaking, these fall into four main categories:

1 Family factors e.g.

- Deprivation, particularly low income, poor housing and large family size;

- Conflict within the family;

- Ineffective supervision;

- Passive or condoning attitudes in relation to antisocial and criminal behaviour;

- A history of criminal behaviour from parents or siblings.

2 School factors e.g.

- Low attainment from primary school onwards, particularly with respect to literacy and numeracy;

- Lack of attachment to formal schooling;

- Organisational weaknesses in the school;

- Aggressive behaviour particularly bullying.

3 Community factors e.g.

- A lack of attachment to the neighbourhood;

- Ready availability of drugs;

- A disadvantaged area and neglected neighbourhood;

- High turnover of the local population.

4 Individual/peer factors e.g.

- Hyperactivity and impulsiveness;

- Attitudes sympathetic to offending;

- Substance misuse;

- Association with delinquent peer groups.

(See pp. 9–13 for more on risk factors).

An early age of onset of criminal behaviour has been shown to be associated with persistent and chronic offending (Farrington 1996). Early offending may itself produce reinforcing effects, which contribute to recidivism. Once involved in offending, a young person may be more likely to associate with other young people engaged in criminal behaviour. A high number of previous convictions, a history of committing more serious offences, and long periods of imprisonment have also been shown to be associated with recidivism (Cottle *et al.* 2001).

A placement away from (the parental) home may be associated with delinquency, perhaps because of the likelihood of associating with pro-criminal peers within a children's home or similar institutional environment (Moore and Arthur 1989), or the reduction of protective factors, such as disruption to school placements. In the UK, recent evidence suggests that young people 'looked after' by local authorities are disproportionately likely to commit offences resulting in a prison sentence (Social Exclusion Unit 2001).

The evidence regarding the impact of factors such as low income and poor housing is somewhat unclear. There is much evidence to show that young people from families experiencing these problems are more likely to be involved in offending than those from affluent backgrounds (Farrington 1992). However, the connection between these factors and offending may not be straightforward. The link between social disadvantage and offending behaviour is likely to be indirect and largely mediated through family stress and poor parenting. Nevertheless, this factor still forms part of the causal chain for antisocial behaviour, and provides a reasonable indicator of an increased risk of offending (Rutter *et al.* 1998).

From self-report data, Graham and Bowling (1995) identified low parental supervision as a key factor associated with the onset of offending. Having delinquent siblings was also strongly associated with offending for males, while nature/degree of attachment to family was significantly associated for females. The Dunedin study (Henry *et al.* 1996) highlighted poor parenting and adverse family situations as being associated with conduct problems persisting through childhood and into later life.

As well as being linked to early onset of offending, poor parental supervision has been shown to be associated with continuing involvement in crime (Wilson 1980). Young people from homes where parents behave aggressively are more likely to engage in violent behaviour themselves as adolescents (Farrington 1991). Clearer results have been demonstrated in relation to the link between juvenile recidivism and substance abuse and/or criminal behaviour by parents (Myner *et al.* 1998; Farrington 2000).

A history of physical or sexual abuse has been found to be associated with recidivism (Cottle *et al.* 2001). The 'family and personal relationships' section of *Asset* also includes questions relating to abuse and loss because of the increasing evidence of a link between these experiences and serious or violent offending by young people (Boswell 1996).

Non-attendance at school is an important factor in relation to starting offending (Graham and Bowling 1995). Young people performing poorly at school are more likely to start offending (Maguin and Loeber 1996). Low grades and dropping out of education are associated with offending (Simourd and Andrews 1994). Being excluded from school is also strongly associated with offending (Budd *et al.* 2005). A study of the effects of permanent exclusion from school on the offending behaviour of young people (Berridge *et al.* 2001) confirmed earlier research findings of persistent offending among a high proportion of those excluded. A history of receiving special educational provision was also identified by Cottle *et al.* (2001) as a predictor of recidivism.

This risk factor has particular implications for young African-Caribbean boys. Ofsted and the then Department for Education and Employment (Barn 2001) showed that they are four to six times more likely to be excluded than their white counterparts. At least some of this difference may be linked to teachers' responses to this group of young people. Therefore, attempts to address educational requirements in this group would need to be particularly sensitive to their experience of education to date, and would need to access resources directed at that experience.

'Children who grow up in economically deprived areas, with poor living conditions and high rates of unemployment, are at increased risk of involvement in crime' (Communities that Care 2001). Various other factors in neighbourhood and community life appear to be relevant to the development and persistence of offending behaviour: levels of disorganisation and neglect (Communities that Care 2001), availability of drugs and weapons (Rutter *et al.* 1998) and high levels of turnover among residents (Hope 1996).

Association with other young people who are involved in offending or antisocial behaviour is a key factor for the onset of offending (Graham and Bowling 1995; Budd *et al.* 2005), particularly for those who begin offending or engaging in antisocial behaviour during later adolescence (Fergusson *et al.* 1996). Delinquent peers and poor use of leisure time have been associated with recidivism (Cottle *et al.* 2001). Even though there are selection effects by which 'antisocial individuals tend to choose friends who are similarly antisocial', the peer group still influences the likelihood of a young person persisting with or desisting from antisocial behaviour (Rutter *et al.* 1998).

While many of the same risk factors may influence the onset of substance use and antisocial behaviour, there are additional ways in which these two types of behaviour influence each other (Rutter *et al.* 1998). Cottle *et al.* (2001) suggested that substance abuse – rather than substance use – is associated with recidivism. Associations between drug abuse and criminal behaviour are most likely to occur as a result of young people stealing to fund an addiction, or as 'an element of a deviant lifestyle in which antisocial behaviour is part of the ethos and provides some of the excitement' (Rutter *et al.* 1998). The prevalence of drug use in a cohort of young people at risk of offending or reoffending is likely to be high (Hammersley *et al.* 2003).

Rutter *et al.* (1998) summarised recent research concerning possible genetic and biological influences on antisocial behaviour (for example, the effects of toxins, nutrients and levels of serotonin). The influence of diet is another area receiving increasing attention (Peplow 2002). While many of these findings are still tentative, the impact of 'hyperactivity' on offending behaviour has been established (Loeber *et al.* 1993), although the attribution of 'hyperactivity' as a label may cover a wide range of behaviours. There is evidence that many of those who display antisocial behaviour also show emotional disturbance and, in particular, that depression (and increased risk of suicide) often accompanies such behaviour (Myner *et al.* 1998). A 'history of non-severe pathology' (defined as experiences of stress and anxiety) in young people who offend has been found to be associated with recidivism (Cottle *et al.* 2001).

Data from the Cambridge study suggested that poor reasoning abilities contribute to criminal behaviour by limiting young people's ability to understand the consequences of their actions (Farrington 1996). Biased cognitive processing, such as misinterpreting social cues, is another factor shown to be associated with offending behaviour (Dodge and Schwartz 1997).

Studies have shown a link between high impulsiveness and criminal behaviour. Difficulty in delaying gratification when aged 12 appears to be (for boys) associated with antisocial behaviour (Krueger *et al.* 1996). Aggressiveness is another trait associated with offending behaviour (Rutter *et al.* 1998). Known school bullies have been found to be significantly more likely to be convicted of criminal offences in adolescence and early adulthood (Olweus 1991).

Young people who 'feel excluded from the mainstream and do not acknowledge responsibilities towards other people' may be at greater risk of involvement in offending behaviour (Communities that Care 2001). Those who have attitudes condoning criminal activity (and drug abuse) are more likely to get involved in such activities (Jessor and Jessor 1977). The early years of secondary school appear to be a significant turning point when young people are most likely to begin to adopt pro-criminal attitudes (Communities that Care 2001).

Protective factors and desistance from crime

The absence of risk factors may help to protect a young person from involvement in antisocial and criminal behaviour, but research has also identified other 'protective factors', which can reduce the negative impact of risk factors. These protective factors can help to explain differences in the frequency or seriousness of offending among young people exposed to similar risks (Communities that Care 2001).

There is obviously an overlap between tackling risk factors and encouraging protective developments. For example, dealing with school exclusion would both remove a risk factor and expose the young person to protective influences as a result of returning to the school community.

The number of studies focusing specifically on the concept of 'resilience' in the context of youth justice is limited. Resilience in general terms has been defined as 'positive adaptation in the face of severe adversities' (Newman 2004). Some commentators (Luther 2003) stress that resilience is a 'process' rather than an innate character trait and that it is not limitless. In situations where adversity is persistent, extreme and unmitigated a young person is unlikely to be resilient (Cicchetti and Rogosch 1997; Runyan et al. 1998). Some factors have been identified which may contribute to a young person's resilience, such as 'personal qualities that elicit positive responses from other people' (Rutter et al. 1998). Other components identified so far include a stable relationship with at least one family member (Rutter 1997), and good experiences at school and experiences that open up new opportunities or provide turning points (Bandura 1995; Farrington 2002). The ability to plan ahead also appears to contribute to a lower risk of antisocial behaviour (Quinton et al. 1993). In addition, the attitudes, expectations and standards of parents, teachers and communities may help to protect young people from risk (Catalano and Hawkins 1996).

A number of other studies have focused specifically on factors relating to stopping offending, although the findings of the literature on desistance are somewhat less clear than that for onset or persistence of offending. Gaining employment has been found to be associated with desistance in some studies (Mischkowitz 1994) but not others (Rand 1987) although it should be noted that these studies focused on adults. Graham and Bowling (1995) found differences in desistance factors between males and females. Factors such as educational achievement, avoiding heavy drinking or using drugs, and avoiding the influence of other young people were associated with desistance for males. For females, the transition to adulthood appeared more important, for example completing education or forming stable relationships.

UNIVERSITY OF WINCHESTER
LIBRARY

47

Desistance factors are difficult to analyse in relation to the age of young people in the Youth Justice System (10–17), because many of the suggested factors (such as marriage or gaining employment) are not necessarily appropriate at this stage in life. Perhaps of the greatest practical relevance for youth justice staff are some of the other identified desistance factors, such as developing a sense of self-efficacy (Bandura 1995) and 'finding a sense of direction and meaning in life, realising the consequences of one's actions on others and learning that crime does not pay' (Graham and Bowling 1995) (see p. 32).

Validity and reliability of Asset

Following the introduction of *Asset*, the Youth Justice Board funded a detailed research study into the validity and reliability of its use. Two evaluations of the use of *Asset* in 39 Yots examined the predictive validity and reliability of the assessment after 12 months (Baker *et al.* 2002) and 24 months (Baker *et al.* 2005). The research team reported that *Asset* had a predictive accuracy of 67 per cent and conclude:

> The results of the study provide further support for the ... Youth Justice Board strategy of putting Asset at the centre of Yot practice. The data suggest that practitioners and managers can have confidence in using Asset as an indicator of risk of reoffending and also therefore of the level and intensiveness of intervention required to address offending behaviour. (2005: 7).

Criticism of Asset

Not all commentators would concur that a 67 per cent rate of predictive accuracy indicates that *Asset* is a robust tool, or indeed that such confidence in using *Asset* as an indicator of risk of reoffending, or the level and intensiveness of an intervention, is justified. Tossing a coin has a predictive accuracy of 50 per cent. Such an outturn still leaves a very high rate of 'false positives' and 'false negatives' (Smith 2006). The question also remains about what happens to the 33 per cent of young people for whom the outcomes of *Asset* profiling have been neither valid or reliable. Critics of *Asset* (e.g. Annison 2005) point to:

- the subjective components within the framework;
- the emphasis on negative risk factors over positive protective factors;
- poor and inconsistent completion rates by practitioners;
- evidence of duplicating (cloning) past assessments of the young person where an updated reassessment is required.

More fundamentally, several commentators have questioned the actuarial approach to assessment, which is embedded in the *Asset* framework (Smith 2006; Muncie 2000; Pitts 2001b; Haines and Drakeford 1998). They argue that the actuarial approach may:

- identify and impact upon risks associated with the young person without necessarily addressing their needs;

- stereotype and demonise young people, thereby facilitating a culture of control;

- dispose with traditional concerns for justice, fairness and due process in the interest of eradicating potential threats;

- promote an oversimplified technical fix to the complex social reality that is adolescent antisocial behaviour.

> Ultimately actuarial principles and methods are incompatible with aspirations towards a Youth Justice System which is rooted in the complex dynamics and systemic inequalities which characterise many young people's lives. (Smith 2006: 106)

Asset's role in informing planning also appears underdeveloped. Based on a sample of plans drawn from Yots, Baker *et al.* (2005) concluded that:

- plans often did not reflect the outcome of assessments. For example, issues identified in *Asset* as being associated with a high risk of reoffending were not always incorporated into intervention plan targets;

- there appeared a tendency to create standard plans, which resulted in targets being set for areas that were not identified in *Asset* as being closely associated with reoffending;

- interventions plans often used 'Yot jargon' and the language would have been difficult for most young people to understand.

Likewise, at a practice level, the first annual report of the joint Yot Inspectorate (HM Inspectorate of Probation 2004) reported on some practitioner aversion to *Asset* and a lack of engagement of children and young people in the process in one quarter of observed instances. The report comments:

> Asset if completed properly provides a useful framework to inform work with the child or young person. Its potential has still, in our view, to be fully realised by the Yots as it could not only inform the work with the child or young person, but also if aggregated, provide much useful management information. We found a few instances where Yots were beginning to adopt this approach ... (2004: 18).

The principles of effective practice and assessment, planning interventions and supervision

Risk classification

At the end of each section on risk factors in *Onset* and *Asset*, practitioners are asked to rate the extent to which they think the issue is associated with the likelihood of further offending (*Asset*) or serious antisocial behaviour (*Onset*) by the young person. This assessment is not of the extent to which the practitioner believes that the risk factor is causing difficulties in the life of the young person in general, rather it is intended to be specifically focused on the risk factor in relation to offending/antisocial behaviour and the link between current risk and likely future behaviour. The following considerations might help a practitioner to establish the level of risk:

- Might this risk factor have been linked to past challenging behaviour? If 'yes', do you think the risk factor is more, less or equally significant now?

- Does there appear to be a direct or indirect link between the risk factor and the young person's behaviour?

- Does the risk factor always appear relevant to the young person's offending or serious antisocial behaviour, or only on certain occasions?

- Is the effect on future offending behaviour likely to be immediate or over a longer period?

- Does the risk factor appear to be strong enough with offending by itself, or is it only likely to contribute to offending behaviour when specific other conditions exist?

These issues may be further clarified by gathering the young person's perspective on risks (and protective factors). This is facilitated by the 'What Do You Think?' (*Asset*) and 'Over to You!' (*Onset*) documentation, which enables young people to record their views and contribute to the assessment process.

In each section, examples are given to illustrate high and low ratings. It may be beneficial for practitioners to compare assessments and the ratings that were given in order to help to create a level of local and individual consistency in assessments (see Baker *et al.* 2005 for an example of this).

The level of intervention should be related to the risk of reoffending, informed by the seriousness of the offence committed by the young person and his/her *Asset* assessment scores. This risk evaluation is intended to be adjusted up or down, where necessary, by an evaluation of the risk of harm to others and the risk of vulnerability.

HIGH	Level 7 HELP/CHANGE + ENSURE COMPLIANCE/ REPAIR HARM	Level 8 CONTROLS + HELP/CHANGE + ENSURE COMPLIANCE/ REPAIR HARM	Level 9 CONTROLS + HELP/CHANGE + ENSURE COMPLIANCE/ REPAIR HARM
MEDIUM	Level 4 ENSURE COMPLIANCE/ REPAIR HARM	Level 5 HELP/CHANGE + ENSURE COMPLIANCE/ REPAIR HARM	Level 6 CONTROLS + HELP/CHANGE + ENSURE COMPLIANCE/ REPAIR HARM
LOW	Level 1 ENSURE COMPLIANCE/ REPAIR HARM	Level 2 ENSURE COMPLIANCE/ REPAIR HARM	Level 3 HELP/CHANGE + ENSURE COMPLIANCE/ REPAIR HARM
	Low (*Asset* score 0–15)	Medium (*Asset* score 16–30)	High (*Asset* score 31–48)

Offence seriousness (using Youth Court Bench Back guidelines)

Figure 2.1 Indicators of level matrix

The evaluation of the level of risk can inform:

- which disposal is relevant in the case;
- the length of order required;
- any additional controls that may need to be imposed to ensure compliance with the order.*

The circumstances in which the probability of risk materialises may change rapidly. Reflection, review and reassessment of risk are thus important components of risk management. This may mean that a risk management plan developed and implemented by practitioners in the first instance may quickly be stood down (to be reassessed and reactivated should the circumstances giving rise to risk re-emerge). Alternatively, risks initially managed within the context of youth justice may be more appropriately managed by partner agencies in the medium to longer term (e.g. by social workers with respect to looked-after children).

*These controls may include tagging, tracking, voice verification, residence requirements, prohibited activities, exclusion requirements and curfew conditions.

A priority context for a change of circumstances which may give rise to risk is where a young person moves from the community into the secure estate and vice versa. An assessment of vulnerability is intended to be a routine component of case planning when a young person enters custody (via remand or sentence) and can be communicated between community-based practitioners and those within the secure estate prior to entry. (Young people entering custody without documentation from the community may be placed on a vulnerability alert until an appropriate assessment is made and/or the documentation arrives.)

An assessment of harm to others may need to be undertaken where the young person is:

- offending persistently;

- charged with a serious specified offence under the Criminal Justice Act 2003;

- subject to a placement in the secure estate, which may contain victims of their offending.

It is a reasonable inference from this principle that the assessment of young people should be linked to a plan for working with them to reduce their likelihood of reoffending. Young people benefit most from interventions that are relevant to their assessed level of need and risk (Andrews and Bonta 1994; McGuire 1995).

Throughout interventions, practitioners may need to monitor changes in young people's levels of risk of reoffending, causing serious harm and vulnerability. Appropriate measures may need to be put in place to manage this process, for example if there is a significant increase in the likelihood of a young person committing a particularly grave offence.

See 'Risk classification' Chapter 1 (p. 22) for more on the limitations of *Asset* as an actuarial approach to the assessment of need in the context of young people who offend.

Criminogenic need

Asset is an interactional tool, which is concerned with the strength of the links between risk/needs and offending behaviour, and with the links among different risks/needs. For example, acquisitive offending behaviour in a particular young person may be very strongly and directly influenced by a peer group, but the choice of peer group may be influenced for that young person by school exclusion. The school exclusion may not in itself lead directly to the offending for this young person, but is indirectly having a very significant effect. In turn, the offending peer group might be encouraging patterns of thinking and behaviour that add to the difficulty of reintegrating into the school community.

A thorough assessment also identifies practical matters that need to be considered when planning interventions (e.g. health problems, transport needs, literacy difficulties). These factors may not be directly related to the causes of young people's offending behaviour, but may need to be addressed or managed in order to give the young people a reasonable chance of completing an order successfully.

Analysis also often identifies issues which are not directly linked to young people's criminal behaviour but which, if not addressed, may prevent effective offending-related work from being undertaken. These issues could include the need for additional support with emotional, social and psychological difficulties.

Assessment, therefore, needs to gather information about individual risk factors, but to do so in a way that is also alert to connections, interrelationships and the strength of the links with offending behaviour.

Responsivity

In the first instance, the principle of responsivity can be applied to the assessment process itself. Young people are unlikely to respond positively to assessment procedures that put them under pressure to perform or when they feel they are being tested in some way. This has implications for the way in which the purposes of assessments are explained to a young person, in particular in terms of explaining the benefits for them and the purposes the assessment outcomes will serve for what is to come. It is clear that in the juvenile secure estate, where young people are subject to a number of assessments on entry to custody, that they do not always know what these are for and may not see the link between these and the programmes of education, training and treatment that follow (ECOTEC 2001a).

Interventions are more likely to engage young people if they have relevance to their lives and employ methods that will motivate and interest them. Interventions are also more likely to be successful if they are delivered in ways that help young people to develop a broader range of learning strategies and are responsive to their capacity to participate (Andrews *et al.* 1990; McGuire 1995). Materials and methods should reflect the different stages of development and maturity of the young people concerned, their gender and/or sexuality, and should take account of their community, ethnic and cultural backgrounds.

Although well-designed, well-delivered interventions are critical to effective supervision, successful outcomes also depend on young people's active participation and willingness to change. The best results are achieved when young people are motivated to take up and engage with interventions (Burnett and Appleton 2002). Practitioners are more likely to actively involve and engage young people if they:

- are aware of young people's perceptions;
- communicate in a way that is appropriate to young people;

- have clear values and purpose;

- give consistent feedback;

- are solution-focused and encourage small steps towards change;

- model problem-solving;

- are open, active, optimistic and realistic.
  (see p. 32)

Effective supervision with adults appears to be that which offers practical and emotional support, together with an understanding of offending, through awareness of individuals' needs and perspectives (Beaumont and Mistry 1996). There is no equivalent research on effective supervision of young people specifically. Addressing concerns which may be indirectly linked to young people's offending behaviour can increase participation and responsivity. For example, if there is a practical obstacle to taking part in an intervention, such as lack of transport, it is important to deal with this problem so that the intervention can take place.

Cognitive-behavioural interventions require young people and others around them to make changes in order to behave differently, in particular with regard to offending. Effective change requires active participation by young people, so they should be fully involved in the assessment and planning processes, jointly identifying problem areas in their lives and how to overcome them (Chapman 2000). In many respects, the responsivity principle as it relates to assessment, planning interventions and supervision implies that the process must be responsive to a young person's needs, whilst enabling them to develop new strategies for responding to situations; in other words to change their behaviours. Drawn from the field of addiction, the cycle of change (Miller and Rollnick 1991) is a widely used and potentially helpful model for assessing a young person's state of readiness to change. This model can be used to help make judgements about an individual's level of motivation, and about the most appropriate interventions to develop and sustain that motivation.

The model suggests that change is a process and, because it is a cyclical model, provides a reminder that progress is always possible. It is based on the premise that practitioners cannot change young people but they can provide them with opportunities that will help them to make changes in their lives for themselves. Practitioners need to be realistic about an individual's attitude to change at a given time and in given circumstances but they should avoid labelling individuals as permanently unmotivated and therefore incapable of change because of past failures or current ambivalence.

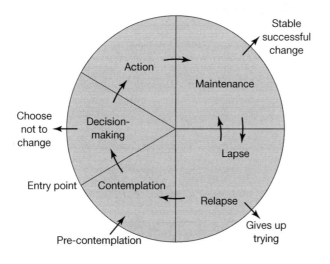

Figure 2.2 The cycle of change
Source: Miller and Rollnick (1991)

The various stages of the cycle can be described as follows:

- **Pre-contemplation** – when individuals do not recognise the need for change. For example, they may see their offending as justifiable, inevitable or the only course of action open to them.

- **Contemplation** – when individuals are ambivalent about change. They may see some of the negatives of their current behaviours and be aware of other more positive alternatives, but be uncertain about their ability to change. One type of example might be young people who are tired of coming up against the criminal justice system, want to move on in life, but fear losing their current peers and group status if they cease offending. Another example might be young people who are unsure whether they have the skills they need to find employment or establish new and more positive friendships.

- **Decision-making** – the process of contemplation is uncomfortable psychologically. People tend to be unable to remain at this stage indefinitely and so move on to decision-making instead.

- **Action** – some young people will be at the point of taking positive action towards change. They may be ready to set goals and take concrete steps towards change, acting on the help given them.

- **Maintenance** – some will already have changed their lifestyle at the outset of involvement in an intervention or during the course of supervision. This change needs to be maintained, so resources and support should still be directed at this group.

55

- **Lapse and relapse** – other young people will revert to problematic behaviour. This may be a further offence or a breach in compliance during a period of genuine and significant reduction in offending behaviour and/or sustained positive attitudes (a lapse). Alternatively, it may be a rejection of the process of change and a reversion to unhelpful patterns of behaviour and thinking (a relapse).

The cycle of change brings together the tasks of assessment, planning, intervention and review. As the model's premise is that change is a process, it serves as a reminder of the importance of continuing assessment and of amending intervention plans to adapt to changes in young people's attitudes, circumstances or levels of motivation. It also highlights the importance of preparing for change, supporting individuals through change, and continuing to provide support beyond the initial period.

The model can be used to assist in identifying how best to target efforts to help individual young people to move through the cycle into stable, secure change. At the 'contemplation' stage, for example, the concept of the 'decisional balance' is very helpful. This is the balance between the factors that motivate young people to change and the factors that demotivate. It may also be helpful to think of this in terms of 'cost–benefit' analysis: what are the benefits for young people in changing their patterns of behaviour and how do these compare with the perceived costs of such a change? The task is to support those factors that tend to support change, and to minimise those factors which militate against it. To achieve this, a clear assessment of the factors on each side of the balance is required.

Further round the cycle, in 'decision-making', the task is to judge whether a young person is ready to make some decisions about change. Practitioners also need to be on the alert for those young people who, perhaps because of an environmental change, have made a decision not to change. These individuals have moved out of the cycle of change and back into pre-contemplation.

A review of progress during the course of an intervention may reveal difficulties at the 'maintenance' stage. Young people may face pressures, which militate against the change being maintained. These pressures may come from their own deep-seated beliefs or habits of thought, or from their circumstances. Situational changes may exert very significant pressure on young people to resume offending behaviour ('lapse/relapse').

Judgements about the above issues should inform the supervision process. For young people at the early stages of the cycle of change, the interventions provided should maximise their chances of beginning the process of contemplation. At the same time, it is important to be realistic and not to place young people who are at this early stage into programmes which require some degree of commitment to the process of change.

In other cases, planned interventions may need to be altered if lapse or relapse occurs and, more generally, if young people move to a different point in the cycle. As well as assessing young people, therefore, it is important to assess the services being provided and judge whether they are appropriate to individual young people's current place on the cycle of change.

Community based

One of the key considerations when planning interventions is ensuring that whatever is arranged keeps young people attached to their communities and helps them to engage with them more effectively. One of the potential difficulties with this is that for those young people most at risk, the communities themselves may be operating in all sorts of ways that isolate them from the mainstream and where certain sorts of antisocial, pro-criminal behaviours are the norm. This begs a question as to how far learning can take place that will develop pro-social behaviours. Alternatively, young people may be so excluded from their communities that attempts to support their re-engagements are hindered by considerable social and structural barriers.

Some critics of the current youth justice system have criticised the design of most interventions because they place too great a responsibility on individual young people and do little to change the broader issues which have led to the social exclusion of young people at risk of offending and reoffending (Pitts 2001b; Muncie 2001). A number of studies have shown that where young people have been exposed to relatively high levels of social exclusion, interventions did little to provide them with the support they needed in order to gain stable accommodation or sustain their attachment to education, training and employment (both indicators of social inclusion) (Gray *et al.* 2003; Dignan 2000; Newburn *et al.* 2002). Gray (2005a) argues that to maximise effectiveness, those planning interventions should take more account of the structural and practical barriers to a young person's social inclusion, enabling them to overcome these. In this sense, a truly community-based intervention would take the wider social and economic circumstances into account when deciding on the best way to build the resilience of a young person in managing their own environment positively.

Gray (2005a) goes further to argue that the 'managerialist imperatives' of meeting Youth Justice Board targets and national standards has meant that the opportunities provided by Yots for accessing the range of expertise and resources required to make changes to the social context of offending has not been maximised. The resulting emphasis, she argues, has therefore been on providing structured, time-limited, correctional programmes which focus on behaviour change by individual young people. The extent to which these two aspects of practice are polarised is debatable, although it is understandable that young practitioners may not feel empowered or indeed able to challenge the fabric of a young person's community even if they wanted to. In addition, there is little in the way of hard evidence of effective practice in achieving the level of social change that this implies, while there would appear to be more to hold on to with regard to working with individual young people.

The community base principle would also suggest that, where appropriate, young people's parents/carers should also be involved in this process of identifying problems and solutions so they can provide informed support during any intervention. In some instances they themselves may need to engage in direct intervention to help meet the needs of the young person (e.g. engaging in a parenting programme).

Intervention modality

Asset and *Onset* are multi-modal in the sense that they ask a number of questions across a range of important domains. The resulting plan ought, therefore, to be multi-modal, responding to the areas of risks and protection identified through the process of assessment.

The risk and protective factors identified through *Asset* and *Onset* also overlap and interact with each other. These interactions present a challenge for practitioners in regard to understanding causality and providing explanations for offending behaviour. It is not the number of risk or protective factors that determines the nature of an intervention, but rather the way in which they interact, reinforce or mitigate each other. An eventual intervention plan would need to take into account those interrelationships in deciding how to target and sequence interventions.

Effective assessment and planning should lead to young people being referred to appropriate interventions designed to prevent further offending and to address the identified risks and needs (Chapman and Hough 1998; Underdown 1998). Inappropriate targeting can be detrimental to individual young people, and reduces the overall effectiveness of intervention work with young people who offend.

This principle applies to the full range of interventions available for young people in community and secure settings: offending behaviour initiatives; personal development; education and training; mentoring; work with families; restorative work; drug and alcohol awareness; health advice; and artistic, dramatic or sporting activities.

Programme integrity

Aside from the issues of problems in participation, co-operation and engagement of the young person (or their parent/carer) in programme implementation, practitioners should be alert to issues of programme integrity (McGuire 2000); did the planned intervention get delivered, were there problems in staffing a programme, were sessions cancelled or otherwise interrupted? Flaws in programme integrity have diluted their potential impact (Pawson and Tilley 1997; Feilzer *et al.* 2004). Problems in this regard should be fed back to strategic managers for their action at an organisational level.

Implementing interventions successfully requires committed and effective management, trained staff who are skilled in pro-social modelling, sufficient resources for continuity, and in-built evaluation and feedback systems (Raynor 2002; McIvor 1990). Interventions are also more likely to be successful if the stated aims are linked to the methods used (Hollin 1995).

Partnership agencies can provide specialist expertise or facilities which may not otherwise be available within a team or unit. In such cases the role of practitioners may be to arrange, co-ordinate and monitor service delivery. It is likely that practitioners who make frequent contact with the providers and the young people will be more able to ensure that interventions are being delivered as specified in the intervention plan, and that young people are attending as required. Monitoring allows practitioners to respond effectively to changes in young people's needs by amending the delivery of services as appropriate (Chapman and Hough 1998).

The findings from Baker *et al.* (2005) (that changes in *Asset* score as a result of an intervention reflect changes in reoffending rates) has an important message for strategic and operational managers of youth justice services. Aggregated *Asset* scores tracked over time may provide the foundation for an evaluation of what programmes, or components of programmes, work. Aggregation of the findings from reviews and case closures provides vital information for the evaluation of the performance of youth justice agencies. Monitoring at a strategic level facilitates:

- building evidence as to which interventions are effective;
- improving the quality of programme interventions;
- providing feedback to practitioners on their impact;
- driving up programme integrity to deliver effective outcomes.

There is little evidence to date, however, that this data is being routinely used by Yot managers, governors in the secure estate or the Youth Justice Board itself to inform planning priorities or service developments.

The final review is very important if cases are to be closed in a positive way. It is a chance for young people to express their views on the work that has been done, and for successes (even small ones) to be celebrated and encouraged for continuation in the future. Changes in ratings are a means of assessing the success of intervention programmes and gauging the progress made by each young person since he/she began the programme. It may be that a young person's circumstances change for the worse during the course of an intervention, leading to ratings increasing rather than decreasing. Alternatively, simply knowing the young person better as a result of programme engagement may alter the scoring, reflecting an assessor's greater understanding of the dimensions of risk and need.

Dosage

The scoring of *Asset* is important with regard to dosage. Clearly, higher scores would indicate that a more intensive intervention might be required than for those areas with lower scores.

One of the key distinctions in terms of dosage is that between what has been arranged for a young person and what they actually receive as part of an intervention. This would imply the need for careful monitoring of attendance as part of the supervision programme. One of the real challenges for practitioners supporting young people through the change process is the high rates of attrition experienced by some projects. The tension and the challenge for practitioners is how to ensure the intensity and duration of a programme is sufficient whilst keeping a young person motivated enough to participate fully and to maintain their attachment to it.

Although dosage is a relatively straightforward principle, relatively little is understood about the actual volume of interventions received by young people who offend, including the amount of individual supervision received (see Chapter 1, p. 26).

The challenges for practice

Assessment can mean very different things to the professionals that work in and around the youth justice arena. In educational terms, for example, assessment is often associated entirely with academic attainment whereas in social work it would be linked to the welfare of a young person and their risk of harm. This represents a significant challenge to practitioners working across agencies and organisations in relation to understanding the outcomes of different assessment systems. The challenges facing practitioners who are attempting to assess need and plan interventions accordingly is explored further in Chapter 1, pp. 9 and 32).

The increasing range of interventions now offered by a variety of service providers (including restorative justice, mentoring, structured programmes and multi-modal interventions such as ISSP) present both an opportunity and a challenge. Differences in the intensity, length, structure and aims of interventions mean that careful decisions must be made about allocating young people to the interventions that are most suitable for them.

While *Onset* and *Asset* are the principal assessment tools they may also act as a gateway process for the identification of:

- broader welfare needs of young people (e.g. social care, education, health);

- the need for specialist assessments and services to meet particular needs (e.g. mental health, substance misuse, sexual abuse).

The challenges for practice here are twofold. Firstly, there is a proliferation of assessment systems, which a young person with multiple adversities can almost simultaneously become subject to. Secondly, the nature and purpose of assessment varies significantly between professions.

Given that these young people frequently cross the agency boundaries of health, social care, criminal justice and education, they can be subject to a barrage of multiple, uncoordinated assessments. Unsurprisingly, the result is considerable duplication of effort, and substantial gaps in the professional knowledge of the learning and other important needs of these young people who are socially excluded.

Each new initiative tends to bring with it a new assessment, planning and review system for practitioners and young people and their parents/carers to participate in. Although the Connexions Service initially promised that it would 'seek to develop a common assessment tool' (DfEE 2000: 43) it ended up developing its own assessment, planning and review system (APIR) so that practitioners and young people had yet another such bureaucratic system to contend with.

Reflecting on the continued failure to gather timely and accurate information in the youth justice system (particularly that relating to education) through assessment, the Audit Commission (2004: 98) recommended that the Government, 'in developing one overall assessment tool for children at risk … should consider having a common core of questions that follow a child, supplemented by specialist sections for different agencies'. This was intended to influence the implementation of the consultation paper Every Child Matters, which recommended the development of a common assessment instrument for all agencies dealing with children and young people at risk. The Audit Commission report recognised that it will prove extremely difficult if not impossible to agree on a common format for all relevant agencies and professionals and to discard all existing procedures.

In fact, the problems around assessment may be far more fundamental than simply improved document design, administrative process and managerial will. Assessment processes lie at the very heart of each profession's practice. Consequently, each assessment process is guarded, as to abandon it may lead to a breach in distinctiveness of each professional grouping and may be perceived by some as a threat to identity and status.

Given the professional cultural value of each assessment process, it is entirely predictable that a common approach that relies heavily on exhortation and goodwill will not be successful. An approach that is too discretionary may be sidelined, or worse will become yet another layer of information gathering and create further transmission problems.

Summary

- Systematic assessment is central to the design, delivery and evaluation of both structured rehabilitative programmes and other types of intervention.

- Assessment is an important opportunity to identify risks that might relate to a young person and a management strategy that may be employed to meet those risks. It may also be useful in identifying protective factors that can reduce the negative impact of risk factors.

- An assessment is likely to cover a wide range of issues, but within the context of youth justice, its primary focus is on risk factors relevant to offending behaviour. A greater number of risk factors appears to increase the likelihood of offending behaviour.

- The actuarial approach to assessment is criticised for its focus on risks rather than needs, its potential for stereotyping and demonising young people who offend and an oversimplification which places the onus of responsibility on young people rather than wider social contexts.

- The validity and reliability of *Asset* as an indicator of risk of reoffending or the level and intensiveness of an intervention is questioned by some commentators.

Further reading

Annison, J. (2005) 'Risk and protection,' in Bateman, T. and Pitts, J. (eds) *The RHP Companion to Youth Justice.* Lyme Regis: Russell House Publishing Ltd.

Baker, K., Jones, S., Merrington, S. and Roberts, C. (2005) *Further Development of ASSET.* London: Youth Justice Board.

Communities that Care (2001) *Risk and Protective Factors for Youth Crime – Prevalence, Salience and Reduction.* Report for the Youth Justice Board for England and Wales. London: Youth Justice Board.

Education, training and employment

The evidence base for education, training and employment

Detachment from education, training and employment is a significant risk factor in relation to offending behaviour. There is no single causal relationship between the two and the relationship between them is a complex one that cannot be defined in simplistic terms. The key challenge for managers and practitioners working with young people in the youth justice system is how to support young people in sustaining any attachment they have to an educational setting and how to help them to become reattached where this has broken down completely.

This chapter outlines some of the key issues with regard to young people at risk of offending or reoffending and education and employment. It highlights many of the systemic difficulties associated with detachment, particularly where young people have individual needs that impact on their capacity to learn at the same rate and in the same ways as other young people around them.

The scale of detachment

Detachment from mainstream education appears to be extensive among young people in the youth justice system. Detachment here is taken to occur through exclusion (permanent, fixed-term, and informal including not being on a school roll), non-attendance (authorised and unauthorised) and the statementing process for special educational needs (particularly for emotional and behavioural difficulties) and potentially culminates in non-participation post-16 (Not in Education, Employment or Training, or Status Zero).

Clearly those young people who have no educational, training or employment provision arranged for them at all can be deemed to be detached, and arguably, so too are those in segregated provision while those on part-time programmes with mainstream schools are at least partly detached. On these definitions the great majority of those entering and leaving custody are detached from mainstream education with between one third and a half having no provision at all (ECOTEC 2001a).

The most recent and most extensive survey (it collected information on 5,568 young people) of the scale of detachment amongst young people in the youth justice system found that:

- the Yots in the sample are struggling with very serious access issues to full-time education, training and employment;

- under half of the young people in the sample may be in full-time provision at any point in time;

- those young people who are older, have been in the care system, have literacy or numeracy difficulties, have previous convictions and have more serious disposals are all significantly less likely to have full-time education, training and employment provision arranged for them;

- only around half of those in the sample of statutory school age appear to have full-time education arranged for them. This is a particularly serious issue for those in their final year of compulsory schooling;

- dubious practices by some schools, coupled with drift and a lack of alternative educational capacity by LEAs were revealed in the census;

- the quarterly percentage in education, training and employment figures reported to the Youth Justice Board were significantly higher than the percentages obtained in the census for all Yots in the sample;

- monitoring of the education and training of those young people in the custodial phase of a DTO appears to be relatively weak by some Yot staff (Youth Justice Board 2006c).

Taking account of non-attendance as few as 35 per cent of young people in the youth justice system may actually be in full-time education, training or employment on a given day. Delay and drift appear to be relatively commonplace and practitioners highlighted cases where young people had received no education for several years, and the negative effects on motivation of part-time provision.

These findings are consistent with other surveys of young people in the youth justice system. For example, out of 2,211 young people engaged in the youth inclusion programme almost one third (695) were not enrolled at a school (Youth Justice Board 2003b). The extensive analysis of the *Asset* data with a sample of 2,613 indicates that 21 per cent of young people of statutory school age had no provision arranged (Baker *et al.* 2002).

The situation for those aged 16 to 18 appears significantly worse, with 39 per cent of a sample of 1,188 being recorded as unemployed and a further 17 per cent having part-time or casual employment in the *Asset* sample of nearly 1,200 young people (Baker *et al.* 2002). Looking specifically at those young people who have been more persistently involved in offending and who are placed on ISSP, even greater proportions are completely detached from mainstream education, training and employment. For those of statutory school age out of a sample of 1,640, over a quarter had no main source of educational provision and only 19 per cent were attending a mainstream school. Again the situation was significantly worse for 16–18 year-olds with 56 per cent being unemployed out of a sample of 1,150 (Youth Justice Board 2006c). The levels of non-participation by 16–18 year-olds is consistently high across different studies of the youth justice system. A survey of Yots in the Greater Manchester area found only 28 per cent of this age group in college or employment (including those with only part-time provision) (Youth Justice Trust 2004a).

The best estimates are that the throughput of young people in the youth justice system is at least 150,000 per annum (Youth Justice Board 2005e).[1] Converting the percentages on lack of access and non-attendance from the above studies means that about 100,000 young people are not in full-time education, training or employment and that of these perhaps 25,000–30,000 have nothing arranged for them at all. Of course, given what is known about the placement instability of the wider population of those not in education, training or employment, and particularly for those in the youth justice system, then even those young people recorded as being in full-time education at any point in time are likely to have had several episodes without any education or training (Hayward *et al.* 2005; ECOTEC 2001a). Allowing for the various assumptions made it is not unreasonable to conclude that perhaps one third of those who have become detached from mainstream education are involved in the youth justice system.

Academic failure at school is widely recognised as being endemic among the population of young people who offend. This is particularly true in the American literature: 'school failure and poor reading performance as early as the third grade, truancy, poor achievement, and misbehaviour in elementary school, and the failure to master school skills throughout schooling are among the most reliable predictors of delinquency and other adolescent "rotten outcomes"' (Schorr 1988, cited in Gemignani 1994: 16).

In terms of the wider population of young people who offend in England and Wales and are known to Yots, *Asset* returns indicated that:

- 1 in 2 Yot clients are under-achieving in school;

- 1 in 3 need help with reading and writing; and

- 1 in 5 has special educational needs.

(Baker *et al.* 2002)

The charity INCLUDE (2000) carried out a small survey for the Youth Justice Board's Basic Skills Initiative of the literacy and numeracy levels of young people with whom Yots were working. This survey revealed reading ages that were lagging several years behind chronological ages. The educational attainment levels of young people who have been involved in serious and persistent offending are even lower. The average reading age of young people starting ISSP schemes is over five years below their chronological age (Moore *et al.* 2004).

The levels of literacy and numeracy of 10–17-year-olds on their entry into custody is very low. For those of compulsory school age (15- and 16-year-olds in this sample) about half had literacy and numeracy levels below that expected of an 11-year-old. Almost one third (31 per cent) had literacy levels at or below that expected of a 7-year-old, whilst over 40 per cent had numeracy skills at or below this level (ECOTEC 2001a). Nine out of 10 young people in one STC were found to have a reading age well below their real age (Social Exclusion Unit 2002). The interim report of a study on improving literacy and numeracy (Hurry *et al.* 2005) amongst a group of young people aged 15 to 18 years who were all on a court order, either in the community or in custody, found that about two thirds were at or below Level 1 (the level expected of the average 11-year-old). Over two thirds of the respondents (69 per cent) in this study had left school without any qualifications compared with about 6 per cent in the general population (Hurry *et al.* 2005).

Interventions to prevent detachment and increase attainment

Much of the evidence for effective interventions that prevent or reverse detachment or low attainment applies to pre-school or primary-age children and often originates in the US.

In his meta-analysis of nearly 400 studies that used control or comparison groups and representing over 40,000 young people aged 12–21 Lipsey (1995) detected an average overall net 10 per cent reduction in reoffending. This modest but significant effect varied significantly according to the type and amount of intervention. Both school participation and academic performance were also seen to improve on average as a result of interventions. The average effect on school participation was a 12 per cent improvement across the 93 studies reviewed. Academic performance improved by 14 per cent on average across the 42 studies reviewed. School participation outcomes were significantly and relatively highly correlated with delinquency outcomes compared to any other outcome category.

More detailed UK-based studies have proven largely unrewarding. A recent Home Office report that examined the findings from four studies on education and offending highlighted this problem as they 'showed the difficulties of providing robust, "evidence-based" findings to inform national policy and practice' (Home Office 2004b: 19). The short duration of the programmes combined with other complexities meant that there was little insight gained into issues of causality and attribution, and other potential influencing factors could not be screened out.

When it comes to research into the effectiveness of UK interventions designed to help lower-achieving children and young people catch up there is a significant gap for those aged 12–18. For children at primary school there are a certain number of high-quality evaluations that have been reviewed (Brooks 2002). In the absence of specific interventions ordinary teaching did not enable children with literacy difficulties to catch up. Brooks (2002) concluded that it was reasonable to expect a doubling of the rate of progress with specific interventions and that these gains were maintained in most of the schemes where progress was followed up.

A systematic review of literacy and numeracy interventions for adults 'found just enough evidence (all of it from the US) to demonstrate rigorously in a meta-analysis that receiving adult literacy and numeracy tuition does produce more progress than not receiving it' (Torgerson et al. 2004: 13). One reading programme accompanied by a 'community-building group process' for adults in a US prison achieved positive results.

Involving parents or carers in their children's education has been found to be a significant factor in strengthening attachment to school and to learning in general (Bynner 2001). This has been demonstrated through evaluation of family literacy projects and usually involves younger children rather than teenagers.

A recent review of the research established a clear and consistent finding that spontaneous parental involvement in education has a large, positive and independent effect on the outcomes of schooling (Desforges and Abouchaar 2003). The research base where planned parental intervention is concerned is flimsy, with findings restricted to participant satisfaction rather than increases in attainment. As with so much of the evidence of 'What Works' there is a significant gap in understanding how to make it work (Desforges and Abouchaar 2003).

Typically most initiatives that have been relatively rigorously evaluated tend to be from the US. The most well-known of these is perhaps the High/Scope Perry project which followed up the children involved to the age of 27. This programme was characterised by a focus on a group of families beset with high-risk factors, a relatively high dosage and length (special classes for two and a half hours daily over 30 weeks supplemented by a weekly home visit from a teacher). Considerable attention was paid to enhancing the academic performance of the children through emphasising active learning, problem solving and concentration on task. Home–school links were emphasised. Teaching staff received specific training and dealt with small groups of children. A number of positive outcomes were found including large reductions in the numbers of lifetime arrests, lower teenage pregnancy rates and large increases in graduation rates. This programme was however classified as promising rather than effective (Mihalic et al. 2001).

The emphasis on school effectiveness in recent years has generated some relevant evidence. Many interventions that have been evaluated have not had the reduction of crime as their main aim although these interventions may directly or indirectly have reduced risk factors associated with offending (Home Office 2004b).

Research findings into what makes an effective school consistently emphasise the importance of leadership, systematic approaches to monitoring attendance and progress, high expectations of young people in relation to both their learning and behaviour, a balanced use of rewards and incentives, high parental involvement, opportunities for young people to exercise responsibility within the school and a positive ethos within the school (Home Office 2004b; Rutter *et al.* 1998). This is in contrast to ineffective schools which 'tend to categorise pupils who behave poorly or persistently truant as deviants, and shift responsibility for their behaviour and welfare to other agencies or institutions' (Home Office 2004b: 19).

One example of an American school-based prevention programme that focused across the school on key organisational issues, and has had a relatively rigorous evaluation, is the Program Development Evaluation method which is a multi-modal organisational intervention implemented by school improvement teams comprising parents, teachers and school officials. This was found to be an effective method of improving classroom management and school discipline with significant decreases in disruption in classrooms (Howell 2003).

Three US programmes for primary-age children that offer a school-based multi-modal approach, have been evaluated and deemed to be effective, or at least to be a promising approach are: Fast Track, the Seattle Social Development Project and the Child Development Project.

The Fast Track programme targets children in their early years of schooling who are from low-income, high-crime communities and are displaying particular behavioural problems at home and school. The programme has six integrated components which match six domains of intervention. The evaluation of the programme involved the random assignment of schools to treatment and control groups. Recipients of the programme displayed decreases in aggression and disruptive behaviour at both school and home. In addition their relationships with peers improved, as did a range of social skills.

Although the collection of robust evidence was a key objective of the Crime Reduction Initiative in Secondary Schools (CRISS) programme in the UK, methodological weaknesses meant that it was only possible to derive recommendations for promising approaches (Home Office 2004b). See Chapter 1, 'Implementation'.

Bullying in school has been linked to an increased risk of offending. A Norwegian programme designed to reduce bullying in schools through establishing behavioural boundaries, with the consistent application of sanctions for rule-breaking and fostering co-operative working with teachers and parents, succeeded in reducing the incidence of bullying. There were also indirect effects such as a reduction in absenteeism, vandalism and theft (Olweus 1993). This programme was also reported to have been implemented successfully in England (ECOTEC 2001a). However, both these evaluations have been criticised as not being particularly rigorous and replication in the US was reported to be unsuccessful (Howell 2003). Anti-bullying programmes operated in Sheffield across 23 primary and secondary schools. In line with evaluations of most school-based interventions greater effect was found in the reduction of bullying in primary schools with relatively small effects in secondary schools (Home Office 2004b).

Individually targeted interventions tend to focus on the reduction of anger, disruptive and violent behaviour by particular individuals. The Social Competence Promotion Programme for Young Adolescents in America is a violence prevention approach that promotes a range of social competencies such as decision-making, social problem-solving, self-control, stress management and communication skills. An evaluation found that compared to controls the participant young people were more engaged with school and less likely to be involved in absenteeism, suspensions and minor delinquent behaviour (Weissberg and Caplan 1998).

Basing probation officers in schools has a long history in certain parts of the USA. This has become a popular approach, with officers operating in both a preventative way and also intervening directly with young people displaying delinquent behaviour. In addition to carrying out probation supervision probation staff in some instances carry out training for teachers and deliver law-related education classes. Studies indicate that attainment and attendance may be increased and antisocial behaviour in the school and also of those on probation is improved (Griffin 1999).

The Safer Schools Partnership (SSP) programme aims to promote the safety of schools and the young people attending them. They vary considerably in structure but generally have active police involvement in schools, often in collaboration with other support staff. The objectives are to improve key behavioural issues in such schools including non-attendance, bullying, antisocial behaviour and offending. The evaluation of the programme (Youth Justice Board 2005d) was later supplemented by an extension of the study to over 1,000 schools (Bowles *et al.* 2006). They found a significant reduction in rates of absence (both authorised and unauthorised) in the SSP schools relative to those experienced in the comparison schools. GCSE performance also improved relative to the comparison schools. Difficulties with the data prevented much examination of changes in levels of bullying and antisocial behaviour in schools. Similarly the data was inadequate to support school-level analysis of convictions or arrest, making it impossible to present any robust findings of the impact of this approach on offending.

Gottfredson's comprehensive review of the evidence for effective school interventions concluded that:

> considerable evidence of positive effects for prevention programmes can be found in the available research, but that implementation, quality and quantity qualify the positive findings. Schools can be a site for effective intervention, or a site for non-intervention or ineffective intervention. Schools have the potential to contribute to the positive socialization of youth. But the range of conditions under which they have been demonstrated to realize this potential is narrow (2001: 258).

Further education colleges

There are a number of promising practice indicators for FE colleges planning to work with young people at risk (Utting 1999) and these include:

- collaborative bridging/access programmes developed with local schools, education authorities and Learning and Skills Councils to create education and training opportunities;

- a student-centred approach with the emphasis on learning as opposed to assessment. Sufficiently flexible curriculum and teaching methods to take account of individual student needs;

- occupational guidance and work experience as an integral part of each course;

- effective support for learning being made available, such as one-to-one tutoring and pastoral support;

- students following a curriculum that is not only relevant to their current and future needs, but also shows them how they are progressing;

- other support services such as help with transport or childcare being made available;

- joint training for school and college staff on working with young people at risk.

Employment

As being unemployed seems to be an independent risk factor, schemes that increase employment or at least employability might be thought to be likely to be effective but again the evidence is sparse and largely confined to adults. For young people who have completed compulsory schooling but have no or few qualifications and will thus struggle to enter the labour markets, successfully gaining post-school qualifications can have a significant impact. One study found that young people with few or no school qualifications but who went on to gain Level 2 qualifications saw a dramatic effect on employment rates. By the time they had acquired Level 3 qualifications they were on a par in terms of finding employment with those young people who went on to achieve A-levels via the academic route (McIntosh 2003).

Previous studies into the efficacy of employment interventions with adults who offend have shown promising results although these may not always be applicable to young people. Bridges' study in 1998 found that adults who were unemployed at the beginning of their probation supervision, but who had an employment intervention whilst on supervision, found employment before the end of their community sentences at twice the rate of those who had no intervention. Reconviction studies suggest that employment interventions can potentially reduce reoffending rates (May 1999; Sarno *et al.* 2000). It is not simply having a job that is associated with reductions in offending but the quality, including the stability, of that employment coupled with levels of satisfaction (Harper and Chitty 2005).

The research challenges are highlighted by the basic skills pathfinder evaluation which sought to measure the progress of adults on basic skills programmes in terms of their basic skills improvements and increased employability, but high attrition rates made this impossible (McMahon *et al.* 2004).

Custodial education

Asking the bald question 'What Works?' of custodial education for young people is simplistic and arguably counter-intuitive given that the evidence suggests that for perhaps the majority of young people custody increases educational risk factors and may reduce protective factors. The best that can be done is to try to assess whether educational programmes within custody have a positive effect within that experience and whether certain approaches can be more effective than others following release.

A number of research studies have been undertaken that try to measure the effectiveness of custodial educational intervention programmes. However, these are bedevilled by relatively weak research design and are usually focused on adults.

Tolbert (2002: 19) identifies the following as being major limitations of studies investigating the relationship between educational intervention and recidivism:

- most do not take into account other services and factors inside and outside prison that may affect recidivism rates, such as drug treatment programmes, post-release services, and family support;

- most of the results are vulnerable to self-selection bias; the methodologies do not adequately account for participant characteristics;

- most do not follow released inmates for a long enough period of time;

- most vary in their definitions of recidivism – a nationally [US] recognised definition of recidivism does not exist;

- most are unable to measure various levels of improvement in inmates' behaviours;

- most are based on correctional educational records that are often poorly kept by institutions.

A few studies, however, do provide some evidence of a positive link between educational interventions and reductions in recidivism, and provide insights into the characteristics of programmes that do seem to be effective, although the studies are North American and deal with adults.

Using three studies that employed a random or matched comparison group design, Porporino and Robinson (1992) concluded that the recidivism rate of participants in the Canadian Adult Basic Education programme was significantly lower than that of the comparison group. Other positive results were achieved in studies in the United States. One longitudinal study involving 3,400 imprisoned adults found that participation in educational programmes reduced the chances of reimprisonment by 29 per cent (Steurer *et al.* 2001). Similarly there was a reduction in recidivism of a third among adult prisoners who participated in vocational and apprenticeship training as part of the Post-Release Employment Project (Saylor and Gaes 1997).

According to Tolbert (2002: 1–2): 'These programmes lead to lower recidivism rates, according to advocates, because they provide inmates with the knowledge, skills, attitudes, and values needed to succeed in society and to avoid future criminal activity.'

Considerable caution should be exercised in extending these more positive findings to younger groups in the UK as they may not be applicable. Not only are they from different countries but the sentence length for adults is much greater and the effects of maturation, stable learning groups and greater dosage of education could be considerable.

Segregated education and training

The history of the education of young people who offend is inextricably bound up with segregated educational provision. This is provided for those young people who, through their antisocial or offending behaviour, or due to perceived differences in their learning needs, are removed from mainstream school. They are seen as being more appropriately placed in 'specialist' environments. There are four broad and overlapping categories of segregated education: separate facilities on the school site, more recently termed learning support units; special schools; PRUs; and, often linked to these, a constellation of initiatives offering formal and informal learning including home tuition.

Special groups or units within schools for young people who are seen to pose behavioural problems in mainstream classes have a lengthy history but have seen a significant expansion in recent years through initiatives such as Education Action Zones and the Excellence in Cities programmes. Despite this the evaluation evidence on their effectiveness is very limited. Their main stated objectives include bringing about behavioural changes so that young people can be reintegrated into mainstream classes and thereby reducing exclusions, increasing attainment and improving attendance.

A study of seven units in Sheffield found no effect on exclusion rates, or on the numbers transferred to special schools, and that the focus tended to be on the perceived problems of the young person rather than the context in which it occurred – 'the half way house fallacy' (Galloway 1985: 162). Reintegration rates into mainstream classes were also found to be low in Inner London units (Mortimore *et al.* 1983).

There is a range of relatively systematic American studies. In reviewing these Topping (1983) found that in certain circumstances both primary and secondary age groups could show substantial academic gains and behavioural improvement although many results were disappointing. Gains appeared to dissipate over the long term when young people were returned to mainstream classes.

The evaluation of Learning Support Units in the Excellence in Cities programme was largely qualitative and there was no systematic evaluation of attainment or behaviour gains (Wilkin *et al.* 2003). While there were abundant positive comments from staff and small samples of young people, only about 22 per cent were fully reintegrated and the majority of these were younger pupils with very few year 10 and no year 11 young people returning to mainstream classes. This provision often was not full-time for all young people. Ofsted (2003) found that a quarter of the LSUs they inspected were not doing sufficient work to help the young people learn more effectively. Other criticisms included 'the use of units simply as "remove rooms" where disruptive pupils were sent at random, weak monitoring and evaluation and a lack of emphasis on staff training and ensuring they were an integral part of the teaching team' (Ofsted 2003: 60).

Pupil Referral Units

Many young people who have offended – particularly if they continue to offend – will end up being referred to off-site provision, usually a PRU. Despite the fact that the use of small segregated units for a range of young people has a long history and very high unit costs there is little evidence on its outcomes. The evidence that does exist is often limited on two counts: there is rarely follow up data and it is characterised by differing educational expectations of the young people on for example curriculum, attainment and attendance. One key issue in assessing the effectiveness of PRUs is agreeing success criteria. There is a lack of clarity about whether this should be progression post-16, qualifications achieved, reintegration into mainstream schooling, desistance in offending, reductions in the behaviours that cause them to be detached from mainstream schooling and a range of softer outcomes such as increases in self-esteem.

Perhaps not surprisingly there is little reference in most studies to the impact of segregated education on offending but there are several inherent characteristics which could lead it to be less effective in terms of reducing risk factors and increasing protective factors. Given that delinquent peer groups are a significant risk factor for adolescents then a concentration in a

73

PRU is likely to be counter-productive. In the same way that it is suggested that learning in such an abnormal environment as custody does not transfer easily to everyday life in the community, similar difficulties may be posed for young people in small units. Positive changes in behaviour or attitudes to learning may well not survive the dramatic shift from a small highly pro-tected environment to the hurly-burly of educational life in a further education college or the workplace.

Defining successful outcomes is divided between those who argue for clear measurable outcomes as a measure (Topping 1983), those who believe this is too narrow (Munn *et al.* 2000), and those who recognise a progression of 'small steps' (Kendall *et al.* 2002; Hustler *et al.* 1998). Views on the measurement of effectiveness appear to lie on a continuum from a reliance on the positive atti-tudes of practitioners from segregated education (Kinder *et al.* 2000), through to the argument that effectiveness should be based on studies that can be gen-eralised producing hard, objectively measurable evidence with a success rate of over 66 per cent (Topping 1983). Partly due to this lack of a consensus over the aims and purposes of segregated education very little attention has been paid to the effects either positive or negative on offending (Munn *et al.* 2000).

Serious weaknesses in segregated – particularly unit-based – provision have been identified:

- Reintegration is the ostensible objective of PRUs, according to guidance issued (DfES Circular 10/99). Each pupil should have reintegration targets for a return to mainstream or special education, further education or employment. The evidence shows that this is achieved for only a minority of children and young people (Parsons and Howlett 2000).

- The curriculum tends to be narrow, and the quality of teaching can be low-ered by the lack of specialist subject teachers (Ofsted 1995).

- Academic achievement and progression into further education, training and employment are often low (Ofsted 1995; Ofsted 2003; Munn *et al.* 2000).

- There is often a wide range of ages in a single unit. This can mean inappro-priate role models for younger pupils and a long-term exposure to an out-of-school culture that hinders their reintegration.

- The cost is at least three times that of mainstream provision (Parsons and Howlett 2000; Audit Commission 1999b).

- There are concerns over the quality of peer group relationships, particu-larly for the small number of young women (John 1996).

- It contributes to a 'double jeopardy' for young people in residential care, who find themselves at a crucial stage in their development outside both family and school environments. This could restrict their ability to acquire the skills to function in normal group settings.

In addition to the definition and formalisation of the status of the unit another symptom of the revitalisation of segregated education is the growth of a wide range of out-of-school educational provision, some of which is delivered by voluntary sector providers. This offers a very diverse mix of formal and informal learning, often with an emphasis on basic skills, personal and social development activities, and work experience. While it very rarely ever takes place on school premises, sometimes separate centres will be used, training premises or youth centres, and there can be access to further education colleges.

A relatively large-scale evaluation was recently conducted for these alternative education projects (Kendall *et al.* 2002). The overall aim of the evaluation was to 'examine the effectiveness of intervention programmes for permanently excluded pupils. Effectiveness is measured in terms of their success in returning pupils to mainstream education, educational attainment, post-16 outcomes and reducing anti social behaviour, including offending' (Kendall *et al.* 2002: 2).

Despite the fact that the six initiatives studied in this research were selected because they displayed some success in the re-engagement of young people, the findings were restricted by weaknesses in the baseline information on young people, the very diverse characteristics of young people referred, and of the projects themselves, coupled with the relatively limited nature of the evaluation.

Although there is no reference to it in the executive summary or in the key findings the reintegration rates into mainstream appear to be low, with only eight (5 per cent) out of 162 young people in the study apparently returning to secondary school.

Analysis of educational attainment was curtailed in that there was apparently no baseline information on the young people and, in the absence of assessment of their literacy and numeracy levels on entry and exit, the evaluation provided lists of qualifications achieved as indicative of progression. There were real problems relating to the information on attendance, which effectively prevents any attempt to compare particular educational or behavioural outputs, in relation to inputs.

This study is unusual in that it did look at offending. In total there was not a particularly high incidence of young people with a criminal record on referral to these projects compared to some out-of-school projects (approximately 50 per cent) but there was a total of 694 offences committed during their time on the projects. While the number of young people (for whom there was detailed information) involved in offending reduced by 11 per cent the number of offences they committed increased by 22 per cent in the intervention year. The study found that young people with undesirable destinations were 20 per cent more likely to offend, and on average committed 32 per cent more crime than those with desirable destinations.

Emotional and behavioural difficulties (EBD)

Another formal route out of mainstream education is for those young people who are labelled as having 'emotional and behavioural difficulties' (EBD). For the overwhelming majority of children and young people categorised as having EBD (95 per cent), a placement in a special school is in effect permanent, whatever the intentions recorded in the individual educational planning process. Reintegration rates are very low. There are very few studies of residential special schools that can yield information on outcomes relating to attainment, detachment and offending. One study of several residential special schools for pupils with EBD found it difficult to collect data there on basic educational skills, and the outcomes in terms of progression to further education and training appear limited. Offending rates appear to have increased significantly following prolonged stays in the schools but this also may have been due to an age effect (Grimshaw and Berridge 1994).

Post-16 training providers

For many young people who offend and are detached from mainstream education, centre-based provision from specialist training providers is one of their main options. They tend to suffer from the same fundamental weaknesses as PRUs but have additional problems related to the length of their programmes and funding regimes. On the other hand the young people receive a training allowance.

Evidence on outcomes is very limited and, where it exists, not encouraging. The National E2E Young Offender's Pilot was an attempt to provide a route into mainstream provision for those young people on DTOs and ISSPs. Despite being partly funded by the Youth Justice Board its explicit aims did not include a reduction in reoffending and the evaluation consequently makes no attempt to assess this. The very limited nature of the data means that it is impossible to judge the intensity and duration of participation and educational progression. The attrition rates appear high with 41 per cent of those who commenced in custody not continuing on release, and out of the remainder 38 per cent were recorded as having a positive exit from the pilot. Although the evaluators acknowledge that the figures 'are not necessarily reliable or robust' they indicate that only 83 young people out of 340 who started this programme had a positive exit (Youth Justice Board 2004b).

The bridge course – a promising approach?

This project has several unusual features: it has been replicated extensively in England and Wales with an apparently high degree of programme integrity, and has relatively comprehensive quantitative information on the antecedents of young people, their attendance, qualifications gained, changes in literacy and numeracy levels and subsequent destinations. It was evaluated recently as part of the Youth Justice Board's review of the education, training and employment projects that it has funded and the data has been further analysed in a recent article (Youth Justice Board 2003g; Hurry *et al.* 2006).

There were nearly 500 young people in this evaluation with an average age of 17, from 16 projects in a variety of locations. Most were completely detached from education and training, just over one fifth were or had been looked after by the local authority. Over two thirds had literacy and numeracy levels assessed at below Level 1 (that of the average 11-year-old) on referral. The great majority of them (83 per cent) were referred by the Yot. Nine out of 10 were repeat offenders (88 per cent) with an average of 12 previous convictions and an average gravity score of 5.3.

There appears to have been a relatively low rate of attrition with a correspondingly high dosage of received hours of education. On average young people were on the project for 17 out of the potential 24 weeks and undertook 22 hours per week of education with an average total of 370 hours received for each young person.

In terms of educational outcomes those who remained for more than 15 weeks recorded modest but highly significant gains in both literacy and numeracy. About 50 per cent gained qualifications while a significant proportion were continuing to work towards them. If those who were removed to custody (9.5 per cent) or moved out of the area (2.2 per cent) are discounted then 72 per cent of young people on the project had initial destinations of education, training or employment.

With regard to offending there was a 67 per cent reconviction rate in the year after entry to the project but this was accompanied by statistically significant reductions in offending both in terms of the number of offences and the gravity of offence. The average number of offences per young person dropped by 25 per cent from 5.1 to 3.8 comparing the year before and the year after being on the project.

In order to examine the potential effect of the programme on reoffending, three educational outcomes were assessed: positive destination; qualifications gained; and literacy and numeracy improvements. Each of these outcomes was significantly related to reductions in offending. While there was a 72 per cent reconviction rate for those who did not have a positive destination this fell to 57 per cent for those who did. There was a similar reduction for those who gained qualifications compared to those who did not. Reductions in the average number of offences per head were even greater with a fall of a half for those who gained qualifications compared to a tenth who did not.

A further study analysed the data using regression analysis to explore predictors of reoffending. Controlling for previous offending and background factors (gender, school leaving age, living situation, number of sessions attended and drug use) it was found that literacy and numeracy gains were significantly associated with lower rates of reoffending. The study concluded that: 'It would appear that improving participants' literacy and numeracy skills may be an effective way of reducing their offending behaviour' (Hurry *et al.* 2006).

The quantity and quality of data garnered by this evaluation means that there can be much closer scrutiny of the costs incurred by this programme. Instead of simply giving a per capita cost of a place, which is the normal method, costs can be calculated per contact hour. This yields interesting results. The per capita cost of the bridge course model appeared to be more than double that of similar projects funded by the Youth Justice Board, but on a cost per contact hour basis it was up to half the cost of other projects. Again, better recording practices bring benefits in that headline costs can be deceptive if the structure, intensity and duration of intervention are not sufficiently intensive to gain high rates of attendance and retention. If there is a more rigorous approach to recording what is actually received by a young person in tandem with the collection of pre- and post-intervention assessment then much more effective cost–benefit analysis will be able to occur in future.

The reasons for the apparent relative success of this project model for young people who often do not get access to or participate extensively in segregated provision may be:

● the use of mainstream environments (principally FE colleges) to dilute delinquent peer group effects and promote behaviour modification;

● intensive supervision (one-to-10 caseload over and above teaching staff);

● multi-modal – the multi-disciplinary project manager worked across social care, health, criminal justice issues;

● the high degree of programme integrity (Stephenson 1996; DfEE 1995).

Incentives for participation

Staying on in education has been considered to be potentially protective against delinquency. The introduction of the Education Maintenance Allowance (EMA) in selected areas enabled a recent quasi-experimental study to examine the impact on juvenile crime (Feinstein and Sabates 2005). The study found that there was a statistically significant decrease in convictions for burglary by 16–18-year-old males (but not for theft or violent offences) in the EMA areas compared to non-EMA areas and compared to older groups in their area. Given that areas of high deprivation tend to attract multiple initiatives from government departments, which could either individually or in concert affect the results, the study looked at the Reducing Burglary Initiative (RBI).

The main effect seemed to occur when both programmes were operated together rather than individually, giving rise to their main finding that there are 'clear grounds that introduction of the EMA together with the RBI programme had significant and substantive effects on conviction rates for burglary offences by 16 to 18 year olds' (Feinstein and Sabates 2005: 4). A further gain over time of staying on in education could potentially be lower unemployment, which is associated with decreases in offending.

Ineffective approaches

It is instructive to examine some examples of educational type projects or approaches that are still supported despite evidence of their ineffectiveness. One very well-known American project highlights this problem – Drug Abuse Resistance Education (DARE), demonstrated as ineffective but widely implemented (see Chapter 1, 'Criticisms of RCTs', p. 15).

The outcomes for those activities with a clear link to more conventional interests, such as hours spent on homework, may well be associated with less delinquency in contrast to involvement in more adult activities, such as motor projects, which are associated with increases in delinquency (Harper and Chitty 2005).

For the whole range of other activities including youth groups, volunteering, sports and individual hobbies little effect on delinquency has been observed in the American research literature (Gottfredson 2001). One study using UK data found that increased leisure activity between ages 8 and 10 was a predictor of both lower levels of self-control between 12 and 14 years of age and of offending between the ages of 14 and 16. It is speculated that supervision exercised in the activity settings was not as effective as that of parents, which possibly reduced self-control.

Arts interventions

The power of the arts to transform the lives of people who offend has often been proclaimed. A recent review found that out of 700 projects catering for both young people and adults who had offended, 400 had used arts-based activities (Hughes 2005). There is a wide range of benefits claimed, including:

- development of self-confidence and self-esteem;
- increased creativity and thinking skills;
- improved skills in planning and organising activities;
- improved communication of ideas and information;
- raised or enhanced educational attainment;

- increased appreciation of the arts;

- enhanced mental and physical health and well-being;

- increased employability of individuals;

- broadened outlook;

- reduced offending behaviour.
(Jermyn 2004)

The quality of the research underpinning this impressive list of claims tends not to be high. Common limitations include evaluations with small sample sizes, a lack of baseline information, lack of control groups, few appropriate measures, over-reliance on anecdotal evidence, difficulties accessing information relating to offending, and unsupported assumptions about the links between intervention and outcome (Hughes 2005). Much of the evidence relates to behavioural changes, usually of adults, within custody such as a reduction in adjudications following an arts intervention. There is a plethora of indirect and testimonial evidence often adduced to support the effectiveness of the arts in the criminal justice system, most of which does not come close to the rigorous methodologies required by the Home Office. Research sponsored by the Youth Justice Board and Arts Council England is currently being undertaken focusing on the links between engagement in the arts, educational participation and progression and offending.

The principles of effective practice and education, training and employment

Risk classification

In the context of devising appropriate education and training programmes it should be noted that being detached from mainstream education, particularly when combined with low attainment in literacy/numeracy, is often highly associated with persistent offending. Suitable full-time education and training in order to accelerate learning are very likely to be salient features of high-level interventions.

This principle should not be taken to mean that only those young people committing the most serious offences or offending persistently should have full-time education or training. Participation in full-time education is a very significant protective factor for all young people. Those young people most at risk however will probably need an intensity of education such as one-to-one learning support and/or a greater volume of learning.

Risk classification is impossible without rigorous assessment of the educational status of individuals and management analysis of the numbers and offending profile of those detached from mainstream education in a given Yot area. This information in tandem with aggregated risks taken from the relevant part of *Asset* will be potentially important in influencing the LEA and the local Learning and Skills Council. Developing this risk classification approach can assist with emphasising the duty of educational institutions and individual teachers in preventing offending.

Criminogenic need

Programmes must focus on those factors that contribute most directly to offending as opposed to more distantly related causes. For obvious reasons, managers and practitioners in education may not willingly accept that their actions, such as a permanent exclusion or part-time provision in a PRU, could actually be directly contributing to offending. Similarly staff who are not teachers feeling that access to education and training is outside their authority may pay less attention to this area than it merits in terms of its contribution to offending behaviour. This may be compounded by the feeling among some practitioners that education is 'best left to teachers', which can lead to an underestimation of risk factors. For instance, there is evidence from the *Asset* data that both practitioners and, to a lesser extent, young people themselves are understating just how low the literacy and numeracy attainment levels are for many individuals (Baker *et al.* 2002).

In this area, as in most areas of youth justice, the evidence base does not allow us to give unequivocal answers as to direct causes or to the detailed transmission mechanisms that turn risk factors into offending behaviour.

Individual practitioners could argue strongly that being detached from suitable full-time education is much more likely to lead a young person into associating with delinquent peer groups or reducing their employability significantly. Similarly, the fact that over half of young people leaving custody have no education or training immediately available on release is probably a powerful contributory factor to the very high and fairly immediate reoffending rates of many of these young people. This would indicate that ensuring that such provision is available ought to be a priority for practitioners.

In terms of associated need, there is evidence demonstrating that young people who have experienced low attainment at school and the consequent sense of failure have a significantly higher rate of substance misuse.

Responsivity

It used to be claimed that the learning styles of most young people at risk of offending require active, participatory methods of working (McGuire 1995) but the latest research commissioned by the Youth Justice Board (Youth

Justice Board 2005a) has found little evidence for this (see Chapter 1, pp 27–29). This claim may be related to the more pervasive belief that, as many of these young people have not succeeded in mainstream school (or that mainstream school has not met their needs appropriately), then they will usually require learning in more active settings, probably vocational.

It is striking that many discussions by educationalists or non-educationalists turn to the need for more vocational training for young people who offend or are seen to be academically underachieving. This may be derived from observations of other countries whose education systems place more emphasis on a vocational education and appear to have fewer problems with engagement, and possibly higher-skilled workforces. It can also be driven by a belief that traditional 'chalk and talk' teaching methods have alienated these young people. This issue has been thrown into relief as the virtually automatic transition from school to labour market has withered away. The UK, unlike countries such as Germany and Denmark, does not offer a high-status vocational training route as an alternative to continuing with academic studies. Given the popularity of the vocational remedy reiterated recently by the Audit Commission (2004) and by the Tomlinson review of 14–19 education (DfES 2004b), it is worth examining the evidence base.

The underlying hypothesis is that learning that is more obviously associated with the world of work will provide much greater motivation to young people with low attainment and limited or no attachment to school. Vocational subjects could also offer greater opportunities to link to their out-of-school interests and hobbies than the academic subjects. Accordingly there has been a range of experimental educational programmes from the early 1990s onwards targeted at 14–16 year-olds attempting to improve motivation and engagement through an emphasis on work-related learning. The evaluations of these initiatives have lacked RCTs, had limited comparison groups and struggled to find an appropriate and consistent approach to measuring progress (Steedman and Stoney 2004).

A review of evaluations of a range of initiatives including those arising from the disapplication of the national curriculum at Key Stage 4, GNVQs, vocational GCSEs, the Connexions Service, the Increased Flexibilities Programme and other work-related initiatives found that for those who were disengaged:

- there was little effect on attainment;
- motivation may have increased but was not necessarily translated into greater attainment;
- careers guidance and information appears to be a major weakness;
- contact with the workplace could sometimes reduce the likelihood of remaining in education and training.

(Steedman and Stoney 2004)

The evidence so far does not indicate better outcomes for a vocational route post-16 for these young people. Drawing on extensive Labour Force Survey data, McIntosh (2003: 14) came to the conclusion that 'it does not appear that post-school vocational qualifications have been at all successful in raising those who failed at school to the generally accepted desirable level (Level 3), or even, for that matter, to Level 2'.

The latest research findings advise youth justice practitioners to take full account of the specific learning environment and the considerable variation in preferred approaches to learning between individual young people in tailoring how they facilitate learning.

While this has specific implications for teachers who will usually be aware of the need to differentiate their teaching according to the needs of individual young people, it is equally important for non-educational practitioners.

The effectiveness of offending behaviour interventions, for example, is likely to be increased if Yot staff ensure that attention is paid to the individual levels of literacy and numeracy attainment, the nature of the learning environment and their own approach in terms of the structure, content and resources used in each session.

There is abundant evidence that the educational expectations of young people in both the care and criminal justice systems are often very low and therefore may be self-fulfilling. The evidence also suggests that this is often compounded by the low expectations of professionals and parents/carers in relation to what these young people can achieve in educational terms (DfES/DoH 2000). High expectations of learners, by setting of demanding and progressively more difficult challenges, is extremely important and is substantiated by evidence of the strong links between expectations and attainment.

Community based

It is the transfer and subsequent application of learning that is the crucial test in youth justice of behavioural change having occurred. Many programmes are deemed by research evidence to be ineffective as they have little impact on offending, even though the deliverers feel that the young people were engaged and had benefited.

Evidence suggests that behaviour is very specific to contexts. Therefore, when programmes are delivered in settings that are radically different from the normal experience and everyday challenges, then they are less likely to work. This applies to both the methods of delivering a programme and the resources used. For example, using literacy/numeracy materials that young people find too childish, old-fashioned or not relevant to their experiences is unlikely to stimulate their interest and encourage optimal learning. Custody is perhaps the most extreme example of an abnormal context. It is therefore not surprising that the evidence suggests approaches that emulate certain features of community orders make for a more successful custodial experience in terms of changing behaviours (Tolbert 2002).

Much of the criminal justice approach and sentencing is, by definition, inimical to learning and behaviour change. Custody tends to inhibit the development of the essential planning and decision-making skills that are fundamental to changing behaviour back in the community. Evidence from the US indicates that where young people serving custodial sentences experience their education in the community, attainment is higher than in control groups (Coffey and Gemignani 1994).

The practical implications are that Yot supervising officers might be pushing for Release on Temporary Licence (RoTL) to involve young people in mainstream education and training. The continuity of courses and teaching and learning materials between custody and community is of paramount importance. Similarly, home visits to the actual or potential host education institution could be useful in securing immediate placements post-custody and smoothing the transition to the community.

It would be a misinterpretation of this principle to argue for the placement of young people in segregated educational settings on the grounds of common experience, for example in PRUs. There is evidence that the significant protective factor of resilience, i.e. the ability to surmount adversity, is fostered by the diversity of normal experiences inherent in participation in mainstream school life. Young people themselves express a desire to engage with mainstream settings (ECOTEC 2001b).

Intervention modality

One of the challenges with wide-ranging programmes is enabling the young person and the allied professionals to appreciate how joined up the approach should be. Most teachers will not know what 'intervention modality' is, let alone accept that their curriculum is part of it.

There are three main threats, particularly where intensive packages are concerned, in relation to education and training:

1 A range of programme interventions may compete with each other and crowd out education as a priority. For instance, in YOIs in particular, education is continually interrupted and is not treated as an absolute priority.

2 There are very real dangers where extensive daytime programmes are arranged by Yots that schools will be happy for young people to attend these activities rather than being a potentially disruptive influence within the school. The evaluation of youth inclusion programmes found a very significant deterioration in attendance at school, which may be partly explained by the pull of these activities and possibly the push of the school (Youth Justice Board 2003b).

3 Yots will be tempted into establishing their own education programmes. While this may keep young people occupied, the track record of such activities is very poor, particularly in terms of progression into further education or full-time training.

Even if some elements are skills-based and with a cognitive-behavioural approach, learning can still be inhibited if there are inadequate linkages or continuity of experience with the opportunities to apply the learning. For example, outward bound type courses may appear to fit this definition but their outcomes in terms of preventing offending tend to be limited as there is considerable difficulty transferring the learning to meaningful everyday contexts for young people (Lipsey and Wilson 1998).

Yot practitioners need to be working with young people to instil and develop a theory of action to underpin all their learning, and giving shape to the interventions. For example, Offending Behaviour Programmes with their emphasis on actions and consequences and the need to develop decision-making skills can be placed within the wider context of improving attainment (particularly in relation to literacy and numeracy). Improving attainment enables young people to achieve qualifications which in turn may lead to sustained employment and the cessation of offending.

Although the jargon is particularly opaque for teaching professionals, the approach is directly applicable in terms of effective teaching. The main challenge is cultural; gaining the trust and understanding of education practitioners so that they see themselves as part of a much wider programme.

Programme integrity

As has already been shown, it is not known what makes effective education and training programmes. Knowledge in this field, as in others, is still so limited as to prevent the adoption of a prescribed programme approach.

One of the advantages of education and training is that it tends to have clear objectives and it is possible to measure progress towards them through educational assessment and accreditation of learning outcomes. This rigour is useful and adaptable to the youth justice approach.

One of the key challenges for Yot staff is ensuring programme integrity where others deliver it. Protocols with local education authorities, schools, Connexions and training providers will all help but will also depend heavily on the skills and knowledge of individual Yot practitioners and recognition of these by teaching staff.

Boundaries of professional specialism can be fiercely guarded but this must not put off attempts at brokering or identifying where the staff of provider agencies are not adequately trained and/or supported.

Ensuring programme integrity indirectly through other professionals suggests that monitoring and evaluation become even more important, as it is often a matter of quality assuring others rather than delivering directly.

Clearly, one of the keys to ensuring programme integrity is the collation and monitoring of data about how far young people at risk of offending and reoffending are accessing, participating in and progressing within education, training and employment. Yet paradoxically very little is known about this. Ofsted for example was withering in its criticisms in relation to young people detached from mainstream school: 'Most significantly, schools and LEAs are not tracking pupils and do not have a comprehensive view of their where-abouts, achievements or destinations. There is insufficient monitoring of the quality and range of alternative provision' (Ofsted 2004: 5). These weaknesses directly affect those young people of most concern to Yots 'indicating a high potential for pupils to be lost to the system, to be accessing minimal education and training opportunities, and to be out of school for a large proportion of the school week without the knowledge of the LEA' (Ofsted 2004: 25).

Within custodial education the paucity of management information partic-ularly with regard to outcomes may even be preventing recognition of some progress. A recent Youth Justice Board review of the implementation of its education reforms in YOIs concluded that 'despite the increased inputs par-ticularly through new posts and increased expenditure on resources the fundamental weakness in monitoring and reporting systems effectively pre-vent this review from establishing equivalent improvements in either outputs (e.g. number of educational hours received by individual young people) or outcomes such as leaving gains' (Youth Justice Board 2005f: 7).

Dosage

While programmes as noted above must have sufficient 'breadth' to match the range of needs of individual young people, they must also have the 'depth' and be of sufficient intensity and duration to achieve programme aims.

While Yot practitioners always have to be concerned with the impact of the totality of interventions, education, training and employment should be con-sidered often the most important single component. 'Sufficient duration' needs to be interpreted as commencing from the moment of sentence and for the full duration of the sentence. Similarly, 'sufficient intensity' means suit-able full-time education, training or employment.

There is no statutory number of hours that represent full-time education for those of compulsory school age, but this is deemed by the Youth Justice Board to be 25 hours per week (30 hours when in custody). For those over compulsory school age it is deemed to be 20 hours per week.

'Intensity' also relates to the quality of the educational experience. Several hours each day simply occupying a young person's time in leisure activities may not be challenging enough, nor fitting within an appropriate curriculum to be deemed of sufficient intensity. If, for example, a young person of school age has had the national curriculum disapplied, the local education authority must still be ensuring a broad, balanced curriculum.

Given that a high proportion of young people who encounter the youth justice system also have difficulties with literacy and numeracy, it is interest-ing to consider the recommendations with regard to dosage for making progress in these areas. Findings of literacy interventions and youth justice interventions suggest that learners usually need to attend at least 100 hours of instruction to make progress equivalent to one grade level (Torgerson *et al.*

2004). Interestingly, a high dosage in youth justice for any intervention is also deemed to be more than 100 hours (Lipsey 1995).

It is essential that Yot staff distinguish between what is arranged (in volume and quality terms) and what a young person actually receives. The dosage is not synonymous with the timetable. The clear implication is that Yot staff need to ensure effective monitoring of attendance and participation.

The challenges for practice

It is recognised that education, training and employment issues pose very different problems for managers and practitioners in the youth justice system than other areas identified by the Youth Justice Board as priorities for guidance on effective practice. Important areas such as final warning interventions or remand management, are specific to those working in youth justice and have a statutory basis. Other interventions such as mentoring or parenting programmes, although used by other agencies, are often provided directly by Yots.

Education and training, in contrast, is delivered by separately constituted agencies. The challenge is therefore that an area containing such important risk factors for the onset and continuation of offending behaviour, and that also provides powerful protective factors, is not under the direct control of managers or practitioners in Yots.

Consequently, managers and practitioners may well feel even more frustrated with regard to education and training issues, feeling they have relatively little effect due to the responses of institutions and professionals beyond their control.

Challenges may also arise as a result of contradictory tensions. Many teachers may feel that colleagues from social work and youth justice do not understand school cultures and their everyday pressures. Equally youth justice or social work practitioners may, all too often, defer to the assumptions and practices of teachers.

Being able to describe what is effective practice in a successful school is however some way from being able to prescribe how to achieve this with all schools. Changing the culture within any institution remains one of the stiffest management challenges, even if systematic evaluations had made clear exactly how this can be achieved – which they have not. The matter is not simply one of the discrete reorganisation of a given school, as – particularly where young people at high risk are concerned – there are all the variable relationships with the other agencies and their professionals to be considered as well as the resources available to the community.

Summary

- Detachment from mainstream education appears to be extensive among young people in the youth justice system. It is estimated that the great majority of those entering and leaving custody are detached from mainstream education.

- Despite the prevalence of and persistent use of segregated educational pro-vision for young people who offend, there is little evidence of its success in terms of key indicators such as reintegration or positive progression.

- Interventions which have been evaluated to a relatively high standard and have been shown to be promising in preventing detachment are the same as for tackling low attainment, and include pre-school education, family literacy, intensive reading schemes, reasoning and social skills education, and organisational change in schools.

- There is some evidence of a relationship between attendance, attainment (particularly in literacy and numeracy) and lower offending rates.

- Most studies that try to measure the effectiveness of custodial educational intervention or resettlement programmes have been compromised by weak research design but do provide some evidence of a link between educational intervention and reduction in recidivism, although this tends to be for adults.

- There is no evidence that young people in the youth justice system require active or vocational learning any more than other young people.

- Maintaining programme integrity is a key challenge for Yot staff due to a lack of useful management information about the educational status of young people and because they are not directly responsible for service delivery.

Note

1 287,883 sentences that resulted in a disposal of some sort were recorded, which may represent about 150,000 young people according to the Youth Justice Board statistics department (personal communication). There is also likely to be a certain number from the previous year's disposals which would increase this total.

Further reading

Stephenson, M. (2007) *Young People and Offending: Education, Youth Justice and Social Inclusion*. Cullompton: Willan Publishing.

Youth Justice Board (2006) *Barriers to Engagement in Education, Training and Employment for Young People in the Youth Justice System*. London: Youth Justice Board.

4

Mental health

The evidence base for mental health

Mental health is a critical issue for all youth justice practitioners. Mental health issues are extremely common among young people who offend; may be associated with self-harm and suicidal behaviour; may be a manifestation of serious physical, or sexual abuse, neglect, or of poverty and deprivation; may lead to self-medication with illicit drugs.

> We are all mental ... mental health is fundamental to us all. (Mental Health Foundation 1999).

Different professions and agencies working in the field of mental health use different terms to describe the range of emotional and behavioural difficulties in children and young people. The language used in the mental health field tends to have a medical bias, 'perhaps because of the rapid advances in research in this area – but this is by no means a complete picture' (National Assembly for Wales 2000). Other sectors and professions use different terminology which youth justice practitioners are likely to come across in their practice.

Educationalists, for example, use the term 'emotional and behavioural difficulties' (EBD) to describe the difficulties children and young people face. The definition of EBD is so broad that it embraces a large number of young people facing multiple difficulties (Stephenson 2007) and refers to a continuum of behaviours from 'behaviour which challenges teachers but is within normal, albeit unacceptable, bands and that which is indicative of serious mental illness' (DfEE Circular 9/94: 7). 'Special educational needs' (SEN) is also commonly used as a label within educational spheres. This can apply to problems with learning as well as to mental health and behavioural difficulties. Given the multiple difficulties that young people who encounter the youth justice system often face and the strong likelihood that they may have detached from education or are at risk of doing so, it is likely that many will already have acquired such labels. The label itself tells us nothing about the nature of their difficulties nor how severe they are.

In this chapter the overall term 'mental health' is used as an umbrella term embracing concepts of mental well-being, mental health problems and mental disorder. These latter terms are used to refer to and describe specific experiences and problems as follows:

- **Mental well-being**: the positive capacities and qualities that enable young people to deal with the ups and downs of life, experience emotions appropriately, make friends and have a sense of identity.

- **Mental health problems**: a broad range of emotional or behavioural difficulties that may cause concern to parents and carers and/or distress to the young person. These difficulties may be short- or long term. Although they affect a young person's day-to-day life, they may not be diagnosable as a mental disorder.

- **Mental disorder**: those problems that meet the requirements of ICD-10 (International Statistical Classificiation of Disease and Related Health Problems, 10th Revision), an internationally recognised classification system for mental and behavioural disorders, usually associated with considerable distress and substantial interference in a young person's everyday life. The distinction between a **problem** and a **disorder** is not always exact but depends on the severity, persistence, effects and combination of difficulties experienced by the young person and those around them.

- **Mental illness**: sometimes used in the mental health sector to refer to the most severe types of mental disorder: 'for example, more severe cases of depressive illness, psychotic disorders and severe cases of anorexia nervosa could be described in this way' (National Assembly for Wales 2000). Practitioners may come across this term in their practice, but it is only referred to in this chapter where it has been used by other authors.

These definitions are underpinned by the assumption that mental health affects all of us in one way or another, and that the mental health of children and young people is an issue that concerns all staff who come into contact with young people in the youth justice system.

As with the educational labels dismissed earlier in this chapter, those broad definitions mask a whole range of distinct difficulties young people are experiencing and describe a continuum of behaviours from those that simply challenge societal norms and authority figures in some way to those that are severe and potentially life threatening at the other end.

It is important to consider mental health within a cultural context, as each culture has its own ideas about well-being and what promotes it:

> Different cultures have varying views about the roles and responsibilities of children within the wider family as well as society – what is seen as 'mentally healthy' behaviour may well differ, therefore, from one cul-

ture to another. Some stress the importance of children acquiring independence from the family, for example, whereas others encourage dependence (Mental Health Foundation 1999).

Definitions of mental health

'Mental' is a word which has for too long been seen almost exclusively in negative terms – as a term of abuse within the playground, the workplace or even the family – and when mental is linked to health, the result is often confusion (Mental Health Foundation 1999).

Many attempts have been made to define mental health in a single sentence or statement. Perhaps the most well-known definition of health, both mental and physical, is that of the World Health Organization (WHO). The WHO defined health as a 'complete state of physical, mental and social well being, and not merely the absence of disease or infirmity'. More recently, and in light of the difficulty of achieving short definitions that are clear and meaningful, contemporary definitions have suggested a range of elements or descriptions that constitute the concept of mental health (Weare 2000).

In practice, the term 'mental health' is often synonymous with 'mental health problems'. Training courses and materials, which are described as being about mental health or mental health awareness, for example, often turn out to be almost exclusively concerned with mental disorders and mental health problems. For this reason, some authors use broader phrases when referring to this area of young people's lives, such as 'mental, emotional and social health'. These terms, familiar to educators, community workers and others, reflect work with children and young people known as emotional, social or personal education. They are seen as less narrowing and negative than 'mental health' on its own (Weare 2000).

The relationship between mental health problems and offending

The relationship between mental health problems or mental disorders and offending behaviour is by no means clear-cut. It is possible that there may be no specific relationship between mental health problems and offending. It may be coincidental that mental health problems and mental disorders are more common among young people who offend than among young people who do not.

Young people who are not experiencing mental health problems before contact with the youth justice system may subsequently experience other life events that could cause anxiety or depression (such as the loss of an important relationship through bereavement or family breakdown) which are not related to their offending behaviour.

It may be suggested that mental health problems and offending behaviour have similar causes. There is a high degree of overlap between the risk factors for developing mental health problems and disorders and for engaging with offending behaviour. Factors associated with both include:

- physical, sexual and/or emotional abuse and neglect;

- poverty and deprivation;

- family dysfunction and discord;

- school exclusion, poor academic attainment and high levels of unemployment;

- individual characteristics, including learning difficulties and hyperactivity.

In the more severe types of mental disorder (mental illness) such as bipolar disorder and psychosis, offending behaviour may be a symptom of mental disorder. Young people who are experiencing delusions (false beliefs) or visual hallucinations, for example, may behave in bizarre or manic ways that bring them into contact with the police.

Mental health problems may be a factor contributing to substance misuse. Young people may try to manage symptoms of a mental health problem by self-medicating with alcohol and drugs (cocaine and cannabis, for example) and then become dependent upon them. This in turn can lead to criminal behaviour for the purpose of obtaining more drugs.

Substance misuse may accelerate or trigger a predisposition to a mental health problem. Research linking substance use with violent or aggressive behaviour shows a clear link between alcohol use and aggression, but is more equivocal with regard to other drugs (Hoaken and Stewart 2003).

Offending behaviour is considered to be a factor in causing mental health problems. For example, some young people who offend attribute their mental health symptoms to 'witnessing violence as part of their criminal lifestyles' (Hagell 2002).

Whether or not young people are experiencing mental health problems before contact with the youth justice system, it is likely that they will be affected by their interactions with it. This is particularly likely to be the case for children and young people in secure settings, given that imprisonment has 'long been recognised as a source of stress' (Hagell 2002).

Remand can be a highly stressful experience for young people, especially where they are expecting to be bailed and/or are remanded away from their home area. It is likely that the uncertainty of remand may increase the risk of suicide (Howard League website 2005, press releases). The question here is whether this can be attributed to a mental 'disorder' or mental health problem of some kind or the additional stress experienced by the young person as a result of the experience. Attributing a mental health label to young people in these circumstances tends to locate the problem and the source of stress within the young person and not in the system that is causing it.

Given the multiplicity of specific difficulties and behaviours subsumed under the various mental health labels described above, it is hard to see how a large proportion of young people who encounter the youth justice system could not be described as having a mental health problem of some kind. There is also a danger in attributing medical labels to young people's behaviours in that it locates the difficulty within the young person and may lead professionals to reach for a medical response. An example of this is the relatively recent phenomenon of Attention Deficit Hyperactivity Disorder (ADHD), a label attached to many young people at risk of offending or reoffending. The bundling together of challenging or 'difficult' behaviours and defining them as a 'disorder' clearly puts the onus on the young person as the one with the problem and not, for example, on the way the school curriculum is organised or the behaviours or others around them, parents/carers, for example. This use of medical terms to describe behaviours also encourages professionals increasingly to reach for a medical solution, the use of drugs for example, to treat ADHD.

The prevalence of mental health problems among young people

A range of studies have been carried out to determine the levels of mental health problems among young people in the general population. It is often difficult to compare these studies as they use different definitions. Some focus just on those mental health disorders that are diagnosable within the ICD-10 classification, while others use broader definitions of mental health problems. With this in mind, the following data are presented to give an overall flavour of current research findings.

In 2000, the Office for National Statistics (Meltzer *et al.* 2000) reported on the findings of a 1999 survey into the mental health of children and adolescents in Great Britain. The survey looked at children and adolescents aged 5–15 living in private households in Scotland, England and Wales. It revealed surprisingly high levels of mental health problems.

Using the criteria that the mental disorder should 'cause distress to the child' or have a 'considerable impact on the child's day-to-day life', the report concluded that 10 per cent of children aged 5–15 had a mental disorder. The survey reported that:

- 5 per cent had clinically significant conduct disorders;
- 4 per cent were assessed as having emotional disorders;
- 1 per cent were rated as hyperactive;
- less common disorders such as autistic disorders, tics and eating disorders affected 0.5 per cent of the sampled population;

- 10 per cent of boys and 6 per cent of girls aged between 5 and 10 had a mental disorder;

- 13 per cent of boys and 10 per cent of girls aged between 11 and 15 had a mental disorder.

Although ethnicity was difficult to interpret as few of those in the sample studied identified themselves as part of a particular ethnic group, the following proportions of the young people were experiencing a mental disorder:

- nearly 10 per cent of white children;

- 12 per cent of black children;

- 8 per cent of Pakistani and Bangladeshi children;

- 4 per cent of Indian children.

(Meltzer *et al.* 2000)

YoungMinds, the children's mental health charity, has used this data to illustrate what this means in concrete terms. For example, 'in a town the size of Derby, about 5,000 children will be suffering from a mental health problem.' In a secondary school with 1,000 pupils, around '50 pupils will be seriously depressed; a further 100 will be suffering significant distress; between 5 and 10 girls will be affected by eating disorders, and 10–20 pupils will have an obsessive compulsive disorder' (YoungMinds 1999).

Bearing in mind the difficulties of comparing different studies in this area and the different definitions being used, Hagell's conclusion is perhaps the most useful for youth justice practitioners. Making extensive use of a range of research projects she concluded that in relation to young people and young adults:

> The rates of mental health problems are at least three times as high for those within the criminal justice system as within the general population, if not higher (Hagell 2002).

Key research in this area has been undertaken by the Office for National Statistics (Lader *et al.* 1997). Approximately 600 young people, both on remand and convicted, were interviewed as part of a survey into mental health problems among prisoners in England and Wales. A very specific range of mental disorders was used in this survey, which concluded that 'a high proportion of all young offenders had evidence of several mental disorders. In all sample groups, at least 95 per cent were assessed as having one or more disorders and a very large proportion, about 80 per cent, were assessed as having more than one' (Lader *et al.* 1997).

More recently, Harrington and Bailey (2005) interviewed 300 people in the youth justice system (50 per cent community, 50 per cent secure estate) using assessments for demographics, mental health and social needs. They found a third of young people had mental health needs, a fifth with depression, a tenth reporting self-harm in the past month and a tenth suffering anxiety and post-traumatic stress symptoms. Hyperactivity was reported in 7 per cent of the young people and psychotic-like symptoms in 5 per cent. Almost a quarter had learning difficulties and a further third borderline learning difficulties.

Drugs, alcohol and substance misuse

The ONS survey by Meltzer *et al.* 2000 found that:

- 41 per cent of 11–15 year olds who regularly smoked were assessed as having a mental disorder, compared with the overall rate of 11 per cent;

- 24 per cent of young people who drank alcohol more than once a week had a mental disorder; this was three times the proportion among the group who had never drunk any alcohol;

- about half of the 11–15-year-olds who frequently used cannabis (i.e. more than once a week) had a mental disorder, compared with one fifth of those who used it less than once a month, and one tenth of those who had never used cannabis.

Hagell also reported a very high correlation between substance misuse and mental health problems among young people in the criminal justice system. For example:

in a study of 111 young offenders referred from court for possible alcohol and drug problems ... 91% were shown to also have conduct disorder, 58% oppositional disorder, 33% aggressive conduct disorder, 32% depression and 23% attention deficit disorder ... Riggs *et al.* (1995) assessed levels of depression in a sample of 90 young offenders who had both conduct disorder and substance use disorders. A fifth had major depression (Hagell 2002).

Similarly, a recent review of young people in custody found that:

- 51 per cent were poly-drug users, using two or more drugs more than once a week;

- 40 per cent had been dependent on a substance at some point in their lives;

- 30 per cent said they had taken drugs not to get high but just to feel 'normal';

- 38 per cent had taken a drug to 'forget everything or to blot everything out';

- 56 per cent were identified as being eligible for a mental health screening interview using the *Asset* mental health screening tool.

(Youth Justice Board 2004g)

Suicide

Suicide and self-harm in young people – and indeed across the whole of the general population – may be related to mental health problems and mental disorders.

Mortality rates have steadily declined in all age groups of the general population since the beginning of the twentieth century, except in relation to young women where this decline has slowed and in relation to young men where it has begun to increase. During the 1960s, 1970s and 1980s, road traffic accidents were the most common cause of death in young adult men. From the 1990s onwards, suicide became the most common cause.

The Office for National Statistics (ONS) uses the term 'suicide' in relation to deaths where the coroner has given a verdict of suicide or an open verdict, on the basis that in most open-verdict cases the harm was self-inflicted but there was insufficient evidence to prove that the person deliberately intended to kill himself/herself. ONS data show that men are far more likely to commit suicide than women.

The rate of self-inflicted death among young people who offend is significantly higher than for this age group within the general population.

Using the term 'self-inflicted death' rather than suicide, the Safer Custody Group has looked at the deaths in prison in England and Wales of young people aged under 21, from 1992 to 2001. In 2001, the rate of self-inflicted death was 119 per 100,000 young people in both the juvenile and young people population (15–20-year-olds) (Safer Custody Group, 2003). This compares with a rate of 13.3 per 100,000 in the general population of young men aged 15–24 and 3.7 per 100,000 in the general population of young women (Office for National Statistics 2004).

The Safer Custody Group usually quotes *rates* of self-inflicted death in order to take into account increases in the population. It is important to note that because of the small numbers of young people involved (see below), small fluctuations in numbers make a big difference to overall rates. For example, in 2003 there were no juvenile (aged 15–17) deaths in custody, so the juvenile rate for 2003 was zero.

The Safer Custody Group found that in the 10-year period 1992 to 2001, there were 668 self-inflicted deaths in the prison population, of which 107 were young people:

- 90 young people (aged 18 to 20);

- 17 juveniles (aged 15 to 17).

In addition, the study found that:

- 95 per cent of the young people and all the juveniles who died from self-inflicted death were male;
- all 107 young people and juveniles died by hanging;
- 71 per cent of incidents among juveniles happened within a month of reception;
- unsentenced young people were over-represented.

Education

In the ONS survey (Meltzer *et al.* 2000) into children and young people's mental health, children with a mental disorder were about three times more likely than other children to have officially recognised special educational needs: 49 per cent compared with 15 per cent. This varied greatly by type of disorder. Children with a hyperkinetic disorder (such as ADHD) were twice as likely as those with an emotional disorder to be diagnosed as having special educational needs: 71 per cent compared with 37 per cent. Among the children with special educational needs, 17 per cent were at stage 5, the level at which the local education authority issues a statement about the child. Among the children who had a mental disorder *and* special educational needs, 28 per cent were at stage 5. Among the children who did not have a mental disorder, but *did* have special educational needs, 13 per cent were at stage 5.

In terms of specific learning difficulty (defined as *'the failure to achieve expected academic progress in reading and spelling despite conventional instruction, adequate intelligence and sociocultural opportunity'*) children with a mental disorder were three times more likely than those with no disorder to have a specific learning difficulty: 12 per cent compared with 4 per cent.

For young people in contact with the youth justice service, where there are higher levels of mental health problems and mental disorders, young people with learning difficulties are also over-represented (Diamond, Floyd and Misch 2004).

Mental health services and effectiveness

An Audit Commission report into specialist Child and Adolescent Mental Health Services (CAMHS) in England and Wales identified a gap in knowledge and understanding about emerging effective practice in mental health interventions. The report concluded: 'There is limited evidence about the efficacy of CAMHS interventions' (Audit Commission 1999a). Efficacy is defined as the ability of a medical or surgical intervention to produce the desired outcome in a defined population under particular conditions.

97

UNIVERSITY OF WINCHESTER
LIBRARY

The report concludes that although some findings are beginning to emerge, 'It is difficult to demonstrate conclusively a cause and effect relationship between interventions and changes, particularly with children and families who have severe and longstanding difficulties' (Wallace *et al*. 1997).

Both studies of Pitcher *et al*. (2004) and Harrington and Bailey (2005) indicate that at the community level CAMHS for young people were patchy. Of health workers seconded to Yots some 40 per cent were seconded by CAMHS, but most of these were not formally members of the service, so did not receive clinical supervision by this route. Few opportunities were found in the studies for formal and regular opportunites for consultation between Yots and CAMHS. Mental health resources within Yots were often stretched and some tensions arose with respect to confidentiality, time-limited working and the extent to which mental health workers should engage in core Yot activities discharging youth justice processes.

In the juvenile secure estate there was found to be no routine mental health assessment of young people on admission, with *Asset* not specifically highlighting this issue. Frequently, mental health services were provided on a sessional basis with a lack of appropriate intervention packages available. Support to secure estate staff to enable them to meet the mental health needs of young people was in short supply. Multi-disciplinary approaches to service provision were uncommon (Harrington and Bailey 2005).

The needs of these young people were often not met while in the youth justice system, largely due to the absence of routine mental health screening and assessment procedures which specifically focused on mental health issues. While there was some evidence that the mental health needs of young people were lower in custody due to the levels of supervision provided, these needs often increased on discharge. Continuity of care between custody and community was poor. In addition there was little co-ordination of interventions between youth justice, mental health, education and social services (Harrington and Bailey 2005).

Benefits to young people

Using information from a range of studies, YoungMinds concludes that mental health problems in young people have been found to be a 'clear predictor of problems in adulthood'. It is likely that 'early assessment and treatment of even the more serious and enduring mental health disorders can reduce problems later on' (YoungMinds 1999). Early intervention may also prevent relatively minor mental health problems from developing into major ones during childhood and adolescence.

Many young people have mental health problems and disorders that are unrecognised and undiagnosed by mental health specialists (Street 2000). In addition, there are insufficient child and adolescent mental health services to treat and support those young people whose mental health needs *have* been identified. Young people need mental health support from the broad range of non-clinical staff who work with them in a range of different roles.

In practice, it is often those young people with the most obvious and/or demanding needs that get the most time and attention from staff. Young people with less obvious mental health needs may not receive the support they need which could prevent a minor problem from developing into a major one.

Benefits to youth justice practitioners

Although practitioners may be concerned that addressing the mental health needs of young people represents an increase in their workload, the evidence indicates the contrary. In schools, for example, promoting mental, emotional and social needs has improved pupils' self-esteem and, in turn, their academic achievement (Weare 2000). There is some evidence in schools that mental health promotion strategies can reduce the workload of teachers rather than add a burden to it (Weare 2000).

Given the prevalence of mental health disorders among young people in the youth justice system, mental health interventions may contribute to reducing crime and the fear of crime.

Mental health promotion

Much of the research evidence about the effectiveness of mental health promotion comes from work with families and work in schools and community settings. What emerged from the evidence to the Bright Futures inquiry into children and young people's mental health (Mental Health Foundation 1999) was a series of features of effective interventions, including the importance of:

- early intervention – intervening early in the problem cycle and early in the life cycle (although this does not preclude later intervention);
- intervening at critical points in parents' and young people's lives – for example, after the birth of a child or when children start school;
- tackling the range of difficulties, not just mental health problems;
- being universally available – to reach all those who will benefit;
- long-term interventions, not 'one-offs';
- directing interventions at risk factors for developing mental health problems.

(Mental Health Foundation 1999)

The inquiry also found evidence that not only the type of intervention but also the manner and location of its delivery affect its outcome. However, the

Mental Health Foundation cautions:

> The enthusiasm for early interventions must be tempered by an under-standing of their limitations. It is unfortunately often those in greatest need who decline their invitations. The challenge is . . . to ensure that interventions are acceptable and appropriate to those most in need. (Mental Health Foundation 1999)

Drawing on a wide range of studies on whole-school programmes on mental, emotional and social health, Weare (2000) identifies four essential factors for ensuring that schools can promote effective academic learning *and* emotional and social learning. Weare sees mental, emotional and social health promotion as being inextricably linked to academic achievement; the one supports and promotes the other. Effective strategies are therefore defined by Weare as those that achieve positive outcomes in both areas. The four key factors that support both social and academic learning are:

● supportive relationships between teachers and pupils, between teachers and their colleagues, and between teachers and the head;

● a high degree of participation by staff and pupils, supported by the values and structures of the school;

● encouragement of autonomy in staff and pupils: supporting staff and pupils to work independently, minimising 'prescription, control and surveillance';

● clarity about rules, boundaries and expectations.

In addition, mental health promotion strategies may need to have a high pro-file within the school, be tailored to the nature and ethos of individual organisations, and take a long-term perspective (Weare 2000).

Specialist interventions

> The absence of a body of information or strong evidence of the effective-ness of psychological and pharmacological treatments for children and young people is well recognised . . . However, substantial progress has been made in identifying the range of interventions that have the poten-tial to benefit children with mental health problems and their families. (Mental Health Foundation 1999)

This is not to say that evidence relating to some interventions with children and young people does not exist. Rather, the knowledge base in this field, and the evidence-based practice deriving from that knowledge base, is still evolving.

Research into specialist interventions with children and young people with mental health problems is less well developed than that relating to young people who offend. This may be because of the wide range of factors impacting on young people's mental health at any one time, and the difficulties of isolating a specific intervention as having a demonstrable impact on the outcome for the young person (Walker 2003). In addition, 'the wide range of professionals from many agencies having some impact on child mental health is so diverse as to make it unrealistic to identify a linear sequence of causality from intervention through to outcome' (Mental Health Foundation 1999).

One of the most comprehensive pieces of research into specialist interventions is by Fonagy *et al.* (2002), reviewing the existing evidence for the range of treatments used in child and adolescent psychiatry. With the aim of informing clinical decision-making, Fonagy *et al.* appraised the findings of hundreds of studies into treatments for specific mental disorders. Owing to the lack of existing research in key areas, the small sample size of most studies, and the inconsistency of outcome measurement and child age ranges across the studies, they conclude that the available evidence is insufficient to identify effective interventions.

While acknowledging these limitations there are, nonetheless, several common features that emerge from the research on treatments for individual mental disorders. These include:

- the importance of early intervention;
- the need to use a range of methods, and combinations of methods, within individual treatment plans;
- the key role of the relationship between therapist and client in treatments;
- the importance of the family context, both in the assessment process and in supporting or thwarting treatment efforts.

(Fonagy *et al.* 2002)

In addition, Fonagy *et al.* identify that though there have been very few drug trials specifically involving young people, there is some evidence that drugs are effective for a small number of disorders.

The principles of effective practice and mental health

Risk classification

High levels of mental health problems are frequently detected in cohorts of young people identified as being at risk of offending or reoffending, particularly when screened using assessment tools specifically developed to ascertain these needs (Audit Commission 2004; Arnull *et al.* 2005). Harrington and Bailey (2005), for example, found 31 per cent of young people so identified in a national cross-sectional study using the Salford Needs Assessment Schedule for Adolescents (SNASA).

> A third of young offenders had a mental health need. This was broken down as follows: almost a fifth of young offenders had problems with depression, while a tenth of young people reported a history of self-harm within the last month. Similar rates were found for young people suffering from anxiety and PTSD. Hyperactivity and psychotic-like symptoms were reported in 7 per cent and 5 per cent of young people respectively (Harrington and Bailey 2005).

This compared with only 15 per cent of young people identified with mental health problems from a cross-sectional study of 600 *Asset* forms sampled from six Yot areas. This finding caused Harrington *et al.* (2005) to conclude that 'Asset is not sufficiently sensitive in identifying mental health needs in young offenders' (see Chapter 2).

To remedy this situation the Youth Justice Board has recently published a mental health screening tool (2006d) for young people in the youth justice system and a screening pathway to improve the identification of mental health needs. Where a young person scores 2 or more in the emotional and mental health section of *Asset*, a Screening Questionnaire Interview for Adolescents (SQIfA) should be completed. This consists of a screen for eight common mental health problems in adolescence and is raised by the practitioner undertaking the core *Asset* assessment:

- alcohol use;

- drugs;

- depression;

- traumatic experiences;

- anxiety/excessive worries/stress;

- self-harm;

- ADHD/hyperactivity;

- psychotic symptoms.

Where the SQIfA yields a score of 2, no immediate action may be required but the practitioner may consider repeating the process in 4–6 weeks or if circumstances change. If the SQIfA score is 3 or 4, a full Screening Interview for Adolescents (SIfA) may need to be undertaken by an appropriately trained youth justice worker. Where the SIfA identifies mental health needs, these may be specifically supported within the Yot, or the young person may be assisted in accessing CAMHS services at tiers 2 to 4.

In respect of the risk of self-harm, this information may be vitally important in ensuring vulnerabilities associated with the young person are identified and responded to. This is particularly important to communicate between youth justice professionals where a young person enters custody or secure accommodation either for remand or sentence purposes.

Criminogenic need

Screening for mental health problems is highly likely to identify allied criminogenic needs, which require recognition and response in the course of an intervention. These are most likely to include the following need areas:

- education (attendance and attainment);
- relationship difficulties (with family members and peers);
- violence (to people and property);
- other risky behaviour (inappropriate sexual behaviour, drug and alcohol abuse).

It may therefore be important that responding to these needs is built into the core components of interventions. Where specific mental health services are to be referred to, assessed for, or provided by CAMHS and allied specialists (i.e. tiers 2 to 4), it is likely that youth offending professionals will have to liaise with mental health professionals as to their co-ordinated working practices. The co-ordination will need to be based on the ethical sharing of information on the young person's needs:

- presenting mental health issue;
- offending history and present position;
- history of alcohol or substance misuse;
- family and social background including history of family mental health issues;
- previous interventions/treatment;
- likely motivation of the young person to change.

Responsivity

Cognitive behavioural and problem-solving based packages for offence reduction and mental health may be more effective if they share common principles. Interventions, for example, that improve self-esteem may also have an effect on depressive symptoms. Some have argued for the introduction of a Care Programme Approach (CPA) to ensure greater responsivity where mental health needs and antisocial behaviour coincide.

The CPA has four main elements:

1 Systematic assessment of need;

2 Formation of a care plan with clear roles for a variety of service providers;

3 Appointment of a key worker to monitor and co-ordinate the programme;

4 Regular review and updating of the plan.

The CPA seeks to address the requirements of both responsivity and continuity of support over time and in different settings.

Community based

Models of mental health provision differ between secure establishments and Yots. In many secure establishments, mental health provision is provided on a sessional basis by a designated mental health professional. To the extent that this reflects professionals' personal interest in the work area, continuity of provision is vulnerable to changes in personnel and priority. Unlike in the community, a multi-disciplinary mental health team working in the secure estate is rare.

Within Yots, mental health provision is usually led by a designated health worker. Available evidence (Pitcher *et al.* 2004) suggests that they are often overwhelmed and unsupported, only infrequently getting clinical support from local mental health provision. Little regular consultation may take place between Yot health workers and local CAMHS (Health Care Commission Report Nov 2006). This tends to be informal or on an individual case basis, although there may be formal protocols signed off with respect to referral pathways for local tier 2 and 3 services.

Problems with the identification and response to a young person's mental health needs include the lack of intervention packages available, poor supervision and support of staff, the need for improved staff training and interruptions in the continuity of care.

Difficulties in maintaining continuity of care may arise from a number of issues such as:

- poor information accompanying young people on entry into the secure estate from the community;

- repeated assessments of the young person as they move through different settings;

- poor information accompanying young people leaving the secure estate for throughcare in the community;

- lack of appropriate services in the community to ensure continuity;

- young people refusing to engage.

Intervention modality

Effective interventions to address the mental health needs of young people at risk of offending or reoffending may not only improve their mental health well-being, but also affect their motivation and ability to engage with offence reduction programmes. Harrington and Bailey (2005) have recently reviewed four different approaches to the treatment of mental health disorders: psychological treatments, pharmacotherapy, systemic/family therapy and multi-modal treatments. Their conclusions identify a six-point approach to the development of interventions.

- Programmes should seek adaptation of a young person's individual circumstances, using cognitive behavioural and problem-solving skills training approaches. These programmes should be based on assessed need, the severity of the need and an appraisal of the young person's motivation and ability.

- Multi-modal approaches should simultaneously focus on the involvement of the young person themselves, his/her family and the young person's peer group.

- Young people should be assisted to engage with interventions by use of motivational initiatives (e.g. motivational interviewing, mentoring).

- Programmes should be delivered by trained staff.

- Young people with moderate and severe mental health problems should be referred to an appropriate professional or agency.

A range of factors impact on young people's mental health – biological, psychological, social and environmental. In monitoring and reviewing specific interventions and programmes, it is therefore important to include *all* aspects of young people's lives, not simply any changes to specific presenting symptoms (Audit Commission 1999a).

The Audit Commission survey of CAMHS states that research has begun to show that:

> The essential ingredient of effectiveness … is not the range of service options, but the human qualities of the individuals who provide these options. If they are not respectful, empathetic and genuine, then little they do will be of value to families. (Audit Commission 1999a)

In monitoring interventions, therefore, it is not only what practitioners do that is important, but how they do it.

Programme integrity

Analyses of recent and past intervention programmes have commented upon the uneven and poor quality of implementation, the ambiguity of the theoretical underpinning of programmes, and poor or flawed evaluation initiatives. In the arena of mental health interventions, a number of recurrent impediments to the integrity of programme delivery can be identified:

- poorly defined referral pathways: 'Even where Asset identified a mental health/substance misuse need associated with offending behaviour, a quarter of these children and young people were still not referred on for specialist assessment and/or treatment' (HM Inspectorate of Probation 2006);
- long waiting times;
- failure to define responsibility for service provision for 16- and 17-year-olds;
- absence of provision for those with dual diagnosis (mental health needs and substance misuse);
- shortage of trained staff;
- requirements of discipline and control in secure environment taking precedence over therapeutic requirements.

Clear case management standards within the context of a local mental health strategy for young people who offend may need to focus considerations on these key impediments to programme integrity.

Young people and their families are often reluctant to engage with mental health services, and quickly cease to be engaged (Audit Commission 1999a; Mental Health Foundation 1999). It is self-evident that where young people withdraw from interventions these are unlikely to be effective. It is therefore important that monitoring and review of interventions are not simply carried out by practitioners and professionals, but include the views of young people and their families about the services they have received.

Monitoring and review of mental health interventions by general and specialist CAMHS are therefore important to the developing knowledge base for interventions across the wider mental health sector. This knowledge base enables practitioners and services to provide interventions that are effective in delivering what young people and their families need.

In involving young people and their families in monitoring and review, a range of factors may need to be considered, including the scope of the review process.

Dosage

Programmes must be of sufficient intensity and duration to achieve their aims, especially with respect to high-risk young people. Several impediments to the delivery of appropriate intensity of support to offending young people with mental health needs have been identified in the research, including inadequacy of resources for intervention; expectation of time-limited work from health staff; the pressures associated with waiting lists; poor co-ordination of support across sectors (custody/community; youth justice/CAMHS) and the non-engagement of young people.

The need for a local mental health strategy engaging Yots, secure establishments, CAMHS, education and social care has been widely canvassed as a vehicle to improve multi-disciplinary service delivery. In line with this, a strategy is proposed to respond to young people who do not attend for intervention. This requires:

- clearly defined procedures for monitoring attendance and engagement in programme elements;

- tight, but supportive, supervision of the young person;

- clear lines of communication between relevant professionals providing the various elements of the intervention;

- support of parents/carers in encouraging the young person to attend and participate;

- a focus on attendance and participation in sentence management review meeting.

The challenges for practice

Multi-disciplinary and multi-agency working

In the history of child and adolescent mental health services there has always been a recognition that multidisciplinary effort needs to be brought to bear on the difficulties of troubled children (Walker 2003).

Working effectively with other agencies appears to be pivotal to the early detection and treatment of mental health problems and disorders: 'A system of care made up of multiple agencies working together acknowledges that troubled children have multiple needs which require, at different times, different combinations of a broad range of health and social care agencies' (Walker 2003). Joint working is underpinned by key principles for synchronised models of care.

Several researchers have, however, described a range of barriers that stand in the way of different practitioners and agencies working together in the interests of prevention, early detection and treatment for young people.

The Mental Health Foundation (1999) found that while it is clear that 'effective multi-agency working within child and adolescent services, and between child and adolescent mental health services and other services is key to effective service delivery', a number of factors were working against this:

- the fragmentation of services, both within and between agencies;

- the lack of priority accorded to children's mental health services in health, social services and education;

- different approaches and lines of accountability across disciplines;

- different conceptual frameworks and language;

- issues of status, salary and training.

(Mental Health Foundation 1999)

Multi-disciplinary training is one of the approaches suggested to overcome these barriers, along with the development of multi-agency screening and assessment tools. A degree of cultural change may also be required, with a commitment from everyone concerned to develop a common language by building on the broad areas of agreement that can be found.

Different services each have their own conceptual framework and language for understanding disturbed and disturbing behaviour in children and young people. This means that:

A Yot team member may talk about a young person engaged in anti-social activity, a teacher about poor concentration and aggressive behaviour, and a social worker or youth worker may perceive a needy, anxious, abused child – all are describing the same child (Walker 2003).

Different agency responses to a specific difficulty may therefore be the consequence of different theoretical models of understanding, working cultures and practices.

The table below shows how youth justice, social services, education and psychiatry respond differently to the same presenting problem.

Table 4.1 Different agency responses to the same presenting problem

PROBLEM: AGGRESSION

Juvenile justice	*Social services*	*Education*	*Psychiatry*
Referral to police: decision to charge	Referral to social services	Referral to education department	Referral to child psychiatrist
Pre-sentence report completed	Social work assessment conducted	Educational psychology assessment	Psychiatric assessment
Sentenced to custody	Decision to accommodate	Placed in residential school	Admitted to regional in-patient unit
Labelled as young person who offends	Labelled as beyond parental control	Labelled as having learning difficulty	Labelled as mentally ill

Source: Walker (2003), adapted from Malek (1993)

Increasingly, however, there is recognition that 'no one agency has the monopoly of understanding and capability when trying to help troubled young people' (National Assembly for Wales 2000).

In the interests of better interprofessional relationships, Walker (2003) argues for:

- shared training across disciplines;

- more integrated provision at tier 1, with staff receiving support to intervene in ways that meet the needs of the local community;

- a community-work dimension to mobilise individuals and groups who can act as grass roots facilitators to help create preventive resources when and where they are needed.

Hagell (2002) reports that while the 'criminal justice system is notoriously bad at detecting (mental health) needs, the NHS is also not good at meeting them even once the right people have been referred'. Hagell urges the need for 'improvement in inter-agency communication, understanding and delivery that is tailored to the stage in the criminal justice system at which the young person is engaged' and an 'end to the confusion about which agency should provide services'.

Agencies involved in delivering substance misuse services experience similar barriers to inter-agency working. These barriers are exacerbated by the absence of working agreements between partners because:

- partners are unaware of each other's roles and responsibilities;

- inaccurate assumptions are made about what is being delivered by the other partner;

- the purpose and potential outcome of another agency's interventions are poorly understood by the other partner;

- there may be cultural differences in relation to the goals of interventions, for example between a focus on preventing offending in youth justice and the minimisation of substance-use-related harm in substance misuse services;

- there is no agreed understanding about information sharing.

Interventions

The nature of the relationship between mental health and offending is not fully understood. More specifically, there is no clear understanding of the impact that mental health interventions will have on a young person's offending behaviour. It is known, however, that there are currently insufficient specialist CAMHS to meet the level of mental health needs among children and young people in England and Wales. In addition, many young people with mental health problems and mental health disorders are not in contact with CAMHS.

From the available research there is a strong correlation on a general level between the characteristics underpinning effective interventions to reduce offending behaviour and those underpinning effective interventions in mental health.

> The greatest chance of positive change in children with conduct problems and emotional difficulties consistent with early signs of mental health problems lies mainly in improvements of their family circumstances, positive peer-group relationships and good school experiences, and less in direct contact with specialist child psychiatric services. (Rutter 1991, quoted in Walker 2003)

The Annual Inspection Report for Yots 2005–2006 summarises the current challenges for mental health services as follows:

- One in five health workers was not able to access the services they required if they were to meet the health needs of the Yot population.

- Access to CAMHS for support, advice and appropriate supervision remained difficult in some Yots. There was limited provision of tier 3/4 CAMHS in some areas, with long waiting times experienced by the young people. Some groups of children and young people, particularly 16- and

17-year-olds, and those with dual substance misuse and mental health needs found it especially difficult to access services (HM Inspectorate of Probation 2006: 41)

Summary

- The mental health of children and young people is an issue for all practitioners who come into contact with young people in the course of their work.

- Mental health problems, as defined here, are prevalent in this population although the link with offending behaviour is not fully established. There is less evidence as to the effectiveness of particular treatments of mental health problems among young people in the youth justice system.

- Mental health appears to be influenced by a range of factors relating to each individual: personality and genetic make-up, family and upbringing, and environmental factors such as poverty and deprivation.

- Young people and their families are often reluctant to engage with mental health services, and quickly cease to be engaged.

Further reading

Hagell, A. (2002) *The Mental Health of Young Offenders.* London: Mental Health Foundation.

Harrington, D. and Bailey, S. (2005) *Mental Health Needs and Effectiveness of Provision for Young Offenders in Custody and in the Community.* London: Youth Justice Board.

5

Substance misuse

There is a high prevalence of substance use amongst children and young people in the UK. While for the majority, this is largely experimental, a significant minority will develop substance misuse problems. Substance misuse problems are correlated with young people who might be described as vulnerable or, put another way, are exposed to a number of other risk factors associated with offending behaviour and social exclusion. For this reason, it is hard to isolate the independent impact of substance misuse on offending behaviour. While the scope and scale of substance misuse amongst children and young people is well documented, there is relatively little evidence relating to effective interventions for preventing substance misuse in the first place and with regard to providing programmes for the treatment of substance misuse difficulties.

The evidence base for substance misuse

Studies of the prevalence of drug use among young people consistently demonstrate that a significant minority engage in such behaviours over time (MORI 2004). Statistics on drug use, smoking and drinking among young people in 2005 (NHS Health and Social Care Information Centre 2006) show:

- 9 per cent of 11–15-year-olds regularly smoke;

- 22 per cent of 11–15-year-olds regularly drink;

- 11 per cent of 11–15-year-olds had taken drugs in the last month and 19 per cent in the last year.

The prevalence of taking drugs and other substances increases with age, but continues to be a minority pursuit. For example, the Home Office Offending, Crime and Justice Survey (OCJS), a household survey of 10- to 25-year-olds, has shown that nearly a quarter (22 per cent) of young people in this age group said they had taken a drug in the previous 12 months. Males are more likely to take drugs than females and the most commonly used drug was cannabis, with only 8 per cent having taken a Class A drug. For those who reported using drugs, the most frequent age of onset was between 10 and 15 years. Drugs generally used first by young people were solvents and cannabis. Only later may they graduate to amylnitrate or harder drugs. Ten per cent of young people were 'frequent' drug users, having taken a drug two or three times in a month or more.

It should be noted though that despite the statistical prevalence of substance use among young people, most will do so without experiencing long-term or significant harm and most will also naturally reach a point of reduction or abstinence from drug use and a reduction in alcohol consumption as they grow older (Keeling *et al.* 2004).

In their survey of 15- and 16-year-olds in England and Wales who had been referred to Yots, Hammersley *et al.* (2003) found that the levels of self-reported substance use were much higher than those in the Youth Lifestyles Survey and the British Crime Survey. The cohort they studied contained relatively few heroin or crack cocaine users: alcohol, cannabis and tobacco were by far the most frequently used. It should be noted, however, that there are also a number of methodological issues with self-report studies. Where surveys are conducted at school, this inevitably excludes a number of young people who are not attending (a particular risk group of substance misuse). In addition, young people may be frightened to reveal the extent of their substance use, fearing punishment or labelling.

Frequent substance use may be associated particularly with young people in vulnerable groups. Goulden and Sondhi (2001), for example, examined rates of drug use amongst the following vulnerable groups:

- young people not attending school;
- young people at risk of offending and reoffending;
- homeless young people and runaways;
- young people living in drug-using families.

In addition, the earlier young people begin using substances, the greater the negative effects are likely to be in later adolescence and into adulthood, in particular with respect to education, making and sustaining relationships and physical and mental health (Kibblewhite 2002, cited in Keeling *et al.* 2004).

There appears to be a link between drug use and crime. The OCJS household survey reported that just over two thirds (66 per cent) of 10–17-year-olds who had taken a drug in the last year had also committed an offence, compared with 23 per cent who had not taken a drug. Frequent drug users were more likely to offend than occasional drug users, although there was no strong association between frequency of drug use and seriousness of offending (Budd *et al.* 2005; Hammersley *et al.* 2003). Among young people known to Yots, some 86 per cent reported to have used a drug (usually cannabis) (Hammersley *et al.* 2005).

> The evidence points to associations between a diverse group of risk factors for drug use. These factors include parental discipline, family cohesion, parental monitoring, peer drug use, drug availability, genetic profile, self-esteem, hedonistic attitudes, reasons for drug use, and the rate of risk/protective factors. (Frisher *et al.* 2007: 19)

For 10–16-year-olds the following factors were associated with increased risk of taking drugs:

- serious anti-social behaviour;
- weak parental attitude towards bad behaviour;
- being in trouble at school (inc. absenteeism and exclusion);
- friends in trouble;
- early smoking.

(Dillon *et al.* 2007; Home Office 2007)

Any association between drug use and crime may not necessarily imply causality. The risk factors associated with drug use problems among young people are very similar to those with offending careers (Lloyd 1998; Hammersley *et al.* 2003). Typically these include:

- disrupted family backgrounds;
- poor supervision;
- delinquent peer groups;
- poor social skills;
- low psychological well-being;
- non-attendance at school;
- having been in care.

When these factors are present then substance misuse and crime tend to develop together, at the same age and within the same peer group. Given the 'normalisation' of drug use amongst young people (Parker *et al.* 1998) – that is that they now culturally accommodate the availability of drugs even if they do not engage themselves – some form of substance misuse among young people who offend should be expected, unrelated to the presence of classic 'risk factors'. Another way of considering the issue of substance misuse problems amongst children and young people is to consider the issue of vulnerability, defined by Drugscope and DPAS (2001) as 'the presence in an individual of one or more factors which may have an influence on them developing a drug problem'.

Hammersley *et al.* (2003) identified three factors for substance use frequency: stimulant and poly-drug; addictive type; and socially acceptable. The last of these categories included alcohol, cannabis and tobacco. The study showed that particular types of offending behaviour were predicted by each type. Shoplifting was more associated with addictive type substance use, for example, whereas stealing from cars and violent assault was more associated with stimulant and poly-drug use.

A number of theories have been advanced to propose reasons why drug use occurs and escalates in some people and not in others, including the 'gathering' and 'stepping-stone' theories (Witton 2001).

The stepping-stone theory argues that cannabis use leads inevitably to the use of harder drugs, culminating with heroin or crack. This is based on predominantly physiological explanations: that cannabis use unleashes chemicals in the brain which desire new drugs, or that cannabis users, after experiencing and getting used to the mild high of cannabis, begin to crave a more intense high and thus move on to other drugs. The stepping-stone theory has proved unsustainable and lacking any evidence base. The 'evidence' – that most heroin users started with cannabis – is hardly surprising, but demonstrably fails to account for the overwhelmingly vast majority of cannabis users who do not progress to drugs like crack and heroin. In respect of young people at risk of offending and reoffending specifically, Hammersley *et al.* (2003) found no evidence of a funnelling towards heroin and crack cocaine, rather that heavy users tended to use alcohol and cannabis frequently and other drugs occasionally.

The gateway hypothesis takes as its starting point the user's environment and behaviour rather than the drug itself. The gateway theory suggests that drug-using careers follow a generally predictable progression in which the individual moves from using legitimate drugs, including alcohol and tobacco, to various forms of illicit drug use. This is different from the stepping-stone theory in that there is no inevitable direction to the drug user's choices. The gateway theory is a metaphor: the individual has access to new gates after entering the first gate or field, but may or may not choose to open those new gates. Individuals may go back to where they started, may stay in the first field, or may decide to open further gates and move on to using other drugs. The gateway theory does not try to determine drug progression; it is simply about access to choices and proximity to drugs.

The weight of empirical evidence suggests that a link between cannabis and more harmful drugs like heroin and crack may exist. The reason for this is not, as the stepping-stone theory suggests, a cause or a chemical process started by cannabis. Rather it is that:

- Some cannabis users have personality profiles or environmental conditions that are in common with those of the users of more harmful drugs.

- Once drugs (be they cannabis, alcohol or tobacco) are used, if the harm ascribed to them is overstated or false, individuals using them will dismiss harm information and are less likely to be concerned about moving to more 'harmful' drugs.

- Cannabis use puts individuals in social situations and supply transactions where they are more likely to experience people using, accepting and supplying more harmful drugs than are others in the population.

The gateway theory does not suggest that cannabis use leads to the use of other, harder drugs. It does stress the relevance of common profiles, environment, experience and access (Home Office Research, Development and Statistics Directorate 2002).

There are a number of interventions designed for young people who are using substances either experimentally or regularly. These have a number of different intended outcomes, ranging from the reduction of harm to complete abstinence. The ways in which they seek to achieve these outcomes are many and varied, including behavioural therapy, counselling, family therapy, 12-step type programmes and therapeutic community and residential treatment programmes. The evidence base for the effectiveness of all these kinds of different intervention is not well established and much of the available research comes from the USA and so should be regarded with caution in relation to its application in England and Wales.

Systematic reviews of the available research on reducing substance misuse (Elliot *et al.* 2001; Health Advisory Service 2001) showed evidence that 12-step programmes are promising in reducing drug use among young people, although this model has not been widely implemented in the UK. Programmes that contained an element of behaviour therapy, in particular cognitive-behavioural approaches, were more effective than those without a behavioural element. School-based and purely educational programmes were found to have weak or no effect on reducing drug use. Family therapy was found to be more effective than individual counselling and group therapy.

In respect of the impact of the effectiveness of interventions aimed at reducing criminal behaviour among drug users, Holloway *et al.* (2005) have undertaken a systematic review of studies which meet Level 3 of the scientific methods scale (SMS) developed by Sherman *et al.* (1997). The main findings from the review were:

- There was no clear evidence that routine monitoring drug testing works.

- Therapeutic communities, probation and parole supervision and drugs courts were the most effective interventions to reduce drug-related crime.

- More intensive interventions tended to produce stronger evidence of success than less intensive programmes.

- More favourable results were obtained for males compared with females, young compared with old and in one study, non-white people compared with white people.

Holloway *et al.* (2005) noted, however, that only a small number of evaluations met the Level 3 eligibility criteria (69) and only a small number originated in the UK (7) compared with the USA. Even in eligible studies few considered the causal mechanisms by which a programme might or might not be effective.

One of the most publicised interventions related to the reduction of substance misuse by young people who offend has been the Drug Treatment and Testing Requirements. However, the report from Matrix Research and Consultancy and ICPR (2007) reached inconclusive findings on the impact of these requirements. Specifically, they found that with regard to arrest referral, which is designed to impact young people's offending through improving their access to relevant support services, there was no change in offending; there was no change in the services young people accessed after arrest referral; and there was no discernible difference between patterns of substance misuse and offending risk in the pilot group as compared to the comparator group. In the case of drug testing, analysis of data from *Asset* 6 showed that very few young people used Class A drugs in either the pilot or comparator areas, and the drug use pattern after drug testing in the pilot area did not vary significantly from that observed in the comparator areas.

Since 2002 ring-fenced funding has been provided to Yots, as part of the Young People's Substance Misuse Partnership Grant, to develop screening, assessment and intervention services for young people involved in substance misuse. Just over 200 substance misuse workers are now deployed in Yots across England and Wales. Overall, positive messages have emerged in respect of the role and deployment of substance misuse workers in Yots (Pitcher *et al.* 2004). The majority of such workers (90 per cent) are physically located within the Yots, providing post-screening assessment of young people and substance misuse interventions both within the Yot and within community settings. High proportions (60 per cent) of young people supervised by the Yot were considered by substance misuse workers to have a substance misuse problem. Many of these issues can be addressed within the Yot by the substance misuse worker themselves providing tier 1 or tier 2 services.

The response to the substance misuse needs of young people entering custody or those seeking continuity of support at discharge has not been as positive to date (Youth Justice Board 2004g). On entry into custody there may be insufficient awareness of a young person's substance misuse needs. While *Asset* assessments may routinely evaluate a young person's risk of reoffending, if their substance misuse is not directly associated with their instance offence their need for treatment may not be properly assessed. Screening for substance and alcohol use on entry into the secure estate may not identify significant issues for young people. Even if it does, only one or two options for substance misuse treatment may be available from within the establishment, or there may be limited resources to access external programme providers (Youth Justice Board 2004g).

All institutions include drug and alcohol education as part of personal, social and health evaluation (PSHE) programmes, but there is a lack of standardisation. There is little evidence that PSHE lessons are used as a means to motivate and move young people into specialised services where necessary. Many young people complained that the lesson content was irrelevant or outdated. They also felt they were being lectured or patronised, and labelled or stigmatised as drug users. The availability of supportive services at tier 2 was inconsistent across the secure estate. Less than half of establishments provide pharmacological assistance for detoxification and withdrawal. There was a lack of structured interventions for alcohol misuse or smoking cessation. There was little appreciation that teaching young people how to manage, reduce or cease their use of primary substances of abuse (smoking and drinking) could give them skills and confidence to resist, understand or better manage their use of criminalised substances (Youth Justice Board 2004g).

Less than 50 per cent of establishments had a formal protocol for cases of dual diagnosis – substance misuse issues and mental health problems. Psychiatric work was generally completed in isolation from drug work, with CAMHS workers frequently refusing to see young people who were still dealing with a substance misuse problem (Youth Justice Board 2004g).

The principles of effective practice and substance misuse

Risk classification

Given the 'normalisation' of substance use amongst young people (Parker *et al.* 1998) it is important to be able to identify where it is a significant risk factor for a young person's offending. This may be a stand-alone risk factor or more usually an interrelated factor with others. For example, persistent substance misuse may cause depression and volatility. This, in turn, may produce low self-efficacy and a failure to engage in academic learning.

The *Asset* core profile specifically explores the nature and extent of young people's substance use (tobacco, alcohol, solvents and drugs) and its links to offending behaviour, including:

● practices which put young people at particular risk (e.g. injecting, sharing equipment, poly-drug use);

- seeing substance use as a positive and/or essential to life;

- noticeably detrimental effect on education, relationships, daily functioning;

- offending to obtain money for substances;

- offending while under the influence, or possessing/supplying illegal drugs.

The challenge for practitioners in completing *Asset*, therefore, is making the judgement about the extent to which substance use by a young person is a significant risk factor in their offending behaviour, and determining a plan accordingly (see 'Intervention modality' below). The key question would seem to be the extent to which current substance use is likely to contribute to the risk of further offending by the young person.

This principle also states that the level and intensity of an intervention should be linked to the seriousness of offending. With regard to substance misuse, this would suggest that a graded approach is taken linked to the *Asset* scores in this area. The HAS four-tier model of care for substance misuse services might provide a framework for ensuring young people receive the type of service that most closely matches their level of need, while avoiding the labelling of young people without serious problems (Keeling *et al.* 2004).

Tier 1: Universal services

Interventions	*Practitioners/Agencies*
- Information/education concerning tobacco, alcohol and drugs within the education curriculum; - Educational assessment and support to maintain in school; - Identification of risk issues; - General medical services/routine health screening and advice on health risks/Hep B vaccination/referral/ parental support and service.	Teacher; Youth worker; Connexions staff; School health.

Tier 2: Services offered by practitioners with some specialist knowledge

Interventions	*Practitioners/Agencies*
- Programme of activities and education to address offending; - Family support regarding parenting and general management issues; - Assessment of risk and protection issues; - Counselling/addressing lifestyle issues; - Educational assessment.	Yot/bail support; Mentor; Social services; Counselling; One-stop shop service; Educational psychology.

Tier 3: Services provided by specialist teams

Interventions	Practitioners/Agencies
● Specialist assessment leading to a planned package of care and treatment augmenting that already provided by tiers 1 and 2 and integrated with them; ● Specialist substance-specific interventions including mental health issues; ● Family assessment and involvement; ● Inter-agency planning and communication.	Specialist YP drug and alcohol services integrated with CAMHS or 'one-stop shops' combined with child mental health, educational assessment and support, Statement of Special Educational Needs.

Tier 4: Very specialist services

Interventions	Practitioners/Agencies
● Short period of accommodation if crises; ● Inpatient/day psychiatric or secure unit to assist detoxification if required; ● Continued tier 3 and multi-agency involvement alongside tier 1 and tier 2.	Forensic child and adolescent psychiatry; Social services; Continued involvement from YP substance misuse services; Substantial support for education.

Criminogenic need

As has been shown from the research on the prevalence of substance misuse and young people at risk of offending and reoffending, Yots can expect substantial numbers of the young people they engage with to screen positive on this measure. The key issue will be the need to assess and analyse whether the presence of substance misuse is a key contributor to the young person's current offence and/or their offending career. Substance misuse issues which primarily provide a lifestyle context for the young person's offending behaviour may require lower tiers of preventive intervention whereas misuse which has a causal contribution may need a more intensive and extensive response.

Community based

Within the context of the Yot, the presence of the substance misuse worker may facilitate direct access to services, either from within the Yot or via protocols to access community-based substance misuse provision. The Annual Inspection Report for Yots 2005–2006 indicates that 'substance misuse workers usually had good access to their parent service for more specialist tier 3 support' (HM Inspectorate of Probation 2006). The key issue is where that support and intervention is required beyond the remit of the Yot worker. In those circumstances it may be important to ensure that local protocols specify the extent to which young people concluding orders are a priority for on-going intervention, and that the needs of the young person with respect to substance misuse are effectively communicated to those who will have continuing contact with them.

A young person's parents/carers and immediate family members may also be a significant support in ensuring the community-based principle is applied. These can be seen as a resource to the young person and staff, but are likely to need support or information in relation to the impact of substance misuse, their own attitudes and patterns of substance misuse, and their role in supporting their child. Hammersley *et al.* (2003) suggest this might be easier to achieve with regard to alcohol, cannabis and tobacco rather than focusing on drugs perceived to be harder. Difficulties are likely to emerge where parents/carers of young people themselves misuse substances, and consideration may need to be given to providing services for them from adult services, contemporaneously with those services provided for young people.

It would seem logical to assume that the community-based principle could also be applied to schools and other educational establishments within a particular community. Education-based programmes though have not been shown to have a particular impact on substance use. The reasons for this are unclear and deserve further exploration. Additionally, Hammersley *et al.* (2003) argue that the zero tolerance policies towards substance use may not be helpful as they encourage young people to conceal rather than deal with their substance use. Ironically, such a policy is also likely to lead to exclusions from school which further place a young person at risk both of substance misuse and offending.

Intervention modality

As has been established earlier, there is a wide diversity in the substance use of young people at risk of offending and reoffending. For this reason, it would seem obvious that responses might need to be tailored to the individual and that funnelling these young people into generic programmes may be detrimental. This implies that substance misuse treatment might include a range of interventions, provided within the context of an overall plan that is focused on addressing the young person's substance misuse.

Even though substance misuse might have been identified as a significant risk factor in relation to a young person's offending behaviour and an appropriate intervention begun, the length of their order may well jeopardise its completion. Ensuring longer-term interventions may entail co-ordination with specialist substance misuse services beyond the young person's involvement with the youth justice system (National Treatment Agency 2005).

The research cited earlier suggests that a more behavioural approach, in particular a cognitive behavioural one, is likely to be more successful (Elliot *et al.* 2001). This would suggest that substance misuse programmes offered within a Yot, or brokered from without, might consider how best to incorporate these elements into the work done.

Responsivity

The responsivity principle would suggest that for substance misuse interventions to be relevant they must engage young people in such a way that they are provided with a range of strategies that enable them to learn a different range of responses. Approaches that hector, patronise, label or stigmatise young people are unlikely to be positively responded to. Initiatives that motivate, foster better understanding, develop skills, confidence and strategies in how to manage, reduce or cease the use of substances (particularly those taken to harmful levels) are likely to have an impact. This suggests that to be responsive, therefore, interventions might need to be:

- structured;
- motivational;
- relevant to the lives of young people;
- provide them with skills to manage challenges; and
- presented by staff with a common purpose and approach.

Dillon *et al.* (2007) suggest that a strategy of providing accurate and credible information, using appropriate language, helps provide young people with the facts necessary to develop a collection of beliefs and attitudes that develops a resilience to drug use. While there is no adequate evidence base establishing the effectiveness of drug and alcohol education *per se*, Dillon *et al.* (2007) suggest that an education strategy needs to be accompanied with help to young people in developing realistic and achievable life goals (e.g. future career) and developing and maintaining strong self-efficacy so that they may resist drug use.

The responsivity principle would also suggest that substance-related advice and information should be culturally and age appropriate for children, young people, parents and carers as appropriate. The principle also raises the question about how to ensure that young people and/or parents/carers who have low levels of literacy, or for whom English is a second language, can be best catered for across the full range of interventions.

Dosage

When young people have significant substance misuse needs which substantially contribute to their offending behaviour it will be vital to ensure that the intervention in the sentence plan is delivered with an appropriate degree of regularity and intensity. When this programme is to be delivered by the Yot substance misuse worker it may be directly monitored as to attendance, punctuality, participation and impact. Where the sentence plan is multi-modal, the worker responsible for the substance misuse element needs to communicate with the case manager and other providers as to the young person's participation (and vice versa).

In custodial settings the inconsistency of provision may mean that assessed need cannot immediately be met. It may be advisable in sentence planning to consider whether substance misuse services unavailable within the secure estate can be quickly assessed once the community part of the sentence is started. Throughcare workers may need to prioritise these elements within cases.

Specific considerations about the delivery of services arise where a young person has a dual diagnosis – substance misuse needs and mental health problems. In these circumstances it may be more effective for drugs workers and CAMHS workers to collaborate to ensure the appropriate sequencing of their respective service inputs.

Programme integrity

The lack of a credible evidence base for the efficacy of the range of substance misuse programmes available, particularly with direct relevance for work with children and young people, presents a challenge in determining what intervention is best for a young person where substance use is identified as a problem. This would imply the need for strict monitoring and evaluation of the outcomes from substance misuse interventions provided directly by a Yot or a secure establishment, and from programmes delivered by third parties. In this respect, Hammersley *et al.* (2003) suggest that specific consideration needs to be given to the impact of intervention on the substance misuse needs of the young person and the impact of changes in the substance misuse needs of the young person on their offending behaviour.

The challenges for practice

While considerable change has taken place over the last five years in the recognition and response to the substance misuse needs of young people at risk of offending and reoffending, a number of outstanding challenges remain.

Keeling *et al.* (2004) argue that substance use interventions in the past were based on the idea that young people did not want to experiment with drugs and alcohol, and those that were doing so wanted to stop. In the light of more recent evidence, services need to recognise the fact that young people do want to experiment with and regularly use drugs and alcohol. This makes the provision of appropriate services and interventions much more challenging. In addition, the 'normalisation' of substance use and its apparent prevalence in the lives of children and young people means that the task of discriminating between what is 'normal' experimentation and what is likely to be deleterious use, particularly in relation to the risk of further offending, is more difficult to determine. In addition, this process of normalisation may also make it much more difficult to get young people to relate to programmes designed to prevent or reduce substance use.

The prevalence of substance use amongst young people at risk of offending and reoffending also has implications for the staff who work with them. It would seem to suggest that all staff require a reasonable awareness of these issues in order to make sensible decisions and to refer appropriately.

Summary

- Studies of the prevalence of drug use among young people consistently demonstrate that a significant minority engage in such behaviours over time.

- Despite the statistical prevalence of substance use among young people, most will do so without experiencing long-term or significant harm, and most will also naturally reach a point of reduction or abstinence from drug use and a reduction in alcohol consumption as they grow older.

- Frequent substance use may be associated with young people in vulnerable groups, in particular those at risk of offending and reoffending.

- The evidence base for the effectiveness of substance misuse interventions is not well established and much of the available research comes from the USA.

- More promising programmes for reducing substance misuse are 12-step programmes (more prevalent in the USA than in the UK), programmes that contain an element of behaviour therapy, in particular cognitive behavioural approaches, and family therapy.

- The response to the substance misuse needs of young people entering custody or those seeking continuity of support at discharge has not been positive.

Further reading

Frisher, M., Crome, I., Macleod, J., Bloor, R. and Hickman, N. (2007) *Protective Factors for Illicit Drug Use among Young People: A Literature Review.* Home Office Online Report 05/07. London: Home Office RDS.

Keeling, P., Kibblewhite, K. and Smith, Z. (2004) 'Evidence-based practice in young people's substance misuse services' in White, D. (ed.) *Social Work and Evidence-based Practice.* London: Jessica Kingsley.

Part II

6

Targeted neighbourhood prevention programmes

Crime does not affect everyone equally, with perhaps 40 per cent of youth crime taking place in 10 per cent of neighbourhoods. These neighbourhoods show up on the Social Deprivation Index and are characterised by high unemployment, lack of investment in physical and social capital, and numerous risk factors, which impact on the lives of young people and the communities in which they live (Hope 2001).

Government policy currently focuses much attention on these neighbourhoods. The Neighbourhood Renewal Unit and Neighbourhood Wardens Scheme, based in the Department for Communities and Local Government; the Antisocial Behaviour Unit, based in the Home Office; Positive Activities for Young People (PAYP) and Splash Cymru, overseen by the Department for Education and Skills (DfES); and the Youth Inclusion Programme (YIP) led by the Youth Justice Board, all point to a commitment to tackling crime and antisocial behaviour at neighbourhood level. More recently, these initiatives and others have been co-ordinated under the 'Respect' agenda led by the Respect Task Force (2006).

This plethora of initiatives is not always seen as benign, with critics pointing to increased surveillance and social control over certain areas and the potential of some of those measures to draw increasing numbers of young people into the youth justice system (Smith 2003; Goldson and Muncie 2006).

In this chapter different underpinning theories to community-based crime prevention and programme approaches are examined, as well as the rationale for targeting and the components of promising programmes.

The evidence base for targeted neighbourhood prevention programmes

The British Crime Survey shows that peripheral council estates and mixed inner-city neighbourhoods are several times more likely to suffer from crime than are more affluent areas. Experts estimate that around 2,000 residential neighbourhoods in the UK are affected by crime rates three to four times higher than surrounding areas; high levels of repeat victimisation; above-average rates of disorder and antisocial behaviour by young people; high incidence of neighbourhood disputes and antisocial behaviour by adults; widespread drug dealing and prostitution.

Depressed neighbourhoods are characterised by high levels of poverty and deprivation, Unemployment rates tend to be high (nearly two thirds higher than more affluent areas). In addition, there is almost one and a half times the proportion of lone parent households, almost one and a half times the rate of underage pregnancy, nearly one third of children grow up in families on income support and 37 per cent of 16-year-olds do not achieve any GCSEs grades A*–C) (Social Exclusion Unit 1998). There is also a high level of environmental deterioration, including run-down or defective housing stock, some of which goes unfilled for long periods (Bramley and Pawson 2002), and physical dereliction, such as graffiti, abandoned cars and boarded-up shops. More specifically, these neighbourhoods tend to be noted for high levels of school disorganisation, often accompanied by high levels of non-attendance and formal exclusions with more than twice as many nursery/primary schools and five times as many secondary schools on special measures (Ofsted correspondence cited in Social Exclusion Unit 1998).

High-crime neighbourhoods demoralise their residents over a sustained period of time, which may in turn create a breeding ground for further crime. High crime levels are likely to divide communities, which further enhances the likelihood and opportunity for crime to take place. High levels of inter-generational mistrust are likely to be present in high crime areas, and this affects how residents view young people. This can be divisive, with many people confident that everybody else's children are at fault. In turn, this can lead to fragmentation in communities and a lack of any general sense of responsibility from adults towards young people.

Bennett (1998) identifies four main theories that have informed community-based crime prevention programmes. Community disorganisation theory (more commonly referred to as social disorganisation) places emphasis on a breakdown of the social order controlled by families, the church, school and community, and youth centres. Community disorder theory has its roots in the 'broken windows' hypothesis of Wilson and Kelling (1982), which states that where there are signals to citizens that an area is unsafe, residents will withdraw from it both physically and from roles of mutual support and community cohesion. Community empowerment theory is concerned with sharing power with residents, particularly in decision-making processes. Community regeneration theory involves building resources in an area. Hope (1996) argues that community empowerment cannot be successful if there is a dearth of resources. Improved resources, it is argued, will contribute to empowerment, help to integrate marginalised young people into the wider community, and enable the community to tackle key risk factors for delinquency.

Tilley *et al.* (2004) identify four main methods that have traditionally been employed to impact upon crime in the community, only the first of which is specifically under the control of the police and other agencies of the criminal justice system. Policing and the criminal justice system provide the traditional response to crime in three main ways: incapacitating young people who offend through the use of custodial sanctions; deterring young people who are known to offend through the threat of punishment; and deterring young people who may potentially offend.

Social crime reduction methods attempt to change the underlying social conditions that permit or promote involvement in criminal behaviour through diverting from crime; improving informal social control: the activation of community, family, school or peer group capacities to exert pressure on young people who offend, or may offend, to behave well; integration into mainstream society by creating social ties. Young people who are known to offend can be provided with interventions that aim to reduce the likelihood that they will reoffend through, for example, reducing drug dependency or changing thought processes by improving cognitive skills. Finally, situational crime prevention modifies the circumstances surrounding specific types of crime event in a variety of ways, for example through manipulating the situation so that the perceived benefits of not committing a crime outweigh the risks of doing so.

The effectiveness of each method, progressed singly or in combination, depends in part on how well it is targeted and implemented. Targeting, in particular, needs to consider the type of problems communities face and the dynamics of the local community. Forrest *et al.* (2005) illustrate the complexity of the issue with the following typology of the relationships between levels of actual crime and levels of fear of crime in different communities. In type A there is high crime and high fear of crime. In Type B, there is high fear of crime but low actual crime. In Type C there is low fear of crime but high actual crime. In Type D both fear of crime and actual crime are low.

	Crime		
		High	Low
High	High	Type A	Type B
Fear	Low	Type C	Type D

Figure 6.1 Crime, fear of crime and community involvement in problem solving
Source: Forrest *et al.* (2005)

Type A is approximated in many high-crime inner-city neighbourhoods. Local residents may understand their problem well enough. They may also know who commits offences. But poverty, low collective efficacy, high levels of intimidation and low levels of trust in the police limit their ability to control or inhibit criminal and antisocial behaviour. If agencies can persuade citizens to co-operate by building trusting relationships and providing them with information, they may be able to tackle crime and build confidence in the police.

Type B describes neighbourhoods or virtual communities (groups with shared attributes, identities and interests but not living in the same neighbourhood) where anxiety about crime is high, but where there are relatively few serious crimes or incidents of disorderly behaviour. Many elderly people and those in middle-class residential neighbourhoods may be found in Type B.

Type C areas are those with high crime rates, but where the victims and, in some cases, the young people who are offending, are not local residents. Examples include holiday resorts, towns with foreign students, stations, motorway service areas, car parks, and dangerous inner-city areas unknown to visitors. Here the at-risk population is not around long enough to get them directly involved. Such areas comprise 'virtual' communities. Moreover, local residents may have little personal interest in the risks faced by the strangers.

Type D describes areas with neither high levels of crime nor high levels of fear of crime. Those living here are relatively safe and feel relatively secure. Many residential areas fall into this category. Many will have social networks of active citizens and formal agencies maintaining both the social and physical fabric of the local neighbourhood.

The national prevention programmes funded by the Youth Justice Board, DfES and Home Office (YIPs, PAYP and Family Support) are all targeted towards high crime and vulnerable neighbourhoods (Type A) as identified under the National Index of Social Deprivation.

It has been argued that successful programmes to reduce risk factors in struggling neighbourhoods have the following components (Communities that Care 2001):

- reduction of the known risk factors;

- ability to strengthen protective factors (through promoting social bonding, setting clear standards for social behaviour, offering children the opportunities and skills to participate and feel that they belong, and showing children that their contribution is valued);

- intervention at the appropriate stage in children and young people's development;

- early intervention (addressing risk before offending behaviour begins);

- reaching those at greatest risk (to be effective, preventative programmes may need to target individual children who are low achievers or behave too aggressively for remedial interventions; however, targeting high-risk neighbourhoods is usually preferable to targeting individuals);

- sensitivity to the needs of different racial, cultural and economic groups;

129

UNIVERSITY OF WINCHESTER
LIBRARY

- ability to make a significant contribution to the overall reduction of risks (programmes are also more likely to contribute to risk reduction if they can be successfully integrated into a comprehensive prevention strategy).

The Youth Justice Board funds a number of preventative programmes which are planned and delivered by Yots and partner agencies at local level. These are outlined below.

Youth Inclusion Programmes (YIPs) and Junior Youth Inclusion Programmes (JYIPs)

YIPs were established in 2000 by the Youth Justice Board in 70 of the most deprived neighbourhoods in England and Wales. Attendance at a YIP is voluntary, although the project aims to focus on the 50 most 'at risk' 13–16-year-olds in the area. Referral criteria include poor attendance or exclusion from school. The programme's targets included reducing recorded crime by 30 per cent and reducing non-attendance and school exclusion each by 30 per cent. Using a youth work approach, YIPs seek to engage this group in a wide range of constructive activities. Activities are also open to other young people who live in the neighbourhood. Each project falls within the overall remit of the Youth Offending Team (Yot). There is also a wide range of managing agents and all projects have a multi-agency steering group with responsibility for targeting, implementation and monitoring progress.

Often linked to senior YIPs, JYIPs are integrated diversionary programmes which concentrate on young people aged 8–12 who are offending or at risk of offending. JYIPs may be either estate-based or school-based (often in school clusters). The programmes are tailored to meet the needs of the target group of young people. These needs are identified in the action plan or Integrated Support Plan (ISP) if referred by the Youth Inclusion and Support Panel (YISP). The YISP is a multi-agency panel with an early intervention and crime prevention role. Young people may be referred to the panel if they are considered at risk of offending. The panel then draws up a programme of early intervention intended to prevent the young person offending. The programme normally includes a menu of activities, such as:

- sports;
- arts and crafts;
- homework, education and information and communication technologies (ICT);
- mentoring;
- trips and residential outings;

- anger management;

- holiday activities.

A national evaluation of YIPs, conducted by Morgan Harris Burrows (2003) showed some positive outcomes, including a 30 per cent reduction in arrests, an 18 per cent reduction in the number of offences for which young people were arrested, and a 33 per cent reduction in fixed-term exclusions. It should be noted though that the figures for arrests and offending were well below the targets set for the programme – a 60 per cent reduction in arrests and a 30 per cent reduction in recorded crime in the area. In addition they also found that non-attendance increased by 40 per cent. Likewise, while their arrest rate by the police decreased, their offending increased by 8 per cent. Stephenson (2007) argues that while this approach might have made common sense from a youth justice perspective, from an educational perspective it may simply legitimise the detachment of young people from mainstream schooling, the decrease in permanent exclusions simply reflecting the increased non-attendance and diversion of particular young people away from school sites.

The researchers also found several issues associated with programme delivery, including:

- poor identification and engagement of the 'top 50' (in some quarters the proportion of the 'top 50' attending YIP was as low as 44 per cent);

- anticipated programme dosage (10 hours per week) not being delivered;

- risk factors associated with their 'top 50'.

Problems with analysing changes in area crime trends within which the projects were located were also cited.

Positive Activities for Young People (PAYP/Splash Cymru)

Funded by the DfES, these schemes run in school holidays and after school. They target the most vulnerable young people aged 8–14, in particular those at risk of offending, by use of a caseworker and the provision of a wide range of activities. Practitioners work with targeted young people in order to achieve the above objectives. They also work with educational and activity providers and other partner agencies, for example Yots, youth services, schools, Connexions/Young People's Partnerships (Wales) and the voluntary sector.

An evaluation conducted by CRG Research (2005) showed that the programme is well targeted in areas of high deprivation, integrating activities for those most at risk with those for other young people. A high rate (80 per cent) of positive outcomes was reported, but the lack of a control group has meant that it was not possible to isolate the effects of PAYP from other interventions the young people may have received. An earlier evaluation of several Summer Splash schemes found that youth crime did not increase dramatically during the summer holidays and that a decline in offending was noted only in areas where there had been little existing summer provision and which had a relatively high rate of incidents reported to the police (Loxley *et al.* 2002).

Powell's (2004) evaluation of the Youth Justice Board development fund prevention projects primarily focused upon the implementation process issues in establishing the projects. Key findings related to the development of multi-agency working, the need to offer a range of interventions and activities, and the need to ensure that the identities of the projects were positive and beneficial and did not 'label' young people as 'young people who offend'. A limited reoffending analysis, tracking 26 participants with previous convictions in projects over a 12-month period and examining their subsequent PNC records indicated that reconviction rates of the young people decreased by 26 per cent. However, the small sample size does not make this a statistically valid result.

The Safer Schools Partnerships (SSP) are an initiative which aims to promote the safety of schools and the young people attending them. See Chapter 3 p. 69, for more on the aims and effectiveness of SSP.

Evaluations of targeted neighbourhood prevention programmes under recent policy initiatives (i.e. YIPs, YISP, Safer Schools Partnerships) have primarily examined the processes employed in establishing and implementing programmes rather than evaluating their impact. These process evaluations do contain some important messages. For example, targeting programmes on priority groups may present a range of problems. Identification of particular risk factors at a disaggregated level may not be easily defined, quantitative data on the target group may not be easily available and comparison groups not easy to ascertain.

Some critics have questioned the validity of such pre-court interventions being delivered by criminal justice agencies on the grounds that they may be counter-productive (Goldson 2005; Bateman and Pitts 2005). Goldson argues for a more 'informalist' approach to preventing offending by diverting young people away from youth justice interventions altogether (2005). Goldson cites research from the US Department of Justice into youth crime prevention programmes (Howell *et al.* 1995) which concludes that some of the most promising approaches were intrinsically informalist in that they were:

> located *outside* of the formal criminal justice system (decriminalisation, diversion); built on children's and young people's strengths as distinct from emphasising their 'deficits' (normalisation); and adopted a social-structural approach to understanding and responding to troubled and troublesome children and young people rather than drawing on individualised, criminogenic and/or medico-psychological perspectives (contextualisation) (Goldson 2005: 240).

Conversely, the argument goes, providing interventions led by criminal justice agencies draws children into the system and rebrands them as 'deviant' or 'criminal'. The attendant stigma attached to this may weaken their relationships with family, peers, neighbourhood and school. It also increases the likelihood of them associating with a group of children and young people carrying similar labels (Bateman and Pitts 2005).

Some critics have also questioned the way such prevention programmes have been targeted and the concepts that underpin their design. With regard to targeting, the use of proxy measures to identify targets (e.g. indices of multiple deprivation) may lead to the targeting of areas rather than individuals and bring into the programme those who may not require or benefit from it (Hughes and Fielding 2006). In this way, unintended 'net widening' may take place and with it the risk of further punitive interventions for behaviour that may fall short of criminal (Smith 2006). Monaghan (2005) has argued that targeting a group of 'at risk' young people may be an infringement of their human rights, in particular the right not to be subject to penal action for behaviour that was not prohibited in law, and the right to be presumed innocent until proven guilty. The emphasis on the early identification of 'risk' and 'risk management' is based on a subjective judgement of those who require social control – 'actuarialism'. The primary emphasis of preventive intervention programmes is on surveillance, control and behaviour management. Meeting the social care and welfare needs of young people can become subsumed to these objectives (Smith 2006). Where crime or antisocial behaviour subsequently takes place there is a significant likelihood that young people (and their parents) may be shunted deeper into the criminal justice system, into custody, for example (Youth Justice Board 2006a). Another argument provided against the concept of targeting 'at risk' individuals in a neighbourhood is that it individualises social problems without tackling the underlying inequalities and difficulties experienced by high-crime neighbourhoods (Muncie 2004).

The underpinning philosophy of the diversionary element of such projects that provide a menu of extracurricular activities can also be questioned on educational grounds (Stephenson 2007). See Chapter 3, p. 79.

The principles of effective practice and targeted neighbourhood prevention programmes

Risk classification

When considering targeted neighbourhood prevention programmes, risk classification applies to both the neighbourhood itself and the individual young people being identified as 'at risk'. Identifying general neighbourhood risks might indicate the nature of the intervention programme designed, particularly with regard to any crime prevention element.

With regard to individual young people, one of the difficulties with such programmes is their universal versus targeted nature. YIP, for example, targets the 'top 50', whilst also opening up the programme to young people outside of this core target group (Morgan Harris Burrows 2003). This means that neighbourhood programmes often include a continuum of young people at risk: young people who have offended, those at high risk, those at medium or low risk, and those who are unlikely to offend. Not only might this be considered as 'net-widening', it would indicate the need for a differentiated approach to those different groups if the risk classification principle is to be achieved. In reality, the design of programmes like PAYP/Splash Cymru and YIPs tends to result in a blanket approach for all young people, which may well dilute the intended preventative impact on the targeted 50. The evaluation of YIPs found no evidence that projects were directly tackling the risk factors identified for each member of the 'top 50' (Morgan Harris Burrows 2003).

In its guidance on implementing YIPs, the Youth Justice Board acknowledges the fact that risk factors for individual young people are likely to change over time and that the group constituting the 'top 50' will also change as a result of this. The evaluation suggested that projects may have repeatedly focused on the same young people or that the repeat risk assessment process had not been repeated as regularly as prescribed in the guidance.

Criminogenic need

Criminogenic need is potentially one of the most challenging principles for targeted neighbourhood prevention programmes, particularly in relation to individual young people. It is very difficult to attempt to disaggregate one risk factor from another as being more directly related to criminogenic needs when no crime has been committed.

It may be more helpful, therefore, to focus on the criminogenic needs within a specific community setting. Building a clear picture of the crime and disorder problems of a neighbourhood might include collecting data about crime, disorder, young people who offend and victims; gathering information on community risk and protective factors; interviewing agency representatives and residents about what is being done to tackle crime problems now, and any perceived gaps (Forrest *et al.* 2005; Tilley *et al.* 2004). In order to unpick these dynamics and develop preventative interventions, many local areas use the SARA problem-solving model (Read and Tilley 2000).

Scanning describes the identification of broad issues that need to be addressed.
Analysis describes breaking down problems and their causes.
Response describes what is done to address the problem, in the light of the analysis.
Assessment involves evaluating the effectiveness of what was put in place.

Feedback occurs between each stage. The community, the police and partner agencies can be involved at any or all stages of the process, to varying degrees.

Community based

Targeted neighbourhood prevention programmes are community based in terms of their location. Where they are implemented faithfully, they should also reflect community contexts and experiences within the range of activity and programme items offered as part of the menu.

Further ways in which the community-based principle might be implemented could be through the use of volunteers to help and support projects. As well as helping to root the experience for young people in their communities, involving other members of the community on a voluntary basis (particularly older people) might go some way to reducing the level of fear of young people that might exist with a high-crime neighbourhood.

Although Parenting Orders currently fall within the remit of the courts and are outside of voluntary prevention programmes, whenever possible YIPs might try to involve the parents and siblings of their client group. Some YIPs offer organised parenting classes, while many seek to involve the parents/carers in supporting their child's individual action plan (Morgan Harris Burrows 2003).

Responsivity

Given the menu of activities usually associated with targeted neighbourhood prevention programmes, there would seem to be ample opportunity to give young people opportunities to acquire new skills and strategies for learning. The danger in this, however, is that the activities themselves may become so focused on ensuring the young people have a good time that they do not actually acquire any new skills or strategies. This has implications for the design and planning of programmes and individual activities.

One of the difficulties with responsivity when a programme is entirely optional is how to ensure that there is sufficient challenge while also providing young people with what they want to do. This would seem to have significance for the way in which staff work to motivate the young person to engage in the first place and then to sustain his/her interest longer term. This is likely to be particularly the case for those programme elements that are less immediately appealing (Morgan Harris Burrows 2003).

As with all other activity-based intervention, the issue of accessibility to activities for young people may also be affected by low levels of literacy and numeracy and poor experiences of formal and group learning. There are also cultural and gender sensitivities that may impact on whether or not a young person will choose to engage in the first place.

Intervention modality

YIPs and PAYP/Splash Cymru offer a menu of activities to young people, including education and training; mentoring; motor projects; sport; environmental projects; family work; arts, culture and media; health and drugs education; outreach and detached work; group development and personal assessment. One of the key issues when offering such a wide range of activities is how to ensure that they are individually contributing (if at all) to the prevention of offending. The evidence base for motoring projects, for example, is not good, being associated more with increases in delinquency rather than preventing or reducing it (Harper and Chitty 2005). The broad category of education, training and employment also conceals a wide range of approaches and programmes, some of which have greater promise in terms of preventing offending (largely those that seek to maintain attachment or reattach young people to mainstream learning opportunities) than others (alternative, part-time provision, for example) (Stephenson 2007). See Chapter 3, p. 66.

From the evaluation data to date, it is also hard to tell how many of these activities contain a strong focus on skill acquisition and problem solving, with a cognitive behavioural approach. The principle would suggest that such an approach may be promising. The key question is how to embed such approaches within the various activities provided as part of the menu.

Programme integrity

Given the wide range of targeted neighbourhood prevention programmes aimed at diverse groups of young people, it may be reasonable to expect them to be susceptible to some degree of programme drift. Monitoring and evaluation of targeted neighbourhood prevention projects pose a number of challenges in the generation of data and the interpretation of results, yet this is important if programme integrity is to be ensured (i.e. what is intended to be delivered is delivered) (Tilley *et al.* 2004).

> Evaluation of even small projects is vital. The feedback may provide lessons about what is and is not workable in the neighbourhood. It will reinforce a sense of achievement where the problem is diminished. It may make the community more confident that it can control its own affairs. It can lead to further problem-solving activities as specific issues are resolved, leading to general improvements in neighbourhood life. (Forrest *et al.* 2005: 17).

It is often difficult to ascertain the impact of targeted neighbourhood prevention programmes as it may not be easy to interpret changes in levels of crime. It is possible that interventions have been effective even where levels of crime have increased. This occurs where the appropriate comparison group's crime problems have risen much more steeply. For instance, if the appropriate comparison group's rate of crime has doubled it would be expected that the target group's numbers would also have doubled. If they have gone up by only 50 per cent, crimes have been 'saved'. So, assuming that there were 100 offences in the before period, it would be reasonable to expect there to be 200 in the after period. With a rise to only 150, 50 crimes have been prevented.

Equally, it is possible that interventions have been ineffective even when the problem declines. This occurs where the appropriate comparison group's problems have fallen much more steeply. In this case, suppose the appropriate comparison group's crimes have halved but the target group's crimes have gone down by 50 per cent. Assuming 200 crimes in the before period, 100 would be expected in the after. If they have reduced to only 150, then somehow, in spite of the appearance of success, the initiative may have unintentionally generated 50 offences that would otherwise not have happened (Tilley *et al.* 2004).

Both displacement and diffusion of benefits are common outcomes associated with targeted community prevention initiatives. Displacement is the substitution of one crime for another in a targeted area; diffusion is a state of positive effects of intervention extending beyond the original target range.

Type	Definition	Diffusion effect	Displacement effect
Geographical	Change by area	Reduction in nearby area	Increase in another area
Temporal	Change by time	Reduction at times not covered by initiative	Increase at times when measures not operative
Target	Change by object of offending	Reduction against targets other than those protected through measure	Increase amongst those not protected by the measure applied
Tactical	Change by method of offending	Reduction in crimes using methods other than those inhibited by measures	Increase in tactics not affected by measures put in place
Crime type	Change by crime type	Reduction in crimes other than those targeted	Increase in crimes other than those targeted
Young people who offend	Change in population of young people who offend	Reduction in population attracted to crime	Switch in young person population as new members move in

Figure 6.2 Displacement and diffusion of benefits in targeted neighbourhood prevention initiatives

Dosage

As with criminogenic need, it is hard to define what an adequate dosage for a neighbourhood prevention programme should be. The Youth Justice Board set the figure at 10 hours per week for the targeted 'top 50' on YIP programmes, but set no expectation for the wider group of young people attending. This proved very hard to achieve, with 9 per cent of all young people attending for an average of 10 hours or more per week and of those only 7 per cent of the 'top 50' getting that minimum dosage. The majority (67 per cent) were attending for less than 2.5 hours per week (Morgan Harris Burrows 2003). It is not clear from the evaluation whether there were any relative reductions in offending for those who had attended for the full 10 hours against those who had not. These figures are not markedly dissimilar to attendance rates for the wider group although there were differences between the two groups in terms of what they attended. The wider group were more likely to participate in arts and sports activities while the 'top 50' participated proportionately more in education/training, mentoring and personal assessment.

Maintaining attendance and dosage on a voluntary programme is clearly difficult as there is no compulsory element to fall back on. This might imply the need for incentives and rewards as a motivational tool to encourage attendance. When considering engagement of young people, it may also be important to address practical matters such as times, venues and family commitments. Religious festivals and community events may also need to be considered. Projects have reported success in the use of outreach workers but also, significantly, refer to the power of peer pressure. They have also pointed out added success in being 'open for business' at times when conventional youth activities are closed.

The challenges for practice

Identification of those young people most at risk within a particular neighbourhood is a significant challenge for a variety for reasons. In the first instance, the reliance on information from a number of agencies and organisations to establish an assessment of risk and protective factors across the full range of domains can prove difficult, as was experienced by some projects in the evaluation of YIPs (Morgan Harris Burrows 2003). Another key challenge presents itself where young people have not offended, in ascertaining the degree to which current risk factors can be taken as predictors of future offending.

Targeting young people who may be deemed to be 'at risk', but who have not yet committed or been caught committing an offence may lead to problems. The key challenge would seem to be how to engage these young people in a menu of activities and interventions that are based on the principles of effective practice without labelling them in any way. It may also result in unintended net-widening, thereby drawing them further into the youth justice system as a consequence.

Given the apparent tendency for some targeted neighbourhood prevention programmes, in particular YIPs, to draw young people away from mainstream schooling, operating as an 'alternative' to this, a challenge for practice would be ensuring synergy between school-based educational programmes and those on offer through the YIP. The outcomes from alternative educational settings of all kinds are not good for young people (Stephenson 2007) and so the emphasis might be more on supplementing mainstream school programmes, rather than replacing them.

While the emphasis on targeted neighbourhood interventions is on tackling risk factors, a number of other, sometimes competing, factors have been identified that may compromise this. The evaluation of YIPs identified a number of competing pressures. The need to provide activities that would attract sufficient numbers of young people was one issue, which may have led to the high levels of sporting activities on offer. Pressure was also felt with regard to providing enough hours to meet the weekly 'dosage' requirement for the 'top 50'. Budget constraints inevitably had an impact on what could be offered, as well as the skills of staff and sessional workers.

Finally, given the number of different initiatives that are likely to target the same neighbourhoods and the same young people, a significant challenge will be in ensuring they are co-ordinated effectively so that individual young people are not stigmatised, subjects of too much surveillance or simply subject to a range of disconnected and, at worst, contradictory, interventions that may actually ratchet them further and faster into the youth justice system.

Summary

- Evidence suggests that 40 per cent of youth crime takes place in 10 per cent of neighbourhoods. These neighbourhoods show up on the Social Deprivation Index and are characterised by high unemployment, lack of investment in physical and social capital, and numerous risk factors.

- There is a wide range of government neighbourhood prevention initiatives, a number of which specifically target youth crime.

- Evaluation of Youth Justice Board funded targeted neighbourhood prevention programmes reveals contradictory and at times weak effects with regard to their overall aims and targets.

- Some critics have questioned the way such prevention programmes have been targeted, and the concepts that underpin their design, in particular their potential to widen the net with regard to young people who encounter the Youth Justice System, and in their capacity to draw young people away from mainstream school.

Further reading

Morgan Harris Burrows (2003) *Evaluation of the Youth Inclusion Programme.* London: Youth Justice Board.

Goldson, B. (2005) 'Beyond formalism: towards "informal" approaches to youth crime and youth justice', in T. Bateman and J. Pitts. (eds) *The RHP Companion to Youth Justice.* Lyme Regis: Russell House Publishing.

7

Parenting

When their children become teenagers, parents may experience demands that they can feel ill-equipped to deal with. Young people themselves are responding to physical, emotional and lifestyle changes that can have a profound impact on them. These challenges, for both parents and young people, have to be faced in the context of major shifts in the last decade in social structures, as well as in political responses to parenting, teenagers and the family (Coleman and Roker 2001). These external factors can exacerbate the internal challenges families are facing. This chapter explores some of these tensions as well as some of the issues resulting from the evaluation of parenting programmes in the UK and in other countries.

Throughout this chapter, the term 'parent' is used, to include birth parents (whether married or unmarried) and guardians or other carers, including step-parents, adoptive parents, foster parents, grandparents, older siblings or other relatives who may undertake a parenting role. Parenting in the youth justice context therefore relates to the parenting support needs of anyone who is involved in the care of a young person, whether they live within the same household or not, as in the case of a non-resident parent.

The evidence base for parenting

There are four major features of family life associated with the offending behaviour of young people (Loeber and Stouthamer-Loeber 1986). These risk factors are:

1 parental and sibling criminality;

2 parental neglect, including lack of supervision;

3 chronic family conflict, either between partners, or between parent and young person;

4 harsh or erratic discipline.

The first two of these – the criminal behaviour of parents or other family members, and neglect – appear to be the most powerful variables which link with the offending behaviour of young people. In considering interventions with parents, therefore, it may be necessary to recognise that not all risk factors are equally amenable to change. A parenting intervention is more likely to impact on parenting styles, communication, ways in which conflict is handled, or types of discipline than on parental criminality, for example.

Rutter *et al.* (1998) identify a number of needs that should be met in order for parenting to be successful in preventing antisocial behaviour. These are:

- effective monitoring or supervision so the parent knows which behaviours are likely to lead to trouble;
- clear setting of standards with explicit and unambiguous feedback;
- skilled diversion or distraction to avoid the development of confrontation and crises;
- responsivity to the child's sensitivities and needs;
- fostering of pro-social behaviour, self-efficacy and social problem solving;
- encouraging the development of internal controls through open communication, recognition of the child's rights and the taking of responsibility.

Parents of 'antisocial children', they argue, fall down on all of these, failing to monitor their child's activities, providing instructions that are often ambiguous, and using discipline methods that result more from their own moods, for example.

Kumpfer and Alvarado (1998) have identified the following parenting behaviours as protective factors against young people becoming involved in offending:

- the use of positive discipline methods;
- active monitoring and supervision;
- supportive parent–child relationships;
- families who advocate for their children;
- parents who seek information and support.

Desforges and Abouchaar (2003) have shown that parental involvement in the form of 'at-home good parenting' has a significant positive effect on children's achievement and adjustment even after all other factors shaping attainment (the quality of schools, for example) have been taken out of the equation. This can be shown to be the case across all classes and all ethnic groups. Given the negative impact low attainment and lack of achievement have on young people, particularly in respect of increased risk of offending, this is a significant finding.

These parenting risk and protective factors need to be seen within the context of other challenges that families face that may also impact on parenting and family functioning. That is, families may be experiencing stress at a community level, for example living in an impoverished neighbourhood; at a family level, such as family poverty and poor housing; and at an individual level, such as social isolation or depression (Ghate and Hazel 2002).

Parenting support provided in the youth justice context is a relatively new development in the UK, although there has for years been a well-established body of knowledge and expertise in supporting parents of younger children. Increasingly, more is being learnt about potentially promising approaches for parents of teenagers, including parents of young people who offend. When focusing on promising practice in working with parents in the youth justice context, it is important to acknowledge the process of building on a range of existing research and practice-based findings, from other areas of parenting support work and from other countries, to inform the development of work in this field.

Parenting programmes now form a major part in the agenda to impact upon social exclusion. The Social Exclusion Task Force Report 'Reaching Out' (2006) lists the following parenting initiatives currently being progressed:

- Early Learning Partnership to support parents of 1–3-year-olds who are at risk of learning delay;

- transition information, making parents aware of how they can support their children during the transitions from pre-school to primary school and from primary school to secondary school;

- Early Intervention Pathfinders – 15 local authorities providing increased support to at risk children aged 8–13 years;

- parent support advisers in 600 primary and secondary schools in the most deprived areas;

- health-led parenting support demonstrator projects from pre-birth to two years;

- Family Interventions Projects providing rehabilitation measures to families that are causing antisocial behaviour;

- parenting programmes funded by the Youth Justice Board used both preventatively and as an intervention of the court.

With particular regard to offending behaviour, Pickburn *et al.* (2005) identify the following broad types of support:

- service delivery: a programme of activities which address areas of the parent–child relationship that are causing difficulty (dealing with conflict and challenging behaviour; constructive supervision and monitoring; and boundary setting, for example);

- family therapy;

- groupwork programmes where groups of parents come together to participate in a programme of activity;

- multi-media cognitive behavioural programmes where a range of media is
used;

- parent adviser, where an adviser offers counselling and guidance in the
home;

- parent mentor, which involves the linking of a parent with a volunteer
mentor.

Some of these interventions may be delivered directly by practitioners in the
Yot, although some of them are likely to be services offered through external
agencies or the voluntary sector.

There are essentially two routes into a parenting programme; one is voluntary referral and the other a requirement of the court to attend through a
Parenting Order. The introduction of the Parenting Order has been controversial and there are a number of arguments that can be cited against holding a
parent responsible for a young person's behaviour.

From a human rights perspective, the Parenting Order could be challenged
as it effectively criminalises a parent when they haven't actually committed a
crime (Henricson 2003). There also remain concerns about the specific
requirements component of the Parenting Order, as Article 7 of the Human
Rights Act (no punishment without law) may be violated by the use of broad
and general requirements specified under Section 8 (4) (a) of the Crime and
Disorder Act 1998. If a parent cannot 'reasonably foresee' what they should
do, or not do, to avoid incurring a criminal sanction through breach of the
Parenting Order, then Article 7 might be contravened (Lindfield 2001).
However, a review by Narain (2001) suggested that they were likely to be
compatible and there have been no successful HRA challenges in the courts.
This is because the rights to privacy and family life enshrined in the Act must
be balanced against the legitimate interests of the state in preventing a young
person's future offending or antisocial behaviour. As a result, Parenting
Orders are assessed on issues of proportionality – whether there is a fair balance between rights and responsibilities.

> It is highly unlikely that it can be argued that a Parenting Order consti-
> tutes an interference with the right to private and family life (Article 8)
> … [as] the parenting order can be viewed as a justifiable interference
> with the right to private and family life in the interests of preventing
> 'disorder or crime'. (Narain 2001)

It could also be argued that the approach places total responsibility for a
young person's behaviour with the parent and ignores the wider community
whilst undermining a young person's agency (Morrow 1999). The majority of

Parenting Orders are made against mothers rather than fathers, as it is mothers who are more likely to attend court and receive the order. This has implications for equal opportunities and equality under the law (Ghate and Ramella 2002; Morrow 1999). Some critics have also argued that compulsion to attend and the stigma associated with a court order may make it less likely that parents will engage fully in the programme (Henricson *et al.* 2000). It is interesting to note that the evaluation of parenting programmes sponsored by the Youth Justice Board found no difference between the level of benefit reported by parents who had come via the Parenting Order and those who had not (it was generally positive), even when they had experienced uncertainty at the start of the programme (Ghate and Ramella 2002).

Promising approaches and parenting

Two reviews of practice from the USA are particularly significant in that they rate programmes in relation to the strength of their research design and the evidence of effectiveness produced. The Strengthening America's Families programme identified exemplary, model, and promising programmes by reviewing each programme on a number of criteria including sampling strategy, data analysis and programme integrity (Kumpfer 1993). The focus was on individual, group and family-based parenting programmes. The Blueprints programme for violence prevention[1] selected 11 model programmes on a number of effectiveness criteria, of which the three given the greatest weight were: evidence of deterrent effect with a strong research design; sustained effect; and multiple site replication. Three programmes were listed in both reviews as achieving the highest rating for effectiveness for programmes designed for parents and families of teenagers who offend. They are: Functional Family Therapy; Multisystemic Therapy; and Multidimensional Treatment Foster Care.

There have been a number of research reviews that have helped to identify a range of promising parenting interventions in the UK as well as in other countries (Sutton *et al.* 2004; Communities that Care 2001; Lloyd 1999; Barlow, 1997; Smith 1996). These include pre-natal services, home visiting services and group-based parenting programmes. They have tended to focus either on parents of younger children or parents of children with special needs such as learning disabilities. The Home Office and DfES have published a review of the international evidence of emerging effectiveness in parenting support (Moran *et al.* 2004). This identifies promising approaches in parenting support, what is still not known about effectiveness in this field and the implications these findings have for policy. In respect of promising approaches in practice, the following are the major messages:

- Both early and later interventions may produce positive outcomes.

- Interventions should have a strong theory base.

- Interventions should have measurable objectives and defined mechanism of change.
- Universal interventions (primary prevention at the community level) should be used for less severe parenting problems.
- Targeted interventions should be used for more complex parenting difficulties.
- Programmes should pay close attention to getting, keeping and engaging parents.
- Programmes should use multi-methods of service delivery.
- Interventions should be delivered by appropriately trained staff, backed by good management and support.
- Behavioural interventions are helpful for changing complex parenting behaviours and impacting on child behaviours.
- Cognitive interventions may help in changing beliefs, attitudes and self-perceptions as to parenting.
- Interventions should work in parallel (though not necessarily at the same time) with parents, families and children.

With regard to reconviction rates among children and young people whose parents have attended a parenting programme, evaluation of Youth Justice Board sponsored programmes found that during the year after parents had left the programme, reconviction rates had dropped to 61.5 per cent (a reduction of nearly one third), offending had dropped to 56 per cent, and the average number of offences per young person had dropped to 2.1 (a 50 per cent reduction). While these look promising on the surface, caution should be exercised. The evaluators themselves acknowledge that it is hard to say whether the programme alone was responsible for this as the intervention was only a part of a range of interventions. Furthermore, there was no control group to provide comparative data for the group studied.

The evaluation did provide information about project implementation issues, about who received services, their level of need, their satisfaction with the services provided and their perception of the changes that had taken place as a result of participating in the programme. On exit from the projects, parents reported positive changes in parenting skills and competencies that were statistically significant, including:

- improved communication with their child;
- improved supervision and monitoring of young people's activities;
- reduction in the frequency of conflict with young people, and better approaches to handling conflict when it arose;

- better relationships, including more praise and approval of their child, and less criticism and loss of temper;

- feeling better able to influence young people's behaviour;

- feeling better able to cope with parenting in general.

(Ghate and Ramella 2002)

Moran *et al.*'s assessment of the available research into parenting programmes highlighted a number of significant gaps in the research literature (2004). In terms of types of intervention, less is known about the impact of some types of open access or universal services than those that target a specific type of user. They also report a significant lack of research that is focused on the views of children and young people, which is ironic given that the ultimate aim of parenting programmes is to effect change that impacts on them. A notable exception to this is the evaluation of the Youth Justice Board sponsored parenting programmes where 300 young people were interviewed, with young people reporting slight but statistically insignificant improvements in communication and mutual understanding; supervision and monitoring by their parents; reduction in frequency of conflict; and better relationships (Ghate and Ramella 2002).

Overall, much less is known about the medium- to long-term impact of parenting interventions, with research tending to focus on the short-term outcomes and outputs. In addition, while there is a substantial focus on parenting support that identifies risk factors, there is much less on support services that focus on building protective factors.

Further, Moran *et al.* highlight some issues relating to diversity in relation to the available evidence base. All the research about who attends parenting programmes indicates that the overwhelming majority of interventions primarily serve white women (Ghate and Ramella 2002). The reasons for this are likely to be complex and reflect certain societal and cultural perceptions about who does the parenting in a family. The impact on the available evidence base is significant as it means that most evaluation samples contain too few men to be able to draw any conclusions about promising approaches for fathers and whether these are different from promising approaches for mothers.

The same is therefore true of ethnically diverse groups of parents. The evaluation of the Youth Justice Board sponsored parenting programmes showed that most of the parents who attended the services were white British (96 per cent). Butt and Box (1998) found a low rate of participation by black families in parenting services offered at family centres that seemed to result from the inability of the services to engage with them. A number of reviews also identify a lack of materials and culturally sensitive programmes (Roker and Coleman 1998; Butt and Box 1998). The Race Equality Unit has worked to develop a UK version of the Strengthening Families, Strengthening Communities Programme and the Home Office Family Policy

Unit has funded projects to work specifically on the needs of black and minority ethnic parents and families (Box 2001).

Based on social learning principles and the subject of a series of controlled evaluations using both intra-subject replication and traditional RCTs, Triple P-Positive Parenting is designed as a multi-level, multi-modal parenting and family support strategy developed at Queensland University in Australia. It incorporates five tiers of intervention offered at increasing levels of intensity for parents of children and young people from birth to 16. Triple-P is not a programme as such and is best described as a model or strategy for how a targeted yet flexible service to parents and families might be organised:

> The rationale for this multi-level strategy is that there are differing levels of dysfunction and behavioural disturbance in children, and parents have different needs and preferences regarding the type, intensity and mode of assistance they may require. This tiered approach is designed to maximise efficiency, contain costs, avoid waste and over servicing, and to ensure the program has wide reach in the community. Also, the multi-disciplinary nature of the program involves the better utilisation of the existing professional workforce in the task of promoting competent parenting. (Sanders *et al.* 2003)

While the different components of Triple-P have mainly been tried and tested with younger children, all studies have shown a significant effect in terms of reductions in unwanted behaviours among children and positive impacts on parents.

Finally, there is very little detailed information about cost-effectiveness or the cost benefits of providing parenting programmes. What research exists in this area is from the USA and focuses particularly on programmes targeting antisocial behaviour by children and young people. These studies highlight the cost-effectiveness of Multi-dimensional Treatment Foster Care (Moore *et al.* 2001) and Multi-systemic Treatment (Borduin *et al.* 2000). Notwithstanding the difficulties of assessing cost-effectiveness where evaluation of other aspects of parenting programmes is also lacking, this would seem to be a significant omission given the government's emphasis on and investment in parenting support programmes.

The principles of effective practice and parenting

Risk classification

It is likely that higher levels of parental stress are experienced by the parents of young people who are committing crimes more persistently or who commit more serious crimes, although this may not be true in all cases. Where it is, it could imply that the more intensive responses to parenting are likely to be required by those parents.

Families of young people with long histories of challenging behaviour, starting in early childhood, may need different interventions from those whose young people commence offending during their teenage years. In practice, the longer the history of difficulty, the more intensive the intervention may need to be and the more it could be necessary to involve the wider family.

Parent assessment and referral are crucial elements in the success of parenting interventions. In particular, the existence of clear and rigorous protocols, which are understood by all agencies involved in the assessment and referral process, may be important for the success of parenting interventions. All involved agencies may need to have a stake in producing, communicating and updating assessment and referral systems (Ghate and Ramella 2002).

As has already been identified, there is a range of risk and protective factors that are specific to parenting. It would seem sensible, therefore, to ensure that these underpin the assessment process for parents about to embark on some kind of parenting programme. While the identification of risk factors is important for establishing the areas where a parent might require specific input, so are the protective factors. Identifying protective factors could help to build parents' confidence and reveal the areas on which parenting support can focus.

The levels and types of stress that families are experiencing at a community, family and individual level could also influence the type of support that parents will find most helpful. Practitioners have reported that they have found that they may need to work with a parent individually, for example on strategies to address a housing crisis, before a parenting programme can be considered (Ghate and Ramella 2002).

A parenting assessment that shows the absence of parenting risk factors and the presence of protective factors may not necessarily mean that parenting support is not relevant to parents. It could be that they are dealing with issues that parenting support may help them to handle with greater confidence. Their child/young person may be being bullied at school or using drugs, for example, and parents might want support in dealing with these issues. A range of services could be useful in these situations, such as advice and information sessions or a parenting group programme to share their experience and learning with other parents.

Criminogenic need

While criminogenic need focuses on young people at risk of offending or reoffending, it can also be applied to the parents of these young people. The issue here would seem to be about the extent to which difficulties with parenting are directly associated with or contribute to the offending behaviour of a young person. The most obvious example here would be where parents or other family members themselves are offending, which can be assessed as having a direct impact on young people.

Where parenting can be seen to be an issue but is more distantly related to the offending behaviour of a young person, there may be a need to refer parents to another agency or organisation for support. This could help to ensure that interventions ultimately aimed at preventing offending are properly targeted and focused.

Community based

In the same way as learning is likely to take place in contexts that are meaningful to a young person, the same is likely to be true for their parents. Parenting programmes are intended to promote behaviour change and it may be advisable for them to be rooted in the experiences and life contexts of the parents taking part and those of the young people they care for. On one level it would imply that how, where and when parenting programmes are offered could be important, particularly with regard to ensuring that parents will turn up in the first place, but also that they will maintain their attendance for the duration of the programme. The evaluation of the Youth Justice Board sponsored parenting programmes also found that a home visit prior to starting work with a parent was felt to be important in terms of dispelling hostility and any anxieties parents were experiencing about attending a programme (Ghate and Ramella 2002).

The other issue that arises from the community-based principle is the potential for focusing too heavily on parenting and family interventions. This may serve to place a burden of responsibility on a family that ignores the impact and influence of the wider community on a young person's offending behaviour and any difficulties families may be experiencing (Morrow 1999).

The principle of community base may pose particular difficulties when applying it to young people who are in custody, where ties with home are fractured, often physically (young people are removed from the home), geographically (many young people are in facilities a long way from home which militates against regular family visits) and emotionally (the stigma and shock of a young person going to prison provides added stress to many parents/carers). In addition, parents may have high expectations that things will have changed when a young person returns from custody, which is contrary to available evidence about the impact of a custodial intervention on a young person after they have returned to their communities (ECOTEC 2001b; Hazel *et al.* 2002). There is little evidence that parenting support is deeply rooted in secure estate culture, where the focus is mainly on dealing with young people and not their parents. The active involvement of parents in planning and review meetings held in the secure estate could go some way towards ameliorating this. Where geographical distance is a significant issue, video conferencing services may provide an opportunity for parents and young people to communicate and for joint planning sessions to take place.

Programme integrity

Many of the parenting programmes sponsored by the Youth Justice Board appeared to experience difficulties in recruiting and training sufficiently skilled staff to work directly with parents (Ghate and Ramella 2002). The evaluation also found that practitioners working on parenting programmes had most success when they were freed from other responsibilities and when there was strong support from the Yot managers. This may be a consideration with regard to ensuring programme integrity is maintained for parenting interventions offered directly by a Yot.

Another issue with maintaining programme integrity arises when parenting services are commissioned by a Yot or brokered through other agencies. Careful monitoring of inputs, processes and outcomes of these interventions for the parents and families of young people at risk of offending and reoffending would seem important here. In addition, clear protocols and agreements about what these services will provide are likely to be important, particularly with regard to assessment and referral systems.

Once the parenting project has established aims and objectives, a steering group, clear protocols and agreements on working with other agencies, assessment and referral systems, and a range of services for parents and families, it needs to be publicised in order to reach parents and colleagues who will refer to the service.

The lack of promotion of a project may result in:

- too few parents being referred;

- group programmes having insufficient numbers to run effectively;

- ultimately parents not benefiting from support when they need it.

This has happened in some areas where Yots have been in partnership with a voluntary agency to provide parenting services. Without sufficient knowledge or ownership of the parenting project within the Yot, workers have not regularly assessed parents' needs and referred them on to the voluntary agency. Alternatively, they may have referred parents but not known enough about what is on offer to sufficiently motivate and engage the parent to keep appointments with the provider agency. This appears to have resulted in partnership projects breaking down and parents not gaining access to the services that they require (Ghate and Ramella 2002).

At the end of any programme of intervention, it is important to review the progress made and to identify any unmet needs that parent/s and other family members may have. A final review might involve practitioners who have worked with the family (whether from the Yot or partner agency) and the parent/s and other family members who have been involved in the programme. As has already been established, reviews and evaluations sometimes ignore the views of young people. It may be appropriate to carry out one review with a young person and another with their parents plus a joint review involving both parents and young people. This may be necessary when confidential issues that are not shared between parent and child need to be discussed.

Parents' own views, in terms of what has happened as a result of participating in a programme, contribute to decisions about whether change is necessary to achieve the objectives which have been set. Dissatisfaction with service provision could indicate that change is necessary, and responding to views expressed by parents could lead to a more effective delivery of support. Parents participating in a consultation process identified some changes they felt were necessary in order to meet their needs:

- increase numbers in the group as not enough participants;
- facilitators should explore their own values and beliefs with regard to parental responsibility so that their values don't clash with ours as parents;
- programme not to focus on being too educational;
- need for variety in group, i.e. others experiencing similar problems;
- programmes need to be longer and follow-up programmes should be available.

(Elliott *et al.* 2002)

This is also an issue shared with wider parenting services. Some of the reasons identified for the low levels of engagement of fathers are the lack of father-friendly services (Lloyd 2001), undervaluing of the role of fathers (Burgess 2002), and the focus on mothers in assessment of parental need (Cusick 2001).

There is not enough data to be clear about the over- or under-representation of black and minority ethnic parents in Parenting Order figures and in voluntary involvement in parenting programmes provided by Yots. It appears from a survey conducted by the Trust for the Study of Adolescents (TSA) that the proportion of black mothers receiving parenting services reflects the over-representation of young black people in the youth justice system. The lack of comprehensive ethnicity monitoring by Yots and their parenting service is an issue that appears to need addressing.

Intervention modality

It could be argued that there is no one 'correct' model of parenting programme that will address all parents' diverse needs. This suggests that a menu of possible intervention options could be made available to which parents and families can be referred as a result of a thorough assessment of need. The Triple P model might be a useful way for Yots to organise and map the parenting and family support available locally, which would include direct work by the Yot, services commissioned from, for example, the voluntary sector, and from other agencies.

It may be advisable for projects to clarify parents' expectations with them, so that it is clear what they can reasonably expect to be achieved. In addition, parents may need to be informed of the full range of services that is available to them to facilitate their informed participation. They could also be given the opportunity to identify helpful programme content as this may give parents more of a sense of ownership of the programme.

In the early stages of parenting work Yots tended towards the delivery of group programmes for all parents, but over time an array of services has emerged including:

- individual structured programmes;
- systemic family therapy;
- parallel group work with parents and young people;
- groups working with a specific ethnic minority;
- interactive CD-ROM programme;
- telephone support programme;
- parent advisers;
- parent mentors;
- information sessions on drugs and legal issues;
- fathers' groups;
- parent-led support groups.

A wide range of resources has been developed since 1999, including videos, interactive CD-ROMs, a family life photo pack, new group programmes including a programme designed to support black and minority ethnic parents and a programme for parents with literacy issues – so that there are now many more resources to draw on when supporting parents.

> Research into the effectiveness of family interventions in the USA has shown that family-focussed programmes are more effective than programmes that focus solely on the child or the parents. (Kumpfer and Alvarado 1998)

Projects are likely to encounter a variety of family structures, with parenting roles provided by one or two parental figures, step-parents, adoptive parents, non-resident parents, foster carers, grandparents and same sex parents.

Knowing about the way in which a family is structured may be crucial to providing support, since the strengths the family has, as well as the tensions experienced and related needs, may be directly related to its structure. The effectiveness of the support provided to families is likely to be influenced by the ability of the practitioner to work with the strengths of their family structure and to acknowledge and help the family to address the tensions.

There are social, psychological, emotional and relationship pressures that may be linked to the way in which a family has been created and is structured. It is important not to assume that these issues are present, as they may have been successfully managed because of a family's strengths. Understanding the key relationships within families will help parents and practitioners to identify the most appropriate services to provide, as well as who should be involved in any programme.

Responsivity

The primary purpose of a parenting intervention is to enable parents to learn new skills and strategies for approaching their relationships with children and, in some cases, others around them. Interventions may also simply reassure parents that they are doing the best they can. Engaging parents and families in any intervention may be regarded as the key to successful outcomes. If parents are not engaged they are unlikely to participate fully in any change process.

Barriers to engagement identified by parents include:

- negative experiences of 'helping agencies'/holding low expectations with respect to the help on offer;
- negative experiences of education and fear that parenting support will involve 'classes' and being taught 'how to be a good parent' (sometimes fed by media messages);
- the preconceptions or lack of understanding amongst other agencies/referrers about the nature of parenting education and support so that an unclear picture is given;
- anger at 'being punished' or blamed for the young person's behaviour, in particular for those parents on Parenting Orders;
- being ashamed or feeling stigmatised by the requirement to attend parenting interventions;
- reluctance to share sensitive experiences with others/confidentiality/privacy issues;
- programme/facilitator insensitivity to cultural diversity;
- language, literacy, disability issues not addressed;

- lack of clear information about the service, i.e. how to get to the venue, the availability of childcare, transport and so on.

(Elliott *et al.* 2002)

Just as young people present with a wide range of existing skills and needs, so do parents. In addition to a menu of support options available, the responsivity principle would imply that further flexibility is likely to be required in three main areas.

Firstly, the mode of delivery may be important in responding to the needs of parents at particular points in an intervention. Some parents are likely to benefit from working with a group of parents. The added value of such a group approach might be the mutual support of other parents who are experiencing difficulties with their children. For some parents, this group approach may well be threatening. This is more likely to be the case where parents are insecure about their own learning skills, in particular where reading and writing are concerned. For some, one-to-one work, particularly to start with, might be more appropriate in terms of building confidence and responding to significant need.

Secondly, the medium of delivery would seem to be important in terms of ensuring parents can access the programme and have the opportunity to develop a range of new strategies. Evaluation of Youth Justice Board sponsored programmes suggested that parents on the whole preferred approaches that:

- avoided formal, classroom-style delivery;

- avoided over-reliance on written materials;

- used interactive methods such as audio-visual material, role-play, discussion and debate.

(Ghate and Ramella 2002)

Variation in presentational style may be important in maximising the opportunity for behavioural change. 'Information alone has not been found to have an impact on behaviour unless combined with discussion time, experiential practice, role-playing and homework to solidify behavioural changes' (Kumpfer 1993). Varying learning methods also helps to reflect the diversity of participants and their life experiences. Whatever the content of the programme, it may be important to note that 'the factor that is likely to make the programme most effective is the skill of the facilitator in understanding group needs and process and being able to use groupwork skills to provide an optimum environment for learning and change to take place' (Howell and Montuschi 2002).

A significant number of adults experience difficulties with literacy and numeracy (Williams *et al.* 2003). Given the high proportion of young people in the youth justice system who experience such difficulties, and the established correlation with parents who struggle with basic skills, it is likely that the need may well be more widespread and entrenched than in the general population. Careful attention may therefore need to be given to the way in which materials are presented. This extends beyond written materials to the presentational style of practitioners.

Thirdly, the content of support is likely to be an important consideration in terms of responding appropriately to parents' needs. The core elements of many parenting programmes could be categorised under the following headings:

Knowledge:	Skills:
Adolescent behaviour – child development	Communication – active listening
Parenting styles – authoritarian, permissive, authoritative	Conflict resolution – assertiveness, negotiation
Cultural background – influence on parenting role	Boundary setting – 'I' statements, behaviour charts
Resources – accessing all sorts of support, friends, specialist agencies	Problem solving – family meetings, generating options
Attitudes:	**Experience:**
Discipline methods – alternatives to use of physical punishment	Own adolescence – how past impacts on present and connecting up
Being a parent – responsibilities and rights and social context	Sharing own experience of promising approaches– why, what, when, who, where and how
Being a teenager – responsibilities and rights and social context	
Potential for change – belief and indicators that change is possible	

Lindfield and Cusick (2001)

Some of the parents involved in the Youth Justice Board sponsored parenting programmes requested additional topics that it was not possible to cover in the courses they attended. These core elements may, therefore, be supplemented with additional topics relevant to the parents, such as alcohol and other drug misuse, step-parenting issues, divorce and separation.

Group workers may need to consider how their programme will reflect participants' different cultural backgrounds and ethnicity in the way that the programme is structured, in its content and in the materials used. It may also be helpful to provide culturally or ethnically specific groups to engage parents.

Establishing links with different community groups and services may help to extend the range of programmes that can be provided for different groups within a locality. Another issue to consider is how to make programmes accessible and engaging for parents whose first language is not English.

The same consideration will need to be given to fathers, both in terms of attracting them into programmes and also being responsive to them when they do attend. One promising model funded by the Home Office sought to engage fathers through providing sporting activities for fathers and their children. The project provided formal or informal parenting support to the fathers. The evaluation of the project concluded that 'Using sport and recreational activities as a strategy to engage fathers was a successful approach with fathers from different ethnic and class backgrounds' (Richardson and Roker 2002). A note of caution should be sounded here with regard to stereotyping fathers and sons as all being motivated by sport and projects may wish to look more closely at the ways in which fathers would like to learn.

Dosage

As with any intervention, the intensity and duration of a parenting intervention needs to reflect the seriousness of the difficulty being experienced. There is a risk that drawing parents into the youth justice system as part of inappropriately lengthy programmes may create dependency by the parent on practitioners within it. In addition, it may result in labelling of whole families making them the target of more scrutiny than other families. Conversely, programmes that are too short may simply open up issues and difficulties and leave parents feeling they know or can do even less than at the start of it. It is interesting to note that parents taking part in the Youth Justice Board sponsored parenting programmes (Ghate and Ramella 2002) felt that the eight-week courses they were attending were on the whole too short. While this is self-report information, it would indicate the need to consider both the exit strategies utilised at the end of programmes and, in some cases, referral to further support, possibly separate from the Yot.

One of the issues for ensuring that parents get the appropriate dosage (i.e. the intensity and regularity of inputs required to meet the identified need) may be ensuring they attend in the first place and then helping them to maintain their attendance at sessions or appointments. The following have been found to be promising in these respects:

- follow-up reminders by phone or letter can reduce the likelihood of parents not attending a first appointment (Staudt 2003);

- telephone calls to clarify what is going to happen and to discuss concerns both prior to and after an initial visit to a service (Forehand and Kotchick 2002);

- requiring some parents to invest time in completing various forms and assessment questionnaires before a first visit (although conversely for a minority of parents this may also be a barrier to engagement) (Staudt 2003);

- warning parents that they may be demoted to the bottom of a waiting list for services if they miss a specified number of appointments. It is interesting to note that rewards for attendance were less effective in encouraging attendance (Parrish, Charlop and Fenton 1986);

- making attendance mandatory through, for example, a Parenting Order (Ghate and Ramella 2002).

The challenges for practice

A challenge that faces projects at the outset, and in terms of sustaining them, is how to ensure maximum awareness of services to those making referrals to them (Ghate and Ramella 2002). Without such awareness, referrals are likely to be low and may ultimately jeopardise the sustainability of a parenting programme. This would imply that projects need to be pro-active in advertising and readvertising the service. A number of successful strategies have been identified, including practitioners who are working on parenting projects talking directly with court and Yot staff, leafleting and getting the project featured in the local media (Ghate and Ramella 2002).

Another significant challenge is the low numbers of fathers attending parenting programmes. Over the last few years though, there has been an increasing recognition of the positive role that fathers can have in parenting and in family life. Parenting support services have begun to reflect this wider societal change and increasingly to work on engaging fathers in parenting programmes. The challenge for practice remains with regard to finding innovative ways of attracting fathers to programmes and for ensuring their full participation over time.

The challenge relating to accessibility also includes parents from black and ethnic minority groups. Staff working in rural areas may find that resources that are specifically geared to black and minority ethnic groups are harder to access. In this case, it may be important to address the realities and effects of racism and cultural isolation for black and minority ethnic families who may be isolated in a majority white environment.

The concept of providing a menu of options for parents may also have significant resource implications for Yots. Further, the monitoring and evaluation of programmes brokered or commissioned from other agencies/organisations as part of that menu will be a challenge for youth justice practitioners, particularly in ensuring that they are achieving the desired outcomes for parents and ultimately for the young people themselves. Linked to this is the inherent difficulty of how to measure the impact of a parenting programme on a young person.

Summary

- Research has highlighted four major features of family life associated with the offending behaviour of young people: parental and sibling criminality; parental neglect, including lack of supervision; chronic family conflict, either between partners, or between parent and young person; and harsh or erratic discipline.

- A number of parenting behaviours has been identified as protective factors against young people becoming involved in offending: the use of positive discipline methods; active monitoring and supervision; supportive parent–child relationships; families who advocate for their children; and parents who seek information and support.

- There are two routes into a parenting programme; one is voluntary referral and the other a requirement of the court to attend through a Parenting Order. The introduction of the Parenting Order has been controversial and there are arguments against it.

- Evaluation has shown that there appear to be promising outcomes with regard to reconviction as a result of the parents attending programmes, although it is hard to say whether the programme alone was responsible for this.

- A number of research reviews has helped to identify a range of promising parenting interventions in the UK as well as in other countries which include pre-natal services, home visiting services and group-based parenting programmes, although these have tended to focus either on parents of younger children or parents of children with special needs such as learning disabilities.

- Significant gaps in the available research have been identified, including a failure to consider the views or impact of parenting interventions on young people; the impact of more open access services; the impact of parenting interventions over the medium- and long term; and the efficacy of programmes that focus on protective rather than risk factors.

Note

1 www.colorado.edu/cspv/blueprints

Further reading

Ghate, D. and Ramella, M. (2002) *Positive Parenting: The National Evaluation of the Youth Justice Board's Parenting Programme.* London: Youth Justice Board.

Moran, P., Ghate, D. and van der Merwe, A. (2004) *What works in Parenting Support? A Review of the International Evidence.* Research Report 574. London: DfES.

8

Restorative justice

Restorative justice has received much interest and publicity as an intervention for young people who have offended and is often an integral part of a number of specific youth justice orders and programmes. This chapter considers the evidence base for restorative justice from England and Wales and from other countries. It further asks questions about where and when restorative justice approaches might be most useful in relation to the prevention of offending. It also considers the tension inherent in restorative justice interventions with regard to who it is for – the young person or the victim of crime?

The evidence base for restorative justice

What is restorative justice?

There is no single definition of restorative justice. There are a number of programmes and practices that could be described as restorative, from conferencing and mediation to court-ordered reparation, victim-impact statements and victim-awareness programmes. In some ways, these programmes are so diverse, it is difficult to identify what each of them has in common that can be called restorative (Roche 2001).

Perhaps the most useful definition of restorative justice is that suggested by Marshall (1999): 'Restorative justice is a process whereby parties with a stake in a specific offence resolve collectively how to deal with the aftermath of the offence and its implications for the future.'

In broad terms, restorative justice processes bring victims and young people who have committed offences into contact, whether directly or indirectly, so that victims can receive answers to their questions, tell the young person what the impact of their offending was, and receive an apology. Restorative justice gives young people the chance to take responsibility and make amends for their crime through apologising and making reparation either to the victim or to the community.

The aim of restorative justice is to repair the harm caused by crime. The most obvious harm is that suffered by victims of crime. Restorative justice also recognises that crime harms society as a whole, and brings the wider community into decision-making to find a way to repair the harm caused by crime.

Restorative justice has been developing in this country and abroad since the mid-1970s. The government has made restorative justice a key objective of the youth justice system since 1998, because the evidence suggests that this process can meet the needs of victims in a way that traditional justice processes on their own cannot. The Youth Justice Board has a specific target to increase the satisfaction of victims year on year, and restorative justice has a major part to play in achieving this goal.

The Youth Justice Board has defined the key aims and outcomes of restorative justice as:

- **victim satisfaction** – reducing victims' fear and ensuring that they feel 'paid back' for the harm done to them;

- **engagement with the young person** – to ensure that they are aware of the consequences of their actions, have the opportunity to make reparation, and agree a plan for their restoration in the community;

- **creation of community capital** – increasing confidence in the criminal justice system among the public.

The Youth Justice Board has further defined the basic principles of restorative justice as including the following:

- the main objective is to put things right and heal relationships, thereby giving high satisfaction to victims and reducing reoffending;

- those directly affected by crime are to be involved in the process and their wishes given careful consideration;

- positive outcomes for the victim and community to be valid objectives alongside change in behaviour and attitudes of the young person.

The Youth Justice Board's evaluation of restorative justice programmes offered by Yots (Wilcox and Hoyle 2002) suggests that restorative justice approaches are used mostly as part of Final Warnings (33 per cent) or Reparation Orders (30 per cent). This would seem to indicate that restorative interventions tend to be focused on those in the early stages of a criminal career. The same study showed that theft and violent offences (including robbery) accounted for over half of all offences leading to referral and that very few referrals were made for fraud, drugs or sexual offences.

How does it work?

There are a number of ways in which restorative justice might have an impact on reoffending. The restorative process might induce empathy for the victim and counteract any techniques that young people who have offended might use for neutralising feelings of guilt or shame, such as a belief that the victim was not affected by the offence or that the losses were covered by insurance.

The restorative process may also result in young people coming to a better understanding of how their behaviour is upsetting those whom they care about (such as parents/carers) and a strengthening of their resolve to avoid causing such harm in future. It may also result in an agreement, which might make offending less likely (where the terms include regular school attendance or the avoidance of risky situations or people).

Where the offending has arisen out of a conflict, or where there is a prospect of retaliation, the restorative process may result in defused tension and reduced likelihood of the matter flaring up again. Finally, many see it as crucial that restorative justice insists on treating young people fairly and respectfully. They feel that this makes it more likely that young people who have offended in the past will treat others with fairness and respect in future. However, much more research is needed before firm conclusions can be drawn concerning the relative importance of these mechanisms in practice.

Models of restorative justice

Restorative justice is founded on a philosophy about how individuals, societies and criminal justice systems can respond to crime and other issues of conflict. The majority of restorative justice theory has been developed to explain the successful outcomes of various models of practice devised in different countries. Restorative justice is a field largely grounded in practice, although research supporting the effectiveness of that practice is emerging.

The most well-known practice models are:

- victim–offender mediation (direct or indirect);
- restorative conferencing;
- family group conferencing;
- community panel meetings.

All these models have a common aim of repairing the harm caused by the crime through balancing the interests of young people who have offended, with those of victims and communities. This is manifest in the definition of restorative justice proposed by the UK-based Restorative Justice Consortium: 'Restorative justice seeks to balance the concerns of the victim and the community with the need to reintegrate the offender into society. It seeks to assist the recovery of the victim and enable all parties with a stake in the justice process to participate fruitfully in it.'

Whichever model is used, evidence suggests, restorative approaches are appreciated by the majority of those who take part. There is no strong research evidence at present to suggest that any one model of restorative justice is more effective than another in general or in particular circumstances. There is some evidence to suggest that only face-to-face contact with a victim leads to reductions in reoffending. But it is also known that indirect contact through a mediator or facilitator is the only form of restorative justice that is effective for many victims. Examining the benefits of different models of restorative practice is something that needs further research.

There are potential strengths in having a range of models available to meet the needs of particular victims and young people who have offended. All the models of restorative practice appear to be effective in meeting the needs of victims who choose to participate. They are also useful in producing plans, supported by all of the participants, for reparation work to be undertaken for the community or victims. Agreements made following restorative justice processes are more likely to be completed, and in less time, than those simply ordered by the court.

Victim–offender mediation

Also called 'victim–offender dialogue' and historically called 'victim–offender reconciliation', victim–offender mediation was the first restorative justice model to develop in England and Wales. It is a process whereby a neutral or impartial person assists a victim of crime and the young person who has committed that crime to communicate with each other in the hope of reaching some degree of reconciliation. A face-to-face meeting may take place between the parties, but most cases result in indirect mediation, which may provide victims with answers to their questions and give them reassurance about their safety.

In some countries, it is undertaken as a voluntary addition to the formal response of the criminal justice system. In others (England and Wales amongst them), it occurs as the response of the criminal justice system. In the latter case, it sometimes constitutes all or part of a sentence, or results in the case being diverted from the system.

In this model, the actual focus of any indirect or direct mediation session is driven primarily by the parties involved, not the mediators. The mediator's role is to prepare the parties so that they are clear about what it is they wish to discuss, and are able to do so in as productive a manner as possible.

Restorative conferencing

Restorative conferencing was initially developed to provide a more effective cautioning experience for young people in New South Wales, Australia. Conferences tend to follow a similar structure to that suggested for panel meetings, and the facilitator often has a 'script' of questions to follow to guide the discussion. The main differences between this model and victim–offender mediation relate to the role of the facilitator, the use of a set structure or script, and the number of people who are involved in a conference.

Whereas victim–offender mediation tends to focus on the interaction between the primary victim and the young person who has offended only, the conferencing model generally involves more people. This is based on the view that young people need to understand the wider impact of their offence (for example on a victim's family and on their own family), and that these 'secondary victims' also need restoration and can benefit from the restorative process.

Family group conferencing

Developed initially in New Zealand, family group conferencing allows the family (on the basis of information from the victim, young person and professionals at the conference) to create an action plan intended to address the consequences of past offending and prevent further offending. In New Zealand, family group conferences are also used to form the core contents of sentences, or as a means of diverting young people from the criminal justice system. A key distinguishing feature of family group conferencing is the use of private family time to develop plans, which are then brought to the wider conference.

At a restorative justice family group conference, the victim is a key participant and contributor. They must be given advice and support, and helped to attend and present their 'story'. The victim is present during the first stage of the family group conference and withdraws, together with the professionals, to leave the family to plan in private. The family has responsibility for determining the most appropriate responses to offending by a young person and for making proposals for reparation. The victim rejoins the conference, with the professionals, to hear the family's plans.

Community panel meetings

A community panel meeting is a legislative requirement following a Referral Order. A young person is required to attend a panel meeting composed of at least two community volunteers, a member of the Yot and a parent/carer (if the young person is under the age of 16). Victims may also be invited to attend or be asked to contribute in other ways if they want to. An agreement or contract is drawn up and it is an expectation that the agreement will contain an element of reparation.

While these broad distinctions between different restorative approaches are useful, the reality is that programmes offered across the youth justice system in England and Wales vary widely in terms of what is offered and the level to which they might be described as restorative.

Table 8.1 Types and degrees of restorative justice practice

Fully restorative	Mostly restorative	Partly restorative
Family group conference	Victim–offender mediation	Compensation
Community conferencing	Victim support circles	Victim services
Peace circles	Victimless conferences	Offender family services
Restorative conference	Therapeutic communities	Family-centred social work
	Direct reparation to victim	Victim awareness
		Community reparation

Source: McCold and Wachtel (2002)

It can be seen from Table 8.1 that, unlike some other interventions within youth justice, the prevention of offending is not the only aim of restorative justice. The repair of harm, including harm to relationships, is also important. Restorative justice entails a different way of working, with a different focus to other interventions, whereby the measures of effectiveness comprise measures of victim satisfaction as well as measures of recidivism.

Restorative justice and reducing reoffending

Internationally, a number of evaluations have now been conducted of different schemes for restorative justice (see McCold and Wachtel 2002 for a comprehensive review).

In Canberra, Australia, young people who had offended were randomly assigned to court or to a restorative justice conference, thus ruling out the possibility that any difference in outcomes was due to the better risks being selected for conferences. Sherman *et al.* (2000) concluded that the effect of diversionary conferences was to cause a significant drop in offending rates by young people who had committed violent crimes (by 38 crimes per 100 young people per year), a small increase in drink-driving offences (by six crimes per 100 young people per year), and no difference in repeat offending by young people committing offences against property or shoplifting. These findings have been treated by some as justification for 'targeting' restorative justice at young people who commit violent crimes. However, it should not be assumed that findings from one jurisdiction (whether positive or negative) will hold good elsewhere.

Evaluations of family group conferences in New Zealand have shown a positive impact in terms of reducing reoffending, with some areas showing a reduction of a third annually (cited in Masters 2005). There have not been many attempts at family group conferencing in England and Wales, although one project in Essex which mimics the New Zealand model in working with the 20 per cent of young people committing the most serious of offences, has shown reductions in reoffending (*ibid*).

McGarrell *et al.* (2000) studied an Indianapolis experiment in which young people who had committed only one offence were randomly assigned to either a restorative justice conference or to the normal range of diversion programmes. Rearrest was 40 per cent lower in the conference group than in the control group after six months, an effect that declined to a 25 per cent reduction after 12 months.

Studies of various restorative justice programmes in the UK are less conclusive in relation to the impact on reducing offending. In a UK study of restorative cautioning, Hoyle *et al.* (2002) went further than most in that they studied rates of self-reported offending rather than relying on the usual proxy measure for reoffending of reconviction or rearrest. They found a substantial aggregate move towards desistance, calculating that young people who went through a restorative caution were half as likely as those experiencing the traditional police caution to be resanctioned within a one-year follow-up period. This study did not involve random assignment and the sample size was small, ie. below significant levels.

Overall, while reviewers of the available evidence differ in their precise conclusions, they are in agreement that restorative justice programmes rarely make reoffending worse and often achieve more positive results than other types of intervention (Umbreit *et al.* 2001; McCold and Wachtel 2002; Braithwaite 2002; Latimer *et al.* 2001).

In the UK, Wilcox and Hoyle (2002) evaluated 46 restorative justice projects funded by the Youth Justice Board. Here they found a reconviction rate over 12 months of 31.4 per cent for those undergoing restorative justice programmes compared to 33.3 per cent for a comparator sample. While there was no statistically significant difference in outcome between the samples, young people who had met the victim of their offence were the least likely to be reconvicted, as were those who had victim awareness intervention.

A further 12-month follow-up of the cohorts (Wilcox and Hoyle 2004) found the size of the effect much reduced. No statistically significant difference in outcome was found between the two approaches. Moreover, the style of caution used had no impact on seriousness or frequency of subsequent reoffending. Restorative approaches, however, did have substantial benefits for victims and young people who had offended in terms of raising awareness and 'closing' the issue.

The most recent study of restorative justice interventions suggests that in general they seem to reduce crime more effectively with more, rather than less, serious crimes; in particular with crimes involving personal victims and with violent crimes as opposed to property crimes (Sherman and Strang 2007). Their conclusions though are drawn from a mixed sample of adult, youth and international studies. Only one of the examples relating to violent crime featured young people from the UK (young women from Northumbria) and similarly, out of the four RCTs relating to property crime, only one referred to young people under the age of 18 in the UK. It is difficult therefore to draw absolute conclusions as to the efficacy of restorative justice in reducing offending or reoffending by young people in England and Wales, although the evidence would tend to suggest that it is more likely to be effective where crimes are more violent and serious in nature. Given the current emphasis on certain forms of restorative justice as part of very early interventions for less serious crimes, this begs a question as to how useful this approach is.

Although considerable emphasis is given in guidance to restorative approaches to delivering Final Warning interventions, the available evidence as to the superiority of its impact remains equivocal. Wilcox *et al.*'s (2004) two-year study, following up the work of Hoyle *et al.* (2002), comparing the performance of restorative and traditional cautions, found no statistically significant difference on resanctioning outcomes between three police forces. Moreover, the style of caution used had no impact on the seriousness and frequency of subsequent offending:

> Taking the results of these analyses together, there was no evidence to suggest that the restorative cautioning[1] initiative had resulted in a statistically significant reduction in resanctioning. Importantly, neither was there evidence that restorative cautioning had increased resanctioning rates (Wilcox *et al.* 2004: vi).

Again, it should be noted that the sample in this study was combined adults and young people with just over one third being 17 and under. Analysis of the data by age showed no statistically significant benefit of one type of caution over another for this age group.

It is not clear, however, that restorative approaches in England and Wales are always being implemented in the ways that capture and reflect the 'spirit' of restorative justice (Crawford and Newburn 2002; Morris 2002). The involvement of victims in the restorative process remains low across the full range of orders that contain an element of reparation. In Dignan's evaluation of four pilot reparation areas, direct reparation to a victim occurred in only 12 per cent of cases with just 9 per cent resulting in mediation (2002). Victim involvement in the Referral Order process is also low (Newburn *et al.* 2002) and the Wilcox and Hoyle evaluation (2002) points to a reliance on indirect community reparation as opposed to the direct involvement of victims in the restorative process.

Some critics also argue that when emphasis is placed on 'the responsibilisation of young offenders' the principles of restorative justice will always be derogated (Gray 2005b). The literature suggests that in the current climate of youth justice policy greater priority is given to confronting young people to accept responsibility for their criminal and antisocial behaviour than in seeking to make good the loss and injury to the victims and seek a restorative resolution to any conflict. In particular, research which has focused upon discourse analysis of restorative justice conferences and Referral Order panels (Crawford and Newburn 2002; Gray 2005b; Haines and O'Mahony 2006) has highlighted a number of tensions between the spirit of restorative justice and the practice of youth justice decision-making. These tensions include:

- coercive and confrontational approaches used in decision-making forums;
- police-led resolution of the conflict (not victim and young person working out their own resolutions);
- low levels of victim involvement in restorative justice processes;
- lack of resources to deliver effective restorative justice solutions;
- predominant use of community-based reparative schemes rather than individually tailored restorative justice solutions.

Haines and O'Mahony comment:

> The growth in popularity and spread of restorative justice precisely at a time when attitudes towards young people find expression in generally more controlling and/or punitive measures (especially in England and Wales) both rest in, and at the same time expose, the crucial tension within restorative justice to be simultaneously both positive and punitive. In practice, the positive elements are more rhetorical whilst the punitive expressions are more materially apparent. (2006: 119)

Restorative justice and benefits to victims

Many victims of crime would like an acknowledgement from the young person that they have been wronged, combined with steps to put that wrong right (Strang 2001). These steps might include offers of financial or practical reparation, but more usually an apology is sought, coupled with reassurance that the offence will not be repeated. Victims also often value the chance to hear the young person's explanation of the offence, to voice their own questions, views and feelings about the matter, and to be listened to with respect. This can also be true of others affected by the offence, such as people who are close to the young person or victim, and other members of the community who were affected by the offence. Some models of restorative justice seek to involve these wider 'stakeholders'.

An essential feature of restorative justice programmes is to consider and meet the needs of victims, and possibly to bring about some 'closure' for them regarding the incident. International research has firmly established that such effects are regularly achieved (Marshall and Merry 1990; Maxwell and Morris 1993; Strang 2002; Umbreit 1994; and acknowledged by Utting and Vennard 2000). Victims consistently report that a strong feeling of justice has been delivered to them, and that their levels of anger and distress are often greatly reduced.

In the UK, Hoyle *et al.*'s in-depth study (2002) of 31 victims who participated in a restorative conference found that 68 per cent felt the process had helped the young person to understand the effects of the offence; 71 per cent said they felt better as a result of the meeting, and only 3 per cent said that they felt worse. When asked for their overall assessment of the meeting, 97 per cent considered that it had been a good idea. Most of the victims who provided follow-up data in the year following the conference reported a long-term positive (and sometimes substantial) impact on themselves, with none reporting any long-term significant negative feelings. Other participants, including young people who have offended, reported in similarly positive terms, thus indicating that restorative justice can be successful in giving equal weight to the interests of young people who have offended, victims and other participants.

The Oxford University report on the 46 Youth Justice Board funded restorative justice projects (Wilcox and Hoyle 2002) found that 79 per cent of victims had been able to put the offence behind them, and that seven out of 10 thought that the young person better understood the impact of the offence on the victim. The expectations and orientations of victims prior to conferences vary, and there is similar variation in the extent to which they derive benefits from the experience, but few consider it a waste of time (Daly 2003).

Studies also show that there are some kinds of activity that are not valued by victims; in particular, apologies that are made under pressure from facilitators (or courts) or that otherwise appear lacking in sincerity (Maxwell and Morris 1993; Strang 2002; Crawford and Newburn 2003).

Restorative justice in the juvenile secure estate

The Youth Justice Board has recently funded research to establish the scope of restorative work being undertaken within custodial and secure establishments (Curry *et al.* 2004). The main finding was that there was little restorative justice intervention of any kind taking place. Some projects, which had previously flourished, were in decline. This was largely due to the pressure of numbers of young people sentenced to custody and secure conditions, and the resulting inability to allocate places within a reasonable distance of the home area. Staff in custodial and secure settings, however, were broadly sympathetic to the notion of experimenting with restorative approaches to working with young people, especially in relation to tasks such as dealing with bullying and disciplinary matters, and in order to bring home to young people the impact of their behaviour on the victims of crime.

The principles of effective practice and restorative justice

Risk classification

One of the criticisms levelled at the use of a restorative approach has been the extent to which it may draw young people prematurely into the youth justice system. As has already been shown, restorative justice interventions are more likely to be effective with young people who have committed more serious offences (Sherman and Strang 2007), which calls into question its use as part of Final Warnings or Referral Orders.

Risk assessment is also relevant when working with the victim and young person and in considering the appropriate type of restorative justice intervention in a case. Risk assessment factors determine whether it is advisable for the victim and young person to meet face to face, or whether a more indirect form of restorative justice would be suitable.

The principle of risk classification highlights one of the tensions inherent in restorative justice already discussed in this chapter, i.e. are the needs of the young person or the victim of crime to take priority when making decisions about whether or not to instigate a restorative process? Taking into consideration the needs of the victim may argue in favour of a restorative process between victim and young person, even if this is not indicated as necessary to reduce reoffending by the young person. An assessment of both parties may determine that a young person who poses very little risk of reoffending might nonetheless be encouraged to participate in a restorative justice programme because a victim has been significantly affected by the young person's behaviour. It may be harmful to the process if, for example, a person who has been a victim of crime several times over were to blame a young person responsible for only one of those offences for all the harm they have suffered.

Criminogenic need

Again, the contracts made at youth offender panel meetings with young people who have offended should include programmes identified by the *Asset* assessment as addressing the factors linked to their offending. A key aim of the subsequent panel meetings during the course of the Referral Order is to monitor young people's completion of these programmes, as agreed in their contract with the panel.

Similarly, this principle again relates directly to the choice of restorative justice programme and the need to remain flexible over a period of time. A complexity of criminogenic issues in a case might, for example, favour the use of a family group conference or a youth offender panel, which would allow criminogenic factors to be looked at alongside, or as part of, the communication with the victim.

The principle of focusing on programmes to address young people's criminogenic needs must be balanced with a key tenet of restorative justice, which is that participants play an active role in determining how to respond to an offence. The outcomes from research would suggest that restorative justice practitioners should be wary of taking over the process or setting the agenda. Creative ways of dealing with the risk of reoffending often emerge from interaction among the participants if they are given the space and time to discuss these matters, and 'professional interventions' are not always necessary. At panel meetings this can best be allowed to take place by enabling victim and young person to first suggest what should be in the contract, before contributing the advice from the Yot, based on the *Asset* assessment.

From the victim's perspective, there is a danger that focusing on criminogenic needs gives the appearance that the restorative process is weighted too much towards the young person's interests. It may, therefore, be important that a restorative process begins with a clear focus on the victim's needs rather than on the young person's criminogenic needs. It may be much easier for victims to show concern for a young person's future once their own sense of harm and injustice has been acknowledged and addressed. Once this has been achieved, many victims appear keen to help to minimise the risk of reoffending. The structure of restorative conferencing, and suggested structure for mediation and youth offender panels, recognises this need to deal with the effect of the crime, thus meeting the victim's needs, before going on to consider the future.

Responsivity

Restorative justice approaches are suitably flexible that they can be tailored to meet the needs of young people and victims of crime while helping them to develop new strategies for learning and new ways of perceiving things.

A conference with a victim provides opportunities for young people to consider alternative strategies for communicating orally. Writing a letter of reparation can also be a valuable activity if used as an opportunity to develop new strategies for expressing themselves in writing. In order to maximise the learning from these experiences, practitioners will need to prepare young people effectively and to support them without imposing so much support that it makes the restorative aspect of the activity meaningless.

Notwithstanding the warning against relying too much on community reparation schemes as the main restorative justice response provided, such programmes may provide all kinds of opportunities for incidental learning for young people. Programmes might involve, for example, producing a piece of art to enhance the local area, where the learning outcomes are both directly related to making reparation and to learning a range of skills related to the arts.

Many advocates of restorative justice see one of the key benefits as helping victims to see that young people who have offended rarely live up to the media stereotype of the unfeeling, calculating 'yob'. Related benefits for victims may include reduced fear that they will be victimised again by the same young person, coming to terms with the experience of victimisation, and increased confidence in their ability to deal with the aftermath of crime.

Whereas all young people who have offended who are handled within the youth justice system are by definition non-adult, victims may be young children, teenagers, young adults, middle-aged or elderly. Allowing victims to negotiate the restorative process in their own way, for example by allowing them to say as little or as much as they want, at the point and in the manner they choose, would seem to enhance the prospects that victims will take positive lessons away from the process.

Community based

Restorative justice processes hold unique potential for involving the wider community as a support for both young person and victim. For example, the youth offender panel brings in community members as part of the restorative process. Restorative conferencing and family group conferencing also involve the wider community. All these forms of restorative practice recognise that the long-term healing or repair of harm for both the victim and the young person may rely on their being supported in their own social and community context in order to move on from the crime.

The use of restorative justice approaches is minimal in the juvenile secure estate. Despite the logistical difficulties involved in this, restorative justice where young people are encouraged to engage with and make reparation in some way to their communities may have the potential to enable secure establishments to better implement the community-based principle in their work with individual young people. This might be achieved through letters of reparation, through arranging face-to-face conferencing between young people, victims and families during the custodial phase of a DTO and continuing such work during the community phase or, where facilities exist, through video conferencing. Victims might also be encouraged to communicate with young people who have committed crimes through similar channels, giving them the same rights and access to restorative justice as victims of young people who remain in their communities.

At the point of release, restorative processes have also been used as forums to make plans addressing the future needs of young people who have offended in the community. Consideration could be given to inviting victims to participate in such forums (whether directly or indirectly), so that any remaining victimisation needs can be addressed alongside criminogenic needs.

Intervention modality

In relation to restorative practice, processes can be both an intervention in their own right *and* a planning tool for further interventions. For example, the youth offender panel could be seen as a restorative process; it is also a planning tool for further interventions, as the contract can include a commitment to a further restorative justice process with the victim. As indicated above, the implication for effective restorative practice is that the most appropriate restorative process should be deployed in individual cases.

The multi-modal principle can also be applied to victims. Responses to victimisation are complex and vary from victim to victim. Restorative processes should allow for such complexity and be flexible enough to meet as many of the victim's needs as possible. At the same time, it should not be assumed that a victim–young person encounter could possibly satisfy all of a victim's needs. Victim Support has argued that victims are entitled to: compensation; protection from intimidation or harassment; respect and support from criminal justice professionals; clear information about the progress of their case, the procedures being followed, their role in the process, and any rights they may have; the opportunity to give a statement about the full consequences of the offence, which is then taken into consideration whenever decisions are made about their case; and to be free of the burden of deciding what should happen to a young person. This list makes it clear that while restorative justice may have an important part to play in meeting the multiple legitimate expectations of victims, it is unrealistic to expect young people who have offended to repair all the harm suffered by victims.

In some respects, it could be argued that the processes involved in a fully restorative process fit a cognitive-behavioural model. The process is designed to get a young person to confront the consequences of their offending behaviour and change their behaviour accordingly. The reliance on practices that can only be described as 'partly restorative' according to the distinctions made by Wilcox and Hoyle (2002) – community reparation, for example – may call into question the extent to which cognitive-behavioural approaches are being fully utilised as part of restorative justice interventions. Interestingly, Wilcox and Hoyle's research also indicated that it was the cognitive-behavioural elements of victim awareness training that had the most lasting impact and not the increased sensitivity to the victim's point of view.

Programme integrity

A key element of programme integrity in relation to restorative justice is ensuring that restorative justice practitioners, including community panel members, are trained to deliver restorative justice to an appropriate standard, and that some kind of quality assurance is in place. At the same time, an important part of restorative justice is its flexibility to meet the needs of particular victims and young people who have offended. Each panel contract should be unique, reflecting the decision-making process at that particular panel meeting. This presents a challenge in relation to programme integrity, although, with appropriate recording of key data regarding both outcomes for young people and victims involved in the process, this might be overcome. This would provide youth justice staff with a clearer picture of what kinds of approaches are working, with whom and in what circumstances.

As indicated earlier, low levels of victim involvement in restorative justice to date may be seen to have compromised the integrity of programmes. The research indicates that better outcomes can be achieved from programmes where victims are directly involved, and yet more indirect methods of reparation are routinely used.

Integrity in restorative justice is also about monitoring and supporting young people who have offended to complete the action points agreed in their panel contract, or in an outcome agreement with the victim if the restorative process takes place separately to a panel meeting (for example, as part of a Reprimand or Final Warning). Completing the contract or agreement may be regarded as essential, both for meeting the young person's criminogenic needs and, as indicated above, for meeting the needs of the victim.

For managers, the integrity principle implies that adequate resources and monitoring are crucial to successful restorative justice. This suggests that programmes need to be sufficiently resourced to prepare all participants for the process, and have access to adequate interventions to implement the plans drawn up.

Dosage

A restorative justice approach should not be considered as a one-off intervention, but as a flexible process, which adapts to changing situations and need. The Referral Order allows for this in follow-up meetings to review the contract. Restorative justice processes should in part be selected based on an understanding of what type of process is most likely to bring about change in the young person (as long as the victim also sees this process as meeting their own needs). It is worth noting that young people who have offended very often voluntarily agree to comply with restorative justice agreements and interventions for longer than a court sentence may require them to.

UNIVERSITY OF WINCHESTER
LIBRARY

The dosage principle could also be applied to victims. Where a victim has suffered only minor inconvenience as the result of an offence, a simple letter of apology may be all that is needed for the young person to repair the harm caused. Victims who suffer greatly as a result of the offence may require much more by way of support, preparation and reparation if their needs are to be met by restorative justice.

The challenges for practice

One challenge for practice is how to increase the level of involvement of victims in restorative justice interventions. This may involve practitioners in looking critically at some of the community reparation schemes they routinely use and asking, in the first instance, whether these are achieving positive outcomes in terms of reducing reoffending and, significantly, whether these are actually helping the victims of crime and the local community in ways that reduce their fear of crime and resentment towards young people.

The research would indicate that the low level of victim participation is not related to an unwillingness on the part of victims to become involved. Where particular effort has been made to involve victims, 60 per cent participation levels have been shown both in this country and in New Zealand (Masters 2005). What studies have shown, however, is a 'cultural resistance' amongst some youth justice staff who do not see it as a priority in their work and so fail even to contact the victims (Dignan 2002; Newburn *et al.* 2001). This would imply that a shift is required in some areas of organisational culture in order to raise the importance of giving victims the opportunity to participate in some kind of restorative process, both for their own benefit and also to strengthen the potential impact of the experience for young people who have committed crimes. In order to involve victims, Masters (2005) reports that opt-out letters, where the expectation of involvement is made, may be more effective than opt-in letters.

What this 'cultural resistance' might indicate is a lack of appropriate training for staff from both Yots and the juvenile secure estate in restorative justice. In their evaluation of referral orders, Newburn *et al.* (2001) found that less than a quarter of Yot staff involved in contacting victims and preparing them for community panel meetings considered that they had had adequate training.

Further systemic challenges for practice stem from the speeding up of youth justice processes, which may conflict with the time required to adequately prepare a victim, young people and their parents/carers/other supporters for a meaningful restorative intervention. There is also some evidence that police forces may withhold contact information about victims in the spirit of data protection unless they have had informed consent from the victim themselves, although the *Code of Practice for Victims* (Office for Criminal Justice Reform 2005) attempts to circumvent this.

While restorative justice has underpinned much recent work in youth justice and remains set to do so, the evidence for the efficacy of such approaches in England and Wales (while well received by victims, young people, parents/carers and professionals) with regard to reoffending is uncertain. The key question is whether more direct victim involvement and better training for practitioners in how to manage the various models of intervention will lead to the achievement of better outcomes in this respect.

Summary

- Restorative justice is promoted as a core part of youth justice interventions from interventions in schools, referral orders and final warnings through to action plan and supervision orders.

- There are four basic models of restorative justice: victim–offender mediation; family group conferencing; restorative conferencing; and community panel meetings.

- Studies of restorative justice approaches in other jurisdictions, primarily in Australia and New Zealand, have shown promising outcomes with regard to reducing likelihood of reoffending.

- Studies conducted in England and Wales of restorative justice projects and referral orders have shown little impact with regard to recidivism, although evaluations show that they do have a positive impact on and are well regarded by victims of crime.

- There is an inherent tension between the reparative elements of restorative justice approaches and the more punitive elements of the youth justice system which is seen to impose reparation as part of an order rather than a voluntary scheme.

- Despite evidence that suggests approaches that directly involve victims are more promising, levels of victim involvement remain low across the range of restorative interventions.

- Restorative justice interventions seem to reduce crime more effectively when applied to young people who have committed more serious and violent crimes and those involving personal victims.

Note

1 A restorative caution is 'a meeting facilitated by a trained police officer, based around a structured dialogue about the offence and its implications (with active involvement from the offender and the victim, if present)' (Wilcox *et al.* 2004: 1).

Further reading

Crawford, A. and Newburn, T. (2003) *Youth Offending and Restorative Justice: Implementing Reform in Youth Justice.* Cullompton: Willan Publishing.

Sherman, L. and Strang, H. (2007) *Restorative Justice: The Evidence.* London: The Smith Institute.

9

Mentoring

This chapter concerns the mentoring of young people 'at risk' of becoming involved in offending, diverted from court, subject to final warning interventions or where mentoring is used as part of an offending behaviour programme. 'Mentoring' is an elastic term, which encompasses a variety of approaches:

> Helping, coaching, tutoring, counselling, sponsoring, befriending, bonding, trusting, role-modelling, mutual learning, direction-setting, progress-chasing, sharing experience, respite provision, sharing a laugh, widening horizons, resilience-building, showing ropes, informal apprenticeships, providing openings, kindness of strangers, sitting by Nellie, treats for bad boys and girls, the Caligula Phenomenon, power play, tours of middle-class life, and so on and so forth. (Pawson 2006: 123)

It considers some of the issues that have been identified through research, contrasting some very positive outcomes from evaluations of programmes in America with less conclusive outcomes from evaluations of projects in the UK.

The evidence base for mentoring

Mentoring in the youth justice system is a voluntary one-to-one relationship between a young person and a supportive adult, established to help the young person to achieve his or her goals. It is more than befriending and aims for constructive changes in the life and behaviour of the young person. A mentor can be defined as 'someone who helps others to achieve their potential' (Shea 1992). Mentors may provide that help by a variety of modes of relationship (Pawson 2006):

- **Befriending**: creating bonds of trust and the sharing of new experiences so that the mentee recognises the legitimacy of other people and other perspectives.

179

- **Direction-setting**: promoting further self-reflection through the discussion of alternatives so that the mentees reconsider their loyalties, values and ambitions.

- **Coaching**: coaxing and cajoling the mentee into acquiring the skills, assets, credentials and testimonials required to enter the mainstream.

- **Sponsoring**: advocating and networking on behalf of the mentee to gain the requisite insider contacts and opportunities.

Mentoring is not a formal part of a young person's order such as the Final Warning, Action Plan Order, Supervision Order or Detention and Training Order (DTO). However, mentoring schemes are often used as part of youth justice interventions and mentioned within official guidance. For example, the Home Office and Youth Justice Board's 2002 document entitled *The Final Warning Scheme – Guidance for Youth Offending Teams* (Yots) states:

> Youth offending teams may also find that referral to a mentoring scheme can be a useful way of reinforcing the rehabilitation programme – either as part of it or in support. Mentoring schemes are designed to help support young people, assisting them to achieve their goals and resist negative peer pressure . . . Mentors are trained to be supportive and non-judgmental. Some schemes are designed specifically for young offenders. (Youth Justice Board 2002f).

Overall responsibility for the provision of mentoring programmes for young people who offend, lies with Yots although they may be run by agencies outside of the formal youth justice system.

The popularity of mentoring as an intervention with 'at-risk' young people has been growing for some years in the UK, following reports from the US that programmes such as 'Big Brothers Big Sisters' had achieved impressive results, for example in reducing drug/alcohol misuse and school non-attendance and in improving relationships with parents/guardians (Tierney *et al.* 1995; Grossman and Tierney 1998). More recent research in the US (Jekielek *et al.* 2002), which reviewed findings from 10 different mentoring schemes, has concluded that:

> . . . mentoring programs can be effective tools for enhancing the positive development of youth. Mentored youth are likely to have fewer absences from school, better attitudes towards school, fewer incidents of hitting others, less drug and alcohol use, more positive attitudes toward their elders and toward helping in general and improved relationships with their parents.

This study also highlighted factors that can undermine the effectiveness of mentoring. Some of these are to do with the particular circumstances of the young person, and some are concerned with the organisation of the scheme; for instance, the level of supervision and training provided for mentors. Other factors are to do with the contact between the mentor and the young person, such as frequency of contact and having a flexible agenda.

In 2002, Dubois *et al.* provided a meta-analysis of 55 evaluations of a range of differently designed mentoring programmes for at-risk and high-risk youth in the US. In addition, Jekielek *et al.* (2002) conducted a smaller review of 10 evaluations of nationwide and local youth mentor programmes in the US. The Dubois study concluded that programmes that failed to follow promising practice design theory did not achieve significant change in young people and were less successful than other types of intervention. When programmes followed these principles though, significant changes in young people occurred. Key factors of promising practice identified by both studies were:

- initial and on-going training for mentors;
- structured and varied activities for mentors and young people;
- developmentally sensitive goal setting with young people;
- clear expectations for the frequency of contact;
- the support and involvement of parents;
- structured support and supervision for the relationship.

In a further long-term study, Grossman and Rhodes (2002) confirmed that length and intensity of the mentoring relationship were additional key factors for success. The most successful mentoring relationships lasted 15 months on average. Relationships lasting fewer than three months could be damaging to the young person.

Young people facing environmental risk or disadvantage were found to benefit most from mentoring. On the other hand, young people with personal risk factors could be damaged by mentoring unless extensive amounts of specialised assistance were carried out by relevant professionals prior to referral (Dubois *et al.* 2002). In addition, young people with significant personal risk were only able to benefit from mentoring if very careful attention was paid to matching the young person with a mentor, together with on-going support for the relationship.

Research in the UK has been more circumspect on the impact of mentoring on the behaviour of children and young people in general, and antisocial behaviour in particular. St James-Roberts and Singh's study (2001) sought to evaluate the outcomes from the CHANCE (UK) programme, in which trained mentors worked one-to-one with primary school children who exhibited behavioural difficulties and allied risk factors. Early intervention with these children was intended to support and redirect them from more serious long-term problems. The outcome evaluation showed no real impact; 'the mentored children improved in their behaviours but equivalent improvements were found in [a] comparison group who had not had mentors. Both groups continued to show serious problems' (2001: viii).

Shiner et al.'s (2004) evaluation of Mentoring Plus, a voluntary, multi-modular programme comprising a pre-programme residential course, an educational and training programme and mentoring, showed that the programme produced for participants substantial moves from social exclusion to inclusion. Social inclusion was defined as changes in engagement in education, training or employment. The proportion of young people who participated in education, training or employment increased substantially during the course of the programme. There was no such increase evident amongst the comparison group. This may to be largely due to the education and training component of the programme, rather than the mentoring component. Moreover, with respect to reoffending, although some reduction in offending could be observed among the participants while on the programme and during a six-month follow-up, similar, and in some cases more marked, reductions in offending were reported by non-participants in the control group. There was no apparent relationship either between social inclusion and reductions in offending, although it was suggested that there might be longer-term effects. Similarly, changes in self-esteem appeared unrelated to changes in both social inclusion and offending (Stephenson 2007).

Tarling et al.'s (2004) national evaluation of the Youth Justice Board's mentoring projects is the largest study of the impact of mentoring undertaken in the UK. The evaluation involved over 3,500 young people referred to mentoring schemes and over 1,700 mentors. Three hundred and fifty-nine young people were followed up one year later; 55 per cent had been reconvicted in that time frame. This is much higher than the 26 per cent obtained in Home Office reconviction studies for young people who have committed offences nationally. There also seemed to be a slight increase in the rate of offending after the project (an estimated 2.1 offences before, compared with 2.6 afterwards). There was no clear evidence that the seriousness of offending had changed in any way. The study concludes, therefore, that even taking into account some differences between the comparison cohorts, those on mentoring projects had higher reconviction rates.

There were variations in terms of reconviction that are worth noting. The age of the young person at the time they joined the project was found to be significant, with those aged between 10 and 13 less likely to receive a further caution or conviction for a subsequent offence than those aged between 14 and 17. The age at which a young person started offending was highly significant with 62 per cent of those committing their first offence between the ages of 10 and 13 reoffending compared with 42 per cent of those committing their first offence between the ages of 14 and 17. Only 30 per cent of young people who had committed only one offence reoffended, whereas just over 80 per cent of those with at least 10 previous offences committed further crimes. Lowest rates of reoffending were associated with those who had been given a reprimand/caution or a final warning (less than 40 per cent). Young people who had received community orders or a custodial sentence were much more likely to reoffend.

Another Youth Justice Board funded project that focused on providing mentors/personal advisers for young people was Keeping Young People Engaged (KYPE). The main aim of the project was to 'improve education, training and employment provision for all young offenders, but particularly for those subject to intensive supervision and surveillance programmes (ISSPs) and DTOs' (Youth Justice Board 2005b: 4).

The apparent withdrawal of support for this project by the Connexions Service National Unit may have affected the outcomes but in any event they appear overall to have been at best inconclusive. The evaluation report used a comparison in YJB quarterly returns between participating and non-participating clusters of Yots. The first cluster of Yots in this initiative recorded a 2 percentage point increase in participation rates compared to a 1.9 percentage point increase in non-participating Yots. In the subsequent six months non-participating Yots increased their numbers in education, training or employment by 1 percentage point while those in the initiative saw no overall increase. Results for those Yots who joined the project a year later were no more convincing as they recorded an overall increase of one third that of non-participating Yots (0.4 percentage point compared to 1.2 percentage points) (Youth Justice Board 2005b). The limited data available to the researchers may though have hidden some significant local changes as during this period individual Yots recorded both large increases and decreases in the numbers of young people engaged in education, training or employment.

The principles of effective practice and mentoring

Risk classification

The relevant sections of *Asset* can suggest ways in which a mentoring relationship might be useful to a young person. In terms of the principle of risk classification it would imply that the nature and intensity of any mentoring opportunity provided should match the seriousness of the young person's offending behaviour and the risk factors identified. Where, for example, education, training and employment is identified as a significant risk factor, the mentoring relationship might focus on ways of increasing confidence and motivation in relation to going to school or college. The mentor might also have a useful role to play in being an advocate in such circumstances when relationships between a young person and a school had broken down.

A thorough assessment process also enables realistic goals to be set:

- What do you hope the mentoring relationship will achieve?
- What does the young person want from it?

Criminogenic needs

In relation to mentoring, the criminogenic needs principle would suggest that any mentoring offered as part of an intervention to prevent further offending must target criminogenic needs. The Youth Justice Board's mentoring projects did cite reducing offending behaviour in their aims and objectives, recognising the importance of tackling factors that contribute directly to offending behaviour – reducing non-attendance at school, for example (Tarling *et al.* 2004). It is not clear, however, how far individual mentoring plans were driven by the criminogenic needs of individual young people, which would seem to be important here.

Many of the schemes in this study also targeted the personal development of young people through raising their self-esteem and self-confidence. It is important to note though that the link between raising self-esteem and reducing the risk of offending is not established in research. Indeed, a review of research into the causal influence of self-esteem on behaviour suggests that in longitudinal studies of young people low self-esteem is not a risk factor (Emler 2001). Some research would indicate that self-esteem may actually contribute to increases in offending behaviour and result from it (cited in Tarling *et al.* 2004).

Responsivity

With regard to learning new strategies, it would seem that mentoring relationships that help young people to develop a range of skills may have some currency, although Newburn *et al.* (2005) identify some difficulties in achieving what they refer to as an 'idealised action-oriented approach' in the mentoring relationships they studied. They argue that most mentoring models tend to 'overstate the centrality of goal-focused, instrumental activities'. This can lead to an expectation that young people will move more quickly into activities that challenge some aspect of their behaviour or provide skills and strategies they need (literacy and numeracy, for example). What they found was that many rarely moved beyond a basic model of 'contact-meeting-doing' where the doing largely involved relatively mundane everyday activities. Where relationships did move on, this was usually as a result of some crisis in the young person's life, a stage Shiner *et al.* (2004) describe as 'firefighting': 'Relationships may stay in the firefighting cycle, revert to the basic cycle or, in some cases, progress beyond the reactive firefighting stage, to become genuinely action-oriented and closer to what often appears to be the ideal-typical conception of mentoring.' What is not clear from their analysis, however, is whether this was due to inadequate training for mentors in moving things on relatively quickly. It is notable that so many young people in the Tarling *et al.* evaluation of Youth Justice Board mentoring projects grew tired of the mentoring relationship and gave up on it before it was due to end. This might imply a need for greater emphasis in training of mentors on how to motivate and engage young people in new activities that do have elements of new learning but that are non-threatening.

Assumptions are sometimes made that a young person should automatically be matched with someone from the same gender group, ethnic origin, sexual orientation or religious belief. However, there are pros and cons, as shown in Figure 9.1.

Issue	For same-group mentoring	Against same-group mentoring
Perspective – seeing the world from a similar viewpoint	Greater empathy with the young person's issues and experiences	More difficult to help young person take different or broader perspective
	Higher levels of psychosocial support occur in same-race mentoring than in cross-race	Career outcomes for young people are less satisfactory than in cross-race mentoring
	More role modelling occurs between same-gender pairs than in cross-gender.	
Expanding networks	Same race/gender networks can be more close-knit and sociable	Young people's and mentors' networks may be too similar to add value to the relationship
Relationship purpose	Favours relatively new developmental objectives	Favours relatively broad development objectives
Role modelling	Occurs more easily	May not broaden young person's range of responses

Figure 9.1 Arguments for and against same-group mentoring
Source: Clutterbuck and Ragins (2002)

Community based

The community-base principle has a number of implications for mentoring programmes. Shiner *et al.* (2004) identified location as being a significant factor in the success of the Mentoring Plus programmes they evaluated. Only one project had its own premises, which was considered important by the staff working there, particularly with respect to the young people feeling able to participate fully in the programme. The other projects shared premises with other community groups and staff raised concerns that the projects were inaccessible and/or unappealing because they were located a long way from where the young people lived and/or because they were based in unsafe and inappropriate locations.

While it may be important that the mentoring relationship is built around a young person's community, and work done within it is geared towards helping young people engage more effectively with it, this could also limit its scope. A mentor may bring new awareness and knowledge about the community and/or other communities. Raising young people's expectations too high might be equally damaging if they don't have the resources, both external and internal, to realise their aspirations.

The evaluation of the Youth Justice Board sponsored mentoring projects indicated that parents/carers might be important in respect of the on-going success of a mentoring relationship (Tarling *et al.* 2004). There were a number of cases where parental resistance had been a factor that prevented matches from being started or sustained.

Intervention modality

It is unlikely that mentoring alone will help a young person experiencing complex and multiple difficulties (Tarling *et al.* 2004). Where young people are known to be at high risk of further offending, more intensive mentoring support, in combination with other forms of intervention, may be required in order to produce positive results, i.e. the mentoring component is part of a broader programme of activities designed to prevent further offending. The challenge then arises as to how far the effects of the mentoring inputs can be separated from the other aspects of the intervention (Tarling *et al.* 2004).

Shiner *et al.*'s evaluation of Mentoring Plus criticised the mentoring component of the programme for not having any explicit model of change (2004). In the short term the intervention had no significant impact on offending rates of the young people taking part as compared to a control group. The study concluded that a mentoring project offered within a youth justice setting is likely to be more successful at achieving the aim of reducing offending if the approach has a clearly defined model of change – 'Why is it that a particular intervention might be thought to work? By what means will it change the behaviour of programme participants?' (Shiner *et al.* 2004: 72).

The more effective mentoring schemes had well-established relationships with Yots and other local organisations from which to receive referrals and provide services to young people (Tarling *et al.* 2004)

Programme integrity

Areas where the Mentoring Plus programme appeared to be most significant were those where the structured activities related directly to the aims of the programme. With regard to the programme integrity of a mentoring pro-gramme, therefore, this would imply the need to ensure that mentors and the young people taking part are clear about what the explicit aims of the pro-gramme are and how the methods they are going to use link to the achievement of these aims. 'It is all too often the case that work with young people is undertheorised. That is to say, there is often little explicit discussion of the aims of particular programmes – other than the most banal identifica-tion of "reductions in offending" or something similarly general'. (Shiner *et al.* 2004: 72).

This links to the issue of training for mentors. Apart from ensuring that initial training and on-going support for mentors introduces them to the aims of the programme and the methods to be used, it would also imply the need for on-going supervision and monitoring to ensure that the aims have not become confused and/or diluted. Tarling *et al.*'s evaluation of the Youth Justice Board mentoring schemes also highlighted the need for support for mentors via training. Volunteer mentors need to be suitably supported via training, peer group networks and supervision (Tarling *et al.* 2004).

Shiner *et al.* (2004) identified further threats to programme integrity with regard to Mentoring Plus. Firstly, staffing proved difficult and while staff said they enjoyed working at mentoring plus, the 'burn-out' rate was particularly high (nearly half – 49 per cent – had left Mentoring Plus by the end of the evaluation).

A further challenge for programme integrity is the fact that there is a lack of consensus about what the mentoring role is (Gay and Stephenson 1998; Piper and Piper 2000) and that its theoretical basis has not been fully estab-lished (Philip 1999; cited in Tarling *et al.* 2004). This, argue Tarling *et al.* (2004) means that the nature and scope of mentoring relationships can vary widely across schemes but also within an individual scheme, which leads to a variabil-ity in treatment that can compromise the integrity of any research design. Again, this would imply the need for schemes to be clear in the training of mentors about the nature of the mentoring relationship relevant to the stated aims of the scheme.

Dosage

The mentoring relationship is frequently characterised by volatility. With regard to dosage, this can present problems as it means that young people may often not be receiving the level of dosage required to achieve the aims of the mentoring intervention. Tarling *et al.*'s evaluation of the Youth Justice Board's mentoring projects found that 42 per cent of mentoring relationships had been ended prematurely, predominantly by the young people themselves (Tarling *et al.* 2004). The primary reason attributed to this was that the young person had lost interest in the relationship and was no longer interested in having a mentor.

This implies that mentoring schemes might need to think of ways of helping young people sustain their engagement with their mentor over time, whether through incentives or clearer marketing of the long-term benefits a young person might expect from it. Of course, compelling a young person to attend through an order would be one way of achieving this, although many would argue that this seriously compromises the voluntary nature of the relationship.

One of the criticisms made of the evaluation of the Mentoring Plus projects is that there were considerable gaps in the evidence with regard to dosage, in particular the degrees of engagement in education, training and employment (one of the programmes aims) were not able to be measured – commencing a very limited part-time programme apparently counted as much as full-time participation. It follows then that the amount of education, training or employment received is unknown which could have varied widely as a result of how much was actually arranged and differential attendance (Stephenson, 2007).

The challenges for practice

Pawson's (2006) review of the inner mechanisms of youth mentoring raises some significant challenges for practice. Synthesising the findings from nine evaluations of mentoring projects and initiatives, the following conclusions emerge.

The functions of befriending practice, direction-setting, coaching and sponsoring within a mentoring relationship become increasingly difficult to accomplish as mentors attempt to move from the sharing of mundane activities to seeking emotional, cognitive and skills gains. Where such movement does take place, it tends to be with mentees 'who arrive in a programme with in-built resilience and with aspirations about moving away from their present status' (Pawson 2006: 148). Selecting mentees with a motivation to change, or providing opportunities to generate such motivation, would seem to be a key learning point from these findings.

Where mentees are disadvantaged young people, their chaotic lifestyles often militate against them sustaining a mentoring relationship. Mentors need to act as persistent firefighters of the tribulations faced by excluded young people. They must be prepared to rebuild their mentoring relationship with the young person, often over many occasions, in an attempt to regain the mentee's trust and imbue them with resilience. The selection of mentors with this tenacious attitude is a key component of an effective mentoring scheme.

The mentoring relationship in and of itself may have only limited impact on the mentees and their lifestyles. That impact may be enhanced when the mentor is able to support the mentee in their network of social interactions with significant others: family, friends, school, employer, welfare benefits agency, social worker, etc. Having a pool of mentors who are able to network across a range of individuals and agencies that are significant in mentees' lives is a key challenge for effective practice.

The available research evidence suggests that mentoring works well when it is embedded in a programme offering the mentee further supports such as education, training or career development. In working with those agencies seeking to provide additional help, the mentees may well experience problems, difficulties and conflicts. In these circumstances, the mentor potentially may have a significant role to play in peacemaking, fence-mending, trouble-shooting or honest-brokering to secure the continued support and service to the young person. Having knowledge of the agencies and services that seek to support young people and the skills to discharge a role in conflict resolution is a key capacity issue for aspiring mentors.

As Pawson concludes, these challenges for practice inform 'the mechanisms that need to be embedded in the construction of a [mentoring] programme, in the selection and training of practitioners, and in the targeting and motivation of subjects' (2006: 150).

Summary

- Mentoring is now quite a widely used intervention with a relatively long history, particularly in the US where evaluation results for programmes have been positive. However, research into mentoring interventions in the UK has indicated more limited effectiveness.

- In the youth justice system, mentoring is a voluntary one-to-one relationship between a young person and a supportive adult, established with the aim of helping the young person to achieve his or her goals.

- An action-oriented approach in mentoring relationships seems hard to achieve, with typical mentoring relationships taking a long time to move beyond the 'contact-meeting-doing' model where 'doing' largely involves fairly mundane activities.

- There is a high level of early drop-out from mentoring relationships that seek to engage young people at risk of offending or reoffending.

- To increase the likelihood of effectiveness, it is suggested that mentoring interventions need to be informed by an explicit model of change.

Further reading

Newburn, T., Shiner, M., Groben, S. and Young, T. (2005) *Dealing with Disaffection: Young People, Mentoring and Social Inclusion*. Cullompton: Willan Publishing.

Part III

10

Offending behaviour programmes

Offending behaviour programmes are designed to prevent (or at least reduce) offending and reoffending by children and young people. Meta-analyses have determined a number of core principles that may make such programmes more effective. They also highlight a number of interventions that are less likely to work overall. This chapter also urges caution in relying too heavily on these meta-analytical outcomes in providing blanket approaches for young people, on the basis that there are things that are effective for some young people in some circumstances which may not be effective for others in different circumstances. It also provides an overview of cognitive behaviourism as the available research would suggest that such an approach can increase the likelihood of reducing offending. Again, it also offers an alternative view which suggests that an overreliance on these approaches may lead to a position where all the responsibility for change rests with the young person as the problem, ignoring wider social issues.

The evidence base for offending behaviour programmes

In discussing offending behaviour programmes, it is helpful to distinguish three forms of prevention:

- **Primary prevention** – planning and delivery of developmental services to improve the overall life opportunities of disadvantaged communities as a mechanism for long-term crime prevention.

- **Secondary prevention** – intervention with children and families who are considered to be at risk of involvement in offending, on the basis of factors associated with the onset of criminal activity.

- **Tertiary prevention** – intervention with those who have already been involved in offending.

Offending behaviour programmes are directed primarily at those young people whose behaviour has brought them to the attention of the youth justice system. Accordingly, they will have received a reprimand or warning as an alternative to prosecution, or will have been convicted by the criminal courts. Offending behaviour work is thus focused at the level of tertiary prevention; that is, it aims to prevent or reduce the seriousness or frequency of further offending by that group of young people who have already been in trouble.

Such interventions are designed to influence the behaviour of young people in a manner that makes it less likely to give rise to offending. In this respect, offending behaviour programmes offered will need to be capable of responding to:

- a broad array of behaviour from the final warning stage, where the offending is relatively minor and the young person may not previously have come to police attention, to those young people whose offending is sufficiently serious or persistent to warrant custody or the highest levels of intervention available in a community setting;

- the nature of the offences (acquisitive, violent, sexual, minor or serious);

- the context in which offending occurs (e.g. premeditated or planned, committed in groups or alone, committed at particular times of the day, under the influence of alcohol or drugs, targeted or random victimisation, motivated by material gain or excitement);

- patterns of offending (e.g. one-off, out of character delinquent act, occasional minor offending, persistent criminality, infrequent serious offences).

Interventions to address offending behaviour therefore vary significantly according to the local offending profile and the category and particular circumstances of the young people for whom the intervention is intended. On this basis, offending behaviour programmes have usefully been defined, in broad terms, as structured, prearranged sequences of opportunities for learning and change designed specifically to have a positive impact on the subsequent recidivism of those young people who take part (McGuire *et al.* 2002).

It is also necessary to stress the breadth of such interventions. In particular, many offending behaviour programmes include elements of a cognitive-behavioural approach and, towards the upper end of the offending scale, may be closely associated with a particular cognitive-behavioural programme. It is important, however, not to equate offending behaviour interventions with cognitive-behavioural programmes, since the former describe a much wider range of services.

Effective programmes, particularly for those young people whose offending is more serious or persistent, tend to have a core content, which focuses on skills training. This training is designed to improve problem-solving capacity, and has a cognitive element. Cognitive-behavioural approaches have become increasingly identified with effective practice. As the term suggests, the cognitive-behavioural model derives from a synthesis of two traditions within psychology: behaviourism and cognitive theory.

In the former tradition, human behaviour is considered to be a product of learning through interaction with the environment. To explain human behaviour is thus to explain how that learning takes place in interaction with the external world. The model is often described in terms of antecedents, behaviour and consequences: ABCs. In this model, behaviour is influenced by an initial environmental stimulus and previous experiences of the consequences that follow from responding to that stimulus in different ways. Cognitive theory, on the other hand, focuses on the importance of the individual's thought processes, attitudes and beliefs in determining behaviour.

From the mid-1970s onwards, a number of writers began to synthesise the two approaches. This synthesis was supplemented with references to social learning theory, which is concerned with the possibility of learning through observation of others' behaviour. As a consequence, the relationship between individuals' environment, previous experiences and behaviour is understood as being mediated by their thoughts, emotions and beliefs. Before individuals can change their behavioural reactions they need to understand their thought processes and the factors that affect their perceptions and emotions.

It is erroneous to conceive of cognitive behaviourism as a single, unified, theoretical approach. It is best understood as describing a range of methods of interventions. Indeed, McGuire (2000) identified seven different theoretical currents along a spectrum running from behaviour modification (using techniques such as aversion therapy) at one end, to cognitive therapy (which aims to correct cognitive distortions or dysfunctional beliefs) at the other.

Some of the more commonly used approaches with young people who offend include training in (often in combination):

- moral reassessing;

- problem-solving techniques;

- interaction skills;

- self-management;

- self-esteem;

- pro-social modelling;

- victim empathy;

- patterns and consequences of offending behaviour;

- values, beliefs and thinking patterns;

- peers and assertion;

- relapse prevention.

The Youth Justice Board's evaluation of cognitive-behaviour projects (Feilzer *et al.*, 2004) reported some reduction in reconviction rates for young people who participated. However, it should be noted that the sample of young people followed up for reconviction data was relatively small and there was no control group for comparison. The study also showed that there were lower reconviction rates for those who completed programmes. Completion rates across the project were low at 59 per cent overall. Completion rates for young people who committed crimes more persistently were lower overall and significantly higher completion rates were found for the younger age group (63 per cent for those aged 15 compared with 41 per cent for those aged 17). Reasons given for non-completion were related to the length and intensiveness of the projects, which young people found difficult to sustain.

Some critics argue that there has been an overdependence on cognitive-behavioural approaches in youth justice interventions when none of the research shows that they can lead to reduced offending when used in isolation (Pitts 2001c; Gray 2005a). This is the result, it has been argued, of a narrow definition of risk which places all the responsibility on the young person – it supposes that it is their attitudes and lifestyles that are the problem and that should be the primary focus of change (Muncie 2001). Consequently, the principle of reintegration or 'social inclusion' is neglected (Gray 2005a) and few interventions go far enough in addressing the broader social issues that have excluded young people who offend from the mainstream (Muncie 2002).

The principles of effective practice and offending behaviour programmes

Risk classification

Intervention is more effective where there is a relationship between the risk of further offending and the intensity of the offending behaviour work being undertaken. In particular, total contact time ought to be higher for young people whose offending is most persistent or serious. Conversely, overintrusive intervention with young people who represent a lower level of risk can be counterproductive, and may on occasion lead to an increase in offending (McIvor 1990).

On the face of it, this particular message from research appears to be counter-intuitive, since it might reasonably be assumed that young people who are more entrenched in an offending lifestyle would also be more resistant to change. On the other hand, it seems plausible that interventions that focus on offending behaviour may have a labelling effect where participants' offending is at a low level. In other words, such interventions may be more likely to consolidate and confirm delinquent identities which, once established, tend to lead to further offending (Goldson 2000). In addition, where groups bring together young people with a range of offending histories, it is possible that 'contamination' may serve to increase the antisocial behaviour of the least criminal in the group.

There is also the question of how young people perceive the programme. If punitive approaches are ineffective, it might be anticipated that outcomes would be influenced according to whether participants regard the intervention as a 'fair response' to their behaviour. An intensive programme following on from a relatively low level of minor offending is more likely to be experienced as excessive, unjust or perhaps punitive. The research evidence on this point appears to have similar practical implications to the statutory requirement that interventions should be proportionate to the seriousness of the offending. In practical terms, it follows that planning should allow for a range of available programmes, with an incremental increase in intensity. More specifically, offending behaviour programmes at the Final Warning stage, or as part of a youth offender contract, should be limited in both duration and intensity.

Interventions should be planned on the basis of an assessment of those static and dynamic risk factors that are pertinent to the young person's current offending behaviour and likely future potential to reoffend. In classifying risk, therefore, it is important to distinguish between those static and dynamic factors. Around 80 per cent of young people who offend are young men, so being male is a characteristic that may be associated with a risk of becoming involved in criminal activity. Similarly, a history of persistent delinquency in the recent past is a relatively strong indicator that a young person will commit further offences. It is clear, however, that in both cases, these identified risk factors could not be altered by any form of intervention. A young person's previous offending record is a historical fact, unaffected by subsequent developments. These are static factors. The process cannot, however, afford to ignore static variables since these may frequently offer 'clues' to modifiable areas of risk. For instance, examination of a young person's criminal history may provide indicators that the young person tends to associate with an offending peer group, evinces an antisocial outlook, suffers from lack of victim empathy, or has problems with temper control.

Dynamic factors, by contrast, are those that are in principle modifiable and might be successfully influenced by offending behaviour programmes. For example, substance misuse or difficulties with anger management might, in some individuals, increase the risk of offending behaviour. Criminogenic needs of this sort are amenable to change through planned intervention, and are thus described as dynamic.

Assessment for offending behaviour programmes consists, therefore, of identifying pertinent risk factors and planning interventions that would be most likely to have a positive impact on these factors.

The broad range and depth of these social influences serve both to draw attention to the limitations of offending behaviour programmes and to highlight the importance of locating specific interventions which target offending within a wider, holistic approach focusing on welfare issues. From the point of view of assessment, these social influences also indicate a further important issue. Given the extent of chaos that characterises the lives of many young people who offend, the timing of involvement in offending behaviour programmes can be significant. Where lives are in crisis, motivation may simply not be at the level required to engage successfully in a highly structured programme.

Criminogenic need

Offending behaviour programmes ought, by definition, to focus on criminogenic needs, that is those that are more directly related to risk factors for offending as identified through the *Asset* profile. One of the tensions here is how to provide bespoke programmes that meet the individual criminogenic needs of each young person while providing a range of programmes for groups of young people. The most recent research into the reliability and validity of *Asset* (Baker *et al.* 2005) studied a number of intervention plans and found that they often did not reflect the outcome of assessments and that issues identified in *Asset* as being associated with a high risk of reoffending were not always incorporated into intervention plan targets. Attitudes to Offending, Substance Use and Education were the areas with the highest proportion of relevant targets. Some areas were unexpectedly low – family and personal relationships, and lifestyle, for example. Baker *et al.* (2005) suggest that this may be because practitioners find it more difficult to think of appropriate targets for working with a young person when the problems identified involve other people (e.g. parents/carers or friends and peer groups).

Conversely, this research showed that in some plans intervention targets were often given for areas that had a low *Asset* score. Education, Training and Employment, Thinking and Behaviour, and Attitudes to Offending were areas with particularly high instances of intervention plan targets being set where the *Asset* score for these areas was 0 or 1. One conclusion that can be drawn from this is that some plans for tackling offending behaviour may be conforming to a

stock response where interventions such as victim empathy, community reparation and referral to Connexions/Careers Wales for example are included as
standard, regardless of any link with the *Asset* profile (Baker *et al.* 2005).

Research into young people and offending behaviour has focused on identifying risk and protective factors for offending (Communities that Care 2001,
for example). Establishing direct causality between risk factors and offending
is notoriously difficult. In terms of ensuring offending behaviour programmes tackle criminogenic need as a priority, therefore, thorough analysis
of the risk factors identified may be required in order to establish the most
appropriate response. If detachment from education, training and employment was deemed to be a significant risk factor for a young person, for
example, further analysis of the reasons for that detachment may be required
in order to provide the most appropriate response. Is it, for example, that the
young person does not have the literacy skills to manage the curriculum
effectively that is the main barrier to attachment, or is detachment more
closely related to bullying? The response required to address detachment as a
criminogenic need in each case will be different.

Another challenge for practitioners when working with young people with
multiple difficulties and barriers to social inclusion is to distinguish which
needs are most salient in terms of the risk of further offending, and which are
less directly related to an individual's offending behaviour. Where a need
exists that is serious but less directly related to the offence a young person has
committed, referral to other agencies may be the most appropriate response.

Conversely, where certain behaviours are highly prevalent in a particular
area, substance misuse for example, there is a risk that this is given too high a
priority in responses to young people in that area. The behaviour, although
causing some problems, may not be as closely related to a young person's
offending as other risk factors. Where certain risk behaviours are prevalent in
a population, the ready availability of programmes to tackle that issue may
also influence responses to young people at the expense of providiing fully
individualised interventions.

Responsivity

The principle of responsivity suggests that the content of offending behaviour
programmes should be structured into discernible units appropriate to the conceptual level and concentration span of participants. Material should be
sequential, building on what participants have already learned, with elements of
reinforcement to sustain what has been achieved to date.

In order to succeed in challenging deeply held attitudes, which may give
rise to antisocial behaviour, programme deliverers also need to give guidance
on what would be appropriate, pro-social responses in particular circum-

stances. The extent to which the young people accept such guidance depends in large part on the quality of programme delivery and the relationship between participants and practitioners.

A wide-ranging approach to understanding and attempting to address the offending behaviour is essential. Measures focusing directly on the offences may be appropriate in some circumstances. In others, a more indirect approach dealing with environmental issues, improving problem-solving skills or empathy for others, may be more useful. In particular, any programme needs to take account of:

- the age, maturity and level of understanding of the young person;

- the nature and extent of any previous intervention. There is little point in delivering the same programme to a young person within a short space of time;

- the level of engagement and motivation to change;

- broader environmental factors, which are likely to have an impact on the young person's behaviour and response to any form of work to address offending.

One of the key issues in ensuring the responsivity principle is achieved is the literacy level at which offending behaviour programmes are pitched. Home Office research into the accessibility of general offending behaviour programmes delivered through probation services to adults found that the literacy demands of the programmes offered was in advance of the literacy skills of a large number of participants, Davies *et al.* 2004. While 57 per cent of those taking part had reading skills well below what is expected of an 11-year-old (Level 1), the reading demands of the programmes were often at or above this level. Things were even more extreme with regard to speaking and listening, with the programme demands at Level 2 (GCSE A*–C equivalent) or Level 3 (A Level equivalent) in some cases while 37 per cent of participants were assessed to have speaking and listening skills below Level 1. While this was an adult-focused study, it is well known that a considerable number of young people in the youth justice system have literacy levels well below what is expected of them. This has considerable implications for the way in which practitioners present materials as part of offending behaviour programmes, but also, and perhaps more significantly, the way in which they deliver the programmes to young people.

In addition, consideration might be given to whether it is feasible to run the programme on a rolling basis as opposed to a closed-entry basis. Closed programmes have a single entry point and exit point. Accordingly, they have (at least in principle) a stable group of participants and sequential programme design. Building learning experiences on to what has been tackled in previous sessions is therefore facilitated. Rolling groups, on the other hand, may allow entry at any point or, perhaps more practically, at a number of pre-determined points in the life of the programme. This arrangement lends itself more readily to reintegrating young people who have, for whatever reason, missed one or more sessions (Merrington 1998).

More generally, group work offers certain advantages; and not simply in terms of resource management. Many of the problems common to young people who offend are experienced in the community in a group setting. Learning solutions may therefore be more effectively developed in the company of others. Young people with similar needs can provide mutual support in the problem-solving process and may increase each other's motivation to change. Group dynamics are powerful, and emotions, beliefs and attitudes may be more amenable to change in a group setting.

At the same time, there are individuals for whom group work is difficult or inappropriate. Accordingly, provision should be made to ensure that materials, which would generally be used within a group setting, can also be delivered on a one-to-one basis where the characteristics of particular young people or the details of their offending behaviour make this desirable. It must be borne in mind though that grouping deliquent young people may actually increase the risks of offending (Stephenson 2007).

Community based

Attention has already been drawn to research which suggests that offending behaviour programmes delivered within the community are likely to have greater success than those provided in a custodial setting. This should not, however, be taken to imply that effective practice is not possible within secure settings. But it suggests that 'boot camp' approaches or regimes associated with 'short, sharp shocks', physical drilling and training are unlikely to prevent offending behaviour (Farrington *et al.* 2002).

The limited research available on this topic suggests that, for young people serving custodial sentences, similar principles of effectiveness apply as those that ought to govern community interventions. However, within a custodial setting, programme characteristics and design appear to play a greater role in influencing outcomes. Conversely, young people's individual attributes have rather less impact than they do where the intervention is delivered in the community (Youth Justice Board 2000b)

In some respects, this is unsurprising since choice as to whether to attend sessions is more tightly circumscribed in custody. Moreover, given the limited activities frequently available within an institution, offending behaviour programmes are more likely to be seen as a welcome diversion.

The value of pro-social modelling as an approach is again emphasised in the literature. One recent review suggests that this approach is currently more highly developed in Secure Training Centres and Local Authority Secure Units than within Prison Service establishments (Youth Justice Board 2000b).

To a considerable extent, long-term success depends on any positive learning experiences being carried over into the community. In this context, it is clearly important to have effective sentence planning in order to establish an integrated programme where the community supervision part of the sentence builds on what has gone before. Co-operation and exchange of information between staff in the secure estate and responsible officers working within Yots is a prerequisite of such continuity.

Even where this is achieved, however, major obstacles remain. Almost 30 per cent of those released from custody do not return to the parental home, and many of them will have problems with accommodation. Similarly, there are frequently substantial delays in arranging and starting education and training.

In a very real sense, effective work within a custodial setting depends on the Yot and the secure estate being able to access services through interaction with other parts of the criminal justice system and beyond (Hazel *et al.* 2002).

Intervention modality

A fully multi-modal approach requires that Yots and secure facilities have access to a wide range of interventions to address the variety of risk as reflected in individual need. Service managers should therefore aim to develop a portfolio of services, which can be combined to create tailor-made programmes for the assessed needs of their target population.

It should be acknowledged that this is by no means an easy task. There is an obvious risk of building up costly services, which prove to be unsustainable. Conversely, there may be a temptation to rely on a small number of proven projects into which a wide variety of need must then be channelled. The most promising strategy for avoiding both pitfalls might be to develop services on the basis of an audit of local need. Such an audit would build on information derived from *Asset*, and other forms of assessment, to provide an aggregate picture of the needs of young people to whom offending programmes are to be offered. The data derived in this manner need to be updated on a regular basis to ensure a continuous match of service provision to the local needs profile.

In broad terms, such a portfolio might be structured around the four-level framework developed in the *Key Elements of Effective Practice*, representing varying levels of intensity of involvement in a young person's life. This allows a proportionate response to a range of offending behaviour, and a graduated intervention with young people who continue to offend after the Yot has commenced work with them. Such an approach is also consistent with evidence about effective interventions.

Recent evidence would suggest that despite the significant advances made with the introduction of multi-agency Yots and the concomitant revisions to the youth justice system, engaging service partners to provide for the full range of the needs of young people who offend continues to present significant problems (Audit Commission 2004; Arnull *et al.* 2005; Gray *et al.* 2005; Stephenson 2007).

Clearly, a multi-modal approach to offending behaviour requires planning derived from the assessment of need previously undertaken when considering the young person's eligibility for engagement. However:

- there should be more consistency in linking assessed needs to planned interventions (Baker *et al.* 2005);

- interventions do not routinely focus on common criminogenic needs or risk factors (Arnull *et al.* 2005);

- recording of anticipated outcomes and delivered outcome from interventions are not robustly documented (Arnull *et al.* 2005).

Programme integrity

Programmes should be informed by a clear theoretical base, which spells out the relationship between the methods employed, the objectives set and the ultimate aim of reducing or preventing offending. Clarity in this respect:

- assists in developing appropriate referral criteria for offending behaviour programmes;

- ensures that programme design is internally consistent;

- assists staff in the delivery of material;

- allows proper evaluation of outcomes.

Programmes are more likely to prevent offending if the following elements are present.

It is sometimes thought that programme integrity requires that the complete content of each session should be scripted, that every module of the programme should be undertaken in a pre-ordained order, and that staff should follow the manual without deviation. Given the disorganisation and chaos in the lives of many young people who offend, and the multiplicity and depth of their welfare needs, 'integrity' understood in this rigid manner may well contribute to the failure of those at the highest risk to complete the programme. Flexibility to deal with crisis or other pressing matters, which

young people bring with them to the programme, is a prerequisite of successful work with young people who offend.

Of course, this is not to deny the validity of integrity where it is construed as
the design of programmes to meet stated aims with a clear methodology. There
should, however, be room within the programme to allow practitioners an element of flexibility so that they can depart from the script where circumstances
make it necessary within an overall framework of standards for delivery.
Ultimately, it is a question of staff exercising discretion in a skilled manner.
Achieving the right balance depends on proper planning and review, proper
management supervision and the quality of practitioners (there is a further discussion of practitioners' discretion later in this section; see pp. 206–8).

It is important for the development of evidence-based practice to ensure
that evaluation of interventions is an integral and on-going aspect of programme delivery. An integrated model of evaluation would be
multi-dimensional, looking at both quantitative and qualitative aspects of
performance, including:

- programme conceptualisation;

- programme delivery;

- cost effectiveness;

- outcomes.

Dosage

To date, one of the most intractable problems associated with offending
behaviour work has been that significant numbers of those who are referred
fail to complete the programmes. Evidence from the adult arena indicates
that dropout rates for the one-to-one programme range from 25 per cent to
40 per cent in some areas. For others, the equivalent figure is closer to 80 per
cent (Hollin *et al.* 2002). Evidence from the Youth Justice Board's evaluation of
cognitive-behaviour projects (Feilzer *et al.* 2004) would suggest that similar
rates of attrition are endemic for programmes offered to young people, particularly those who are older and those who are more persistently involved
in offending behaviour. Indeed, one might be led to expect higher rates of
attrition for young people than for adults, because of adolescents' impulsiveness and inability in some cases to appreciate fully the consequences of their
actions (particularly those who are most at risk of offending) (Grisso and
Schwartz 2000).

One of the dangers with consistently high levels of attrition is that it might
lead some services to be withdrawn. Some evidence to support this expectation
derives from London, where the Probation Service has decided to close a day

centre running a 'Reasoning and Rehabilitation' programme for young people. This decision has been made on the basis that completion rates of between 15 and 24 per cent are not cost-effective (National Probation Service 2003).

Effectiveness in relation to offending behaviour programmes relates, therefore, to what inputs are received by young people, not just what is arranged for them. This would suggest that programmes should have clear strategies in place for fostering participation and engagement. This might include:

- clearly defined procedures for monitoring attendance and punctuality in all programme elements and across all phases of a sentence;

- tight, supportive supervision;

- clear lines of communication among relevant staff members;

- enlisting the support of parents/carers in encouraging regular and sustained attendance and punctuality;

- discussion about attendance and punctuality at all review meetings.

Programme providers might also employ mechanisms which encourage or facilitate attendance. As a minimum, young people's fares may be reimbursed, or, given the financial circumstances of many families, could be advanced where this is feasible. Where transport can be arranged for participants, attendance at the right time can be maximised. Encouragement might also be provided through inducements, such as linking attendance to leisure activities or other rewards. Providing refreshments or building in an element of recreation as part of the session can also act as a motivator.

It may be important to address potential barriers to attendance. Where young people are parents or have responsibility for dependants in other ways, allowance should be made for this fact and facilities provided so that they are not disadvantaged. In rural areas, where distance is a significant issue, it might mean delivering programmes on a one-to-one basis in the young person's home.

To reinforce the importance of compliance, information should be provided to young people and their families in a variety of forms and at regular intervals.

The information provided should spell out the expectations of staff, participants and participants' carers during the life of the programme. Information giving might include oral and written explanations at the outset of the intervention, reminders by telephone and letter in advance of any appointment, and diaries for the young people showing where they are expected to be on a day-to-day basis.

Particular care should be taken to ensure that information is given in a form that young people can readily understand. Where literacy is an issue, consideration should be given to how diaries might be used to provide a visual representation of appointments. As a matter of course, all information provided for young people should also be explained and provided in writing to parents and carers.

Programmes are very likely to be disrupted by the impact of young people's lifestyles. Participation in a group might be interrupted by court appearances, breach action, the impact of subsequent orders, attending under the influence of drugs or alcohol, late arrival and simple non-attendance. Wherever possible, programmes may attempt to anticipate and allow for such difficulties without suspending the service. This might mean providing 'catch up' sessions, repeating modules, covering the same learning points at a variety of points in the programme, or using one-to-one work at certain points during the life of a group.

While it is appropriate to focus on expectations and the consequences of non-compliance, it is also important that information giving should be experienced as motivational rather than threatening (Morgan 2006).

The challenges for practice

In recent years, there has been a considerable literature on the nature of effective interventions. However, less attention has been paid to the importance of skilled staff for effective delivery of offending behaviour programmes. In many ways, that oversight is regrettable, since it encourages a tendency to see programme content as the defining feature of effective practice.

In reality, content, without the human resources to ensure skilful delivery, is unlikely to maximise the potential for a positive impact on recidivism. Who delivers the programme and how they do it are just as important as the programme itself; the two dimensions are opposite sides of the same coin.

This suggests that practitioners should:

● have a good knowledge of the youth justice system;

● appreciate the links between risk factors and offending, and protective factors and desistance;

● understand the rationale behind interventions and be committed to the programme;

● be trained in delivery of effective practice.

But skilled staff must also be able to engage and motivate the young people with whom they work. The relationship between young people and the practitioners who supervise them is increasingly recognised as having an impact on young people's:

- engagement in the supervisory process;
- motivation to undertake and persist in programmes;
- desire to desist from offending.

This is unsurprising, since if young people are not engaged or motivated, the opportunity to deal with offending behaviour is lost. Moreover, attendance at a programme in no way guarantees that a young person pays any attention to what is going on, or understands what is being said.

But the issue of relationship appears to go deeper than this. Cognitive approaches may only carry conviction with the young people to whom they are addressed if they feel some form of obligation or loyalty to staff who seem committed, and whose ideas make sense. Motivation is thus in part a consequence of what those who are supervised consider to be a display of interest in them as autonomous individuals (Rex 1999). This provides echoes of some rather older research in a therapeutic setting, which suggested that 'people variables' might be as important as 'method variables' in determining success or failure. In this context, people variables were defined as empathy, genuineness and 'non-possessive warmth' (Truax and Carkhuff 1967). In practice, this means that young people whose offending is persistent may need to be won over by persistent workers (McNeill and Batchelor 2002; Gray et al. 2005).

The success of the Freagarrach project for young people who offend persistently in Scotland is testimony to the importance of such an approach. The evaluation pointed out that what set this project apart from others, which were less effective, was the high quality of work delivered by staff. This was in terms of both the content and (importantly in the current context) the style of what was delivered:

> A vital stage ... was the initial process of engagement. The staff succeeded in conveying to the majority of young people that it was worth making a commitment to the project and what it had to offer. They communicated an attitude of respect and care, which many young people – and their parents – contrasted favourably with their experience of other adults in positions of authority. (Lobley et al. 2001).

From a slightly different perspective, it has been noted that young people generally enter offending behaviour programmes for *extrinsic* reasons. That is, they attend in the initial stages because they are subject to a court order. Failure to comply can result in breach action, return to court and, frequently, a custodial sentence.

Lasting behavioural change, however, is more likely where there is an intrinsic motivation to engage in the process, for reasons that are not related to compulsion, such as the potential for an improved quality of life (Williams and Strean 2002). Thus, the court order might be regarded as providing a window of opportunity; it requires certain actions of the young people, irrespective of their disposition, but those actions are not in themselves guaranteed to produce the desired change. It is the intervention of the practitioner, and the way in which he or she is able to engage a young person (rather than the programme's content *per se*), which is crucial to effecting the shift from extrinsic to intrinsic motivation. That shift is required if the programme is to maximise the opportunity for change offered by the judicial process.

One approach to intervention in which the relationship is regarded as essential is that of 'pro-social modelling'. This model has been developed at its highest level in Australia. Effective engagement is one of its central principles, and involves the practitioner being:

- non-blaming;

- open and honest;

- able to display empathy and genuine concern for problems;

- reliable;

- friendly and able to use humour appropriately.

One research study, conducted over a four-year period, established that pro-social modelling correlates with higher rates of compliance with supervision, and lower recidivism. Particularly good results have been achieved with high-risk young people who offend (Trotter 1996). In general terms, the skills an individual brings to the task are more important than professional background or qualification. At the same time (perhaps unsurprisingly given the nature of the qualities required by a pro-social approach) there is some evidence that staff with social work training may be predisposed to adopt effective practice skills more quickly (Trotter 2000).

Reference has also been made already to the importance of staff having some scope to exercise discretion to depart from the programme. Staff should be empowered to adopt a flexible approach which makes the best use of the issues that young people bring to sessions, and which can respond to crises. Absence of such discretion discourages initiative and creativity, and is unlikely to engender the required degree of 'responsivity' to programme participants. At the same time, limits of discretion should be clear.

A useful model, developed in a slightly different context by Eadie and Canton (2002), proposes that the tension between discretion and accountability should be understood in terms of four ideal types of practice (see Figure 10.1).

Quadrant C is easily dispensed with. Nobody would seriously suggest that practitioners should be unaccountable for what they do and simultaneously exercise no professional discretion. Effective structured programmes would clearly be impossible in such a context.

Quadrant D 'Constrained practice' High accountability and low discretion	Quadrant A 'Best practice' High accountability and high discretion
Quadrant C 'Worst of all worlds' Low accountability and low discretion	Quadrant B 'The bad old days' Low accountability and high discretion

Figure 10.1 Discretion versus accountability

Quadrant B, it is suggested, represents the early days of youth justice service delivery in which quality standards, programme content and casework decisions were the preserve of professional judgement. Monitoring of outcomes was minimal and consistency a matter of chance. While the delivery of effective offending behaviour programmes would be possible within this quadrant, this would depend on the quality of practitioner and could not be guaranteed. Moreover, in a climate of limited agreement about what, if anything, might constitute an effective intervention, the likelihood of achieving positive outcomes is further reduced.

Quadrant D, on the other hand, represents the converse problem, where innovation and flexibility are stifled. But a degree of creativity and use of discretion is essential for delivering a sensitive response to the problems presented by young people who persistently offend. In many cases, the engagement of difficult young people depends on it. The low discretion found in this quadrant is accordingly likely to inhibit effective practitioners.

The model suggests that best practice is located within quadrant A, where there is a combination of high accountability and high discretion. This would work by allowing a certain discretion to staff delivering offending behaviour programmes. Any departure from the programme should be within agreed permissible parameters of variability and would have to be justified (and justifiable) by the practitioner concerned.

Given the centrality of skilled staff to the effectiveness of programmes, it is incumbent on managers to select with care the practitioners who are to be responsible for service delivery. Selection should be made on the basis of evidence that staff have an understanding of the task, are confident in the role, have a commitment to effective work with young people, and possess a highly developed ability to form effective relationships with young people. Baseline training can go some way towards ensuring staff development in this context.

However, not all recipients of training will benefit equally from the input. Managers should elicit feedback from those providing the training on the ability of participants to deliver offending behaviour programmes effectively.

Under- and over-representation of particular groups

Another significant challenge for practice is the potential for differential treatment and outcomes for particular groups. Monitoring of gender and ethnicity is key to ensuring that offending behaviour programmes are delivered to all potential participants within an anti-discriminatory framework. In practice, girls and young women are frequently excluded from certain types of programme, thereby limiting the range of court disposals available to them relative to those used for boys and young men. There is also sometimes a tendency to require relatively higher levels of intervention with females, on the basis of perceived welfare need, in circumstances where this is not warranted by considerations relevant to their offending behaviour (Gelsthorpe and Sharpe 2006)

It is well established that black young people are over-represented at every stage of the youth justice system, and this is especially marked among those who are sent to custody (Feilzer and Hood 2004). Well-delivered and targeted offending behaviour programmes have the potential to divert some of those young people from custody. In these circumstances, the importance of monitoring referrals and completions rates by ethnicity is patent.

Summary

- Offending behaviour programmes can be characterised as being designed to influence the behaviour of young people in a manner that makes it less likely to give rise to offending. They vary significantly according to the local offending profile and the category and particular circumstances of the young people for whom the intervention is intended.

- There are three forms of prevention – primary prevention (designed to improve overall opportunities in communities); secondary prevention (intervention with children and families deemed to be 'at risk'); and tertiary prevention (intervention with those who have been offending).

- Effective programmes, particularly for those young people whose offending is more serious or persistent, tend to have a core content, which focuses on skills training. This training is designed to improve problem-solving capacity, and has a cognitive element.

- Some argue that there has been an over-dependence on cognitive-behavioural approaches when none of the research shows they have any impact when used in isolation.

Further reading

Feilzer, M., Appleton, C., Roberts, C. and Hoyle, C. (2004) *Cognitive Behaviour Projects: The National Evaluation of the Youth Justice Board's Cognitive Behaviour Projects.* London: Youth Justice Board.

Roberts, C. (2004) 'Offending behaviour programmes: emerging evidence and implications for practice,' in R. Burnett and C. Roberts (eds) *What Works in Probation and Youth Justice: Developing Evidence-based Practice.* Cullompton: Willan Publishing.

11

Intensive Supervision and Surveillance Programme

The Intensive Supervision and Surveillance Programme (ISSP) is the most robust community programme available in England and Wales for young people who offend. It is targeted at young people who persistently offend, or those who have committed more serious offences. It can be used for those who are on community sentences or on bail, or for young people in the second part of a DTO. ISSPs are intended to be multi-modal and highly rigorous. They combine supervision with surveillance in an attempt to ensure programme completion and to bring structure to the young people's lives. The goal is to ensure that the risks posed by the young people are managed, and that their needs are met and continually reassessed over time.

This chapter explores the impact ISSP has had in the UK on reducing recidivism. Further than that, it looks at the available evidence for what appears to be promising with regard to particular aspects of ISSP and the tensions that may arise as a result of combining supervision with surveillance.

The evidence base for ISSP

When ISSPs were first launched in 2001, the Youth Justice Board stated that the aim of the programme was to:

- reduce the frequency and seriousness of offending in the target groups;
- tackle the underlying needs of young people which give rise to offending, with a particular emphasis on education and training;
- provide reassurance to communities through close surveillance backed up by rigorous enforcement.
  (Youth Justice Board 2004d)

  ISSPs are thus expected to contribute to the Youth Justice Board's more general objectives to reduce offending by young people and to promote interventions that reduce the risk factors associated with offending (Youth Justice Board 2000a).

A further objective has been for ISSPs to reduce the number of custodial sentences imposed on young people. This is demonstrated by the introduction of eligibility short-cuts to counter any increase in the use of custody resulting from other policy initiatives, and by the Youth Justice Board's stated preference for ISSPs over short DTOs (Youth Justice Board 2002a). Furthermore, one of the Youth Justice Board's targets for 2003/04 to 2005/06 was to 'ensure that, by March 2005, at least 4,000 young offenders a year are intensively supervised in the community to reduce reoffending and reduce the number of under-18s remanded and sentenced to secure facilities by 10 per cent from the October 2002 level' (Youth Justice Board 2003a).

Diverting young people from custody is an objective of the 12-month ISSP. The Youth Justice Board has stated that the key objectives of the longer programme are to:

- reduce the number of young people eligible for ISSP going into custody;

- deal more effectively with the problems of those young people with the most entrenched offending-related problems, with a particular emphasis on accessing on-going activities;

- provide reassurance to the community that the behaviour of these young people who repeatedly offend is being closely monitored and that any relapse will be effectively and swiftly dealt with;

- inform the development of the Intensive Supervision and Surveillance Order.

The last of these objectives highlights the long-term desire to establish the programme as a specific court order in its own right.

In the majority of schemes, ISSPs are provided predominantly through existing Yot structures. Many of these schemes involve a consortium of Yots. However, some schemes have been subcontracted to non-Yot agencies (e.g. Nacro), which are responsible for co-ordinating and delivering the programme. Other schemes have adopted an alternative theory base, either the Youth Advocate Programme (YAP) or multi-systemic therapy (MST). YAPs promote a strength-based, holistic approach, developing problem-solving strategies by focusing on a young person's strengths. MST, in contrast, combines family and behavioural therapy strategies with intensive family support services.

Targeting

The ISSP targets young people aged 10–17 who offend. Unlike many previous intensive programmes, it targets these young people both pre- and post-custody. More precisely, the three routes onto the programme are:

1 As a condition of bail supervision and support;

2 As part of a Supervision Order or Community Rehabilitation Order (CRO)[1]

3 As a condition of community supervision in the second part of a DTO.

Thus the ISSP is currently not a court order, and no new legislative powers relate specifically to the programme.

ISSPs are targeted towards the small group of young people who are responsible for a disproportionately large amount of offending. Initial estimates of the size of this group were based on research carried out by Graham and Bowling (1995) as the first 'sweep' of the Youth Lifestyles Survey. This was followed by further analysis in the Audit Commission's report *Misspent Youth* (1996) and the second sweep of the Youth Lifestyles Survey (Flood-Page *et al.* 2000). Various complexities associated with this data make it difficult to define persistence precisely and therefore to agree on the target group (Moore *et al.* 2004). Hagell and Newburn (1994), for example, studied a sample of 531 young people who had been arrested at least three times in the previous year, and tested several definitions of 'persistent offending'. Each definition identified a substantially different set of young people, which could also suggest that persistence may be somewhat transitory.

Two eligibility short-cuts were introduced in April 2002 following concerns that government initiatives on street crime, and robbery in particular, could lead to an increase in the use of custody for first-time serious offences, and that implementation of Section 30 of the Criminal Justice and Police Act 2001 might lead to secure or custodial remands for young people with a history of offending while on bail. The driving force was, therefore, the objective for ISSPs to have an impact on custody rates.[2]

The Youth Justice Board has stated that the ISSP is 'unique in both the amount and intensity of supervision and surveillance that is provided' (Youth Justice Board 2000a). While this is certainly true of the current Youth Justice System in England and Wales, the ISSP is by no means the first intensive community programme. In the USA, such programmes are well established and date back to the 1960s. By 1990, Intensive Supervision Programmes had been initiated in every state, and by 1994 it was estimated that over 120,000 people were the subject of such programmes (Altschuler 1998; Corbett and Petersilia 1994; Petersilia and Turner 1992; Tonry 1998). There are indications that those programmes which (i) target those at higher risk of offending and (ii) have a treatment component (e.g. counselling, supervised activities) have successfully produced a reduction in recidivism (Gendreau *et al.* 2000; Bonta *et al.* 2000).

In England and Wales, recent decades have witnessed a general strengthening of community sentences. Notably, the Criminal Justice Act 1982 enabled courts to add further requirements to Supervision Orders, while the Criminal Justice Act 1991 introduced the Combination Order (since renamed the Community Punishment and Rehabilitation Order, combining probation and community service in a single sentence. At the same time, there have been numerous attempts to develop intensive community programmes (e.g. Intensive Matched Probation and After-Care Treatment (IMPACT) in the 1970s, and Intermediate Treatment projects in the 1980s). These initiatives have, however, tended to be short-lived (Moore 2004).

ISSP is designed to be based on the principles of the community base and risk classification. The Audit Commission report *Misspent Youth* (1996) has also proved highly influential in guiding recent policy. It concluded that 'persistent offenders should receive more intensive supervision in the community'.

Characteristics of young people receiving ISSPs

Understanding the profile of young people receiving ISSPs is an important basis for effective delivery. The national evaluation found that the mean age of young people starting ISSPs was 16.4 years, 93 per cent of them were young men, and over 80 per cent were white. Official and self-report data both indicated a high frequency of involvement in offending behaviour. Approximately half the sample had committed a domestic burglary or a robbery in the preceding 12 months (Moore *et al.* 2004).

The Audit Commission (2004) has stated that 'almost all serious and persistent young offenders have complicated lives and most have a variety of problems'. This is certainly the case for young people referred on to ISSPs. From an analysis of *Asset* data the national evaluators were able to determine profiles of young people admitted to ISSPs (Baker *et al.* 2002).

The research indicated that practitioners were more likely to identify a link to further offending for young people on ISSPs than for non-ISSP cases. The nature of both the damage and deprivation experienced by the young people was not uniform. Some showed evidence of mental health problems and others of considerable vulnerability. The importance of tailoring provision in such cases is clearly crucial.

A national evaluation involving analysis of *Asset* scores found that nearly half of the ISSP sample fell within the high-score band, compared with one fifth of the national sample. The corresponding risk of reconviction within 12 months for this score band is 76 per cent (Baker *et al.* 2002). Furthermore, 10 per cent of the ISSP young people scored 35 or more on *Asset*, which corresponds to a risk of reconviction within 12 months of 84 per cent. Such findings appear to justify the more intensive work offered by ISSPs.

Care history

Young people on ISSPs are more likely to have been looked after by a local authority or to have had contact with social services departments than the non-ISSP cases. For example, the national evaluation found that 37 per cent of the young people on ISSPs were currently or had previously been accommodated in local authority care with the agreement of their parents (compared with

213

UNIVERSITY OF WINCHESTER
LIBRARY

18 per cent of the non-ISSP cases). Twice as many young people on ISSPs were or had been subject to a care order (14 per cent compared with 7 per cent), and nearly twice the number had their name on the child protection register (either previously or currently – 18 per cent compared with 10 per cent).

Living arrangements, family and personal relationships

ISSP workers noted that 62 per cent of the young people on ISSPs lived with their mother, but only 25 per cent with their father. Additionally, 86 per cent had contact with their mother and 48 per cent with their father; this latter figure was lower than for the non-ISSP sample, where 60 per cent had contact with their father. Another significant difference was the number of young people on ISSPs who lived in a home or institution (16 per cent), compared with the proportion of non-ISSP cases (7 per cent).

Further to this, 47 per cent of the young people on ISSPs were assessed as currently or usually living in a deprived household, with 36 per cent currently or usually living with people known to offend. This latter figure increased to 45 per cent when considering the criminal activities of people they had contact with (compared with 25 per cent of the non-ISSP sample). Also, 52 per cent of the ISSP sample were assessed as suffering from inconsistent supervision from their family and carers (compared with 24 per cent of the non-ISSP sample).

Education, training and employment (ETE)

In the six months prior to their *Asset* assessment, only 19 per cent of the young people on ISSPs were in mainstream education; the comparable figure for the non-ISSP sample was 59 per cent. In addition, 40 per cent of the young people on ISSPs were assessed as having special educational needs (SEN), and 62 per cent were underachieving in relation to their perceived abilities. Using standardised tests it was found that the average reading age of the ISSP young people was 10.8, five and a half years behind their chronological age. Over 60 per cent were regularly not attending, and 60 per cent were assessed as having a lack of attachment to their school.

For those young people of non-school age, only 4 per cent were in full-time employment; 88 per cent were assessed as having a lack of suitable qualifications for the workplace.

Friends and lifestyle

The young people on ISSPs were more likely to be assessed as associating with pro-criminal peers than the non-ISSP sample (82 per cent compared with 40 per cent). A higher proportion were also assessed as not using their time constructively (84 per cent compared with 53 per cent). Substance use had a detrimental effect on the lives of 34 per cent of the ISSP sample, compared with 14 per cent of the non-ISSP sample.

Attitudes, thinking and behaviour

Thinking and behaviour were more likely to be assessed as difficult for the young people on ISSPs than for the non-ISSP cases. Overall, 90 per cent of the ISSP sample were assessed as being impulsive and acting without thinking (compared with 74 per cent of the non-ISSP sample), and 74 per cent had a constant need for excitement as they were easily bored (compared with 44 per cent). There was a lack of understanding of consequences in 63 per cent of the ISSP young people, and 62 per cent displayed a lack of understanding for other people (compared with 25 per cent of the non-ISSPs). In addition, 62 per cent showed aggression towards others (compared with 42 per cent).

Young people on ISSPs were also assessed as displaying a lack of empathy for others. Lack of understanding of the effects on victims was displayed in 60 per cent of cases, with 52 per cent assessed as lacking an ability to understand the effects of offending on their family.

Differences in ISSP participants

Further analysis suggests that young people receiving ISSPs can be divided into a number of sub-groups with different criminal histories and problems, for whom different solutions might be needed. For example, the national evaluators found that those who qualified for ISSP on the grounds of the seriousness of their offence but not the persistence of their offending had fewer offending-related problems than other ISSP participants, and better problem-solving skills. The evaluators thus concluded that these young people may not require 'the same intensity or range of intervention as persistent offenders' (Moore *et al.* 2004).

Perceptions of ISSP

The introduction of a high-profile initiative such as the ISSP inevitably generates diverse opinions about its value. The Youth Justice Board describes it as a 'robust alternative to custody' which needs to be in place in order to 'punish persistent and serious young offenders, but also to tackle the underlying causes of their offending behaviour' (Youth Justice Board 2003c). The ISSP is seen as having value not just for young people who offend, but also for the communities affected by their behaviour. Referring to the recent national roll-out of ISSP schemes across England and Wales, Hazel Blears, Home Office Minister of State for Crime Reduction, claimed that 'they will make a big difference to the local communities that are blighted by the persistent behaviour of a criminal few' (Youth Justice Board 2003c).

Others have expressed concerns about the potentially intrusive nature of the intervention, particularly the surveillance element (Smith 2003). A further concern is that ISSPs might come to be used as a substitute for other community disposals (instead of as an alternative to custody), with the result that young people become subject to more intensive supervision than is necessary

215

or appropriate. There are instances of diversionary programmes failing to target young people at genuine risk of custody, but targeting instead others who might have been dealt with more leniently (Bottoms 1995). So-called 'net-widening' has accompanied the introduction of intensive programmes in the US (Tonry 1998). More positively, however, the high-tariff Intermediate Treatment projects were viewed as the 'most important factor' in reducing custody rates for young people in England and Wales in the 1980s (Pitts 2002).

The introduction of ISSPs was accompanied by a national evaluation of the first 41 ISSP schemes by the University of Oxford (hereafter referred to as the 'national evaluation') following up young people who engaged with ISSP for 12 months (Moore *et al.* 2004) and then 24 months (Gray *et al.* 2005b). The results of this first evaluation provide detailed information regarding perceptions of ISSPs (Moore *et al.* 2004).

When sentencers were asked about the usefulness of ISSPs as an option for the courts, taking into account the full range of sentencing options, 70 per cent responded that they are 'very useful' and a further 28 per cent that they are 'quite useful'. The Lord Chief Justice (2001) has stated that 'offenders may receive custodial sentences because the judiciary does not believe that there is any credible community alternative' (although a recent study by Hough *et al.* (2003) found that sentencers did not identify a lack of satisfactory community options as a factor 'tipping' towards custody in cases on the cusp). The evaluation found that there is a clear belief that ISSPs have bridged this gap for young people who offend.

> Extremely useful. Absolutely no doubt about that. As far as the magistrates are concerned, they see it as a very sound and supportive sentence. It assists them in thinking that they are going to keep the young person out of custody, but still infringe upon their liberty. It is rigorous, there's no doubt about that. It's very heavy stuff. (*Magistrate*) (Moore *et al.* 2004)

Many practitioners emphasised the value of the programme's 'rigorous' nature. When asked to comment on the most effective aspects of the ISSP, they highlighted the intensity of supervision. The extensive number of hours was perceived to create a comprehensive 'regime' of full days of activities, facilitating the development of relationships and affording staff the flexibility to tailor programmes where possible.

When interviewed at the end of their programme, 82 per cent of the young people thought they had benefited from the ISSP.

A number of parents/carers also reported benefiting from their contact with the ISSP staff.

> It gave us more support and also more information of places to go. Daniel had a few problems and you can take him to this centre, you know? ... And we didn't even know it existed. And when we had a

problem, they were like, yeah, you can go there. You just phone them up and make an appointment. So it's things like that that we still fall back on. 'Cos we know these things exist now' (*Father*) (Moore *et al.* 2004).

Impact of ISSPs

> Most innovative programmes in youth justice are handicapped by unrealistic expectations about what can be achieved. Almost by definition, persistent offending behaviour is extremely resistant to change. (Little *et al.* 2004)

It is clear that ISSP teams are faced with a considerable challenge in addressing these young people's underlying needs and their consequent offending behaviour. Immediate or very short-term changes in attitudes, skills and behaviour are unlikely to occur quickly or easily. Nevertheless, the national evaluation demonstrated that, in a significant number of cases, ISSPs provided an important first step towards positive maturation and development. In particular, significant progress was achieved in areas such as educational provision, employment changes, family relationships, meeting accommodation needs, and attitudes to crime and the victims of it (Moore *et al.* 2004). Access to statutory services for these young people was, though found to be poor and staff felt this undermined the ability of ISSP to meet the needs of young people more permanently (Gray *et al.* 2005).

The national evaluation found a marked reduction in both the frequency (39 per cent) and seriousness (13 per cent) of reoffending for young people on ISSP, particularly for those who completed the programme. Both these figures exceeded the then Youth Justice Board target for ISSP to reduce reoffending of its population by 5 per cent. However, the national evaluation found that comparison groups (young people eligible for ISSP but who received an equivalent sentence without an ISSP) performed just as well. Given the offending histories and complex problems of this group of young people, some failure and relapse is inevitable, and change may be a very gradual process. Furthermore, the improved levels of surveillance involved in ISSP may serve to raise recorded reconviction rates for young people on ISSP (91 per cent). Such improvements in the level and speed of detection can be viewed positively: 'As programs move away from rehabilitation and toward surveillance and control, some might argue that higher arrest rates should be seen as an indication of program success, not failure, especially when dealing with high-risk probationers' (Petersilia and Turner 1992). As pointed out by Worrall and Walton (2000) in their evaluation of a prolific offender project, this results in 'a "win/win" situation, which complicates evaluation and may raise questions about definitions of "success"'.

The Youth Justice Board's intention was that ISSPs would also help to reduce the number of custodial sentences imposed on young people. The national evaluation and the Audit Commission (2004) found that there had been a reduction in the use of custody in ISSP areas (a fall of 17 per cent between the first quarter of 2001 and the third quarter of 2003 in the Audit Commission analysis of YJB statistics), but there had also been a similar fall in those areas which, at the time, did not have ISSPs. There was no significant difference in the rates of custodial remand between Yots with ISSPs and those without (Audit Commission 2004). Drop in custody rates, therefore cannot be attributed directly to the introduction of ISSP. This finding also demonstrates that a multitude of factors may have an impact on custody rates.

In assessing the relationship between ISSPs and custody rates, the impact of breaches also needs to be taken into account. Bearing in mind that imprisonment is a potential consequence of a breach, there is a clear tension between the objective of reducing the use of custody and providing a community penalty which is rigorously enforced. Notably, the Youth Justice Board has emphasised that strict enforcement is crucial to the success of ISSPs and in providing reassurance to the community (Youth Justice Board 2003d). A consequence of such an approach is that even if ISSPs successfully target 'high-risk' cases, a number of initial diversions from custody will reappear in the custody figures following breach (Audit Commission 2004).

The national evaluation stressed the importance of using precise assessments, supervision plans and implementation strategies in work with young people on ISSPs (Moore *et al.* 2004). Collecting accurate evidence and information was identified as crucial for practitioners and managers to plan and deliver effective interventions. There was evidence that not only did young people benefit from such an approach, but also that Yot practitioners, staff in the secure estate, local police officers and others delivered improved interventions and became gradually more confident in delivering the programme.

Surveillance

Community surveillance is perceived to be an important component of ISSPs. The twin objectives of this surveillance are to provide reassurance to the community and to ensure that the young people are aware that their behaviour is being monitored and their whereabouts checked. ISSP teams must provide at least one of the following four forms of surveillance:

1 **Electronic tagging** – the tag is used to reinforce a curfew, usually at night when young people are most at risk of offending;

2 **Voice verification** – the young people's voice prints are checked over the telephone at times specified in a contract schedule, to confirm that they are where they are supposed to be;

3 **Tracking** – ISSP staff check the whereabouts of the young people throughout the week, reinforcing their participation in the ISSP by accompanying them to appointments, providing support and advice, and following up any non-attendances;

4 **Intelligence-led policing** – the police overtly monitor the young people's movements at key times and exchange information with ISSP staff.

In addition, there is electronic tracking, in which the whereabouts of a young person are tracked by satellite 24 hours a day. This method is being piloted by one ISSP scheme with juveniles who persistently offend.

Research in Canada has reported reductions in recidivism resulting from intensive treatments directed at young people who are at higher risk of further offending. Completion of the programme is aided by electronic monitoring (Bonta *et al.* 1999). Similarly, research in England and Wales has highlighted the view of practitioners that a curfew is most effective when it is used to assist the work of other interventions. Curfew Orders can be used constructively alongside other community penalties to:

- support curfewees;

- build on the consequences of being tagged;

- know that a curfewee is not offending during curfew hours;

- develop routines and timetabling skills which can improve attendance on other interventions.
  (Walter *et al.* 2001)

The national evaluation also found that sentencers believed that the supervision and surveillance components of an ISSP complemented each other.

> Supervision is required to challenge behaviour and help develop an alternative lifestyle. Surveillance is a necessary deterrent. Without it, many magistrates would be reluctant to make an ISSP order as an alternative to prison. (*Sentencer*) (Moore *et al.* 2004)

The Youth Justice Board expects all young people on ISSPs to be electronically tagged where appropriate. The electronic tag checks whether a young person is at a specified location during set times. Monitoring is constant during the specified period. The tag acts as a transmitter, sending signals to a monitoring unit which detects whether the tag is in range.

This process has become the most commonly used form of surveillance for young people on ISSPs. The national evaluation reported that 70 per cent of young people had been tagged (Moore *et al.* 2004). The tag's impact on the young people was highlighted by the fact that some referred to their programme as 'the tag'. Tagging was also very popular among sentencers, who saw it as a vital component in ensuring that the ISSP is a tough and credible programme.

> I very much agree with the tag and the curfew whilst they settle down ...
> They've got to be tagged. It gives them the structure that they need.
> Otherwise, it's a watering down of the order. (*Sentencer*) (Moore *et al.* 2004)

Previous research has reported some ethical concerns among practitioners regarding tagging, but also that these concerns can be alleviated with greater awareness of how the tag can be used constructively (Boswell *et al.* 1993; Nellis and Lilly 2001). In the national evalution, ISSP staff highlighted the value of the tag in providing structure and discipline and securing a period of calm in which to work on offending behaviour.

> The tagging gives them some structure. Very few violate the tag, and
> quite a few say that they welcome it, having to be in at a certain time.
> There's no doubt that attending here, having their welfare needs met, is
> far less an infringement of their liberty than being locked up in a YOI.
> (*ISSP manager*) (Moore *et al.* 2004)

Furthermore, the tag may facilitate an improvement in family relationships, because of the stability brought to young people's lives and the increased amounts of time spent in the home (Walter 2002). In certain instances, however, the presence of the young person in the home can cause friction. Parents/carers may also view the electronic monitoring equipment as intrusive.

The suitability of the tag for those with particularly chaotic lives is not always clear cut and must be assessed on a case-by-case basis. While the tag is popular with practitioners and sentencers, some young people find it difficult to comply with its requirements. Evidence from the ISSP national evaluation suggested that some young people were antagonised by the tag, reinforcing their pro-criminal attitudes and leading to further offending while on the programme.

Imposing a tag on young people with serious drug problems can create particular difficulties, although it can also offer the potential for disrupting their habits and prompting them to access treatment (Walter *et al.* 2001). More generally, Home Office research has identified the following factors as contributing to breaches:

- **psychological issues** – motivation is a key issue, with the young person needing to exercise self-discipline to keep to the curfew;

- **housing and domestic issues** – compliance can be hindered by unsuitable housing, unstable tenure or relationship problems, while family support can aid compliance;

- **employment** – for those young people in employment, working shifts, long hours or overtime can conflict with a curfew.
  (Mortimer 2001)

Tracking as a form of surveillance involves ISSP staff in tracking the where-abouts of young people throughout the week, accompanying them to appointments, providing support and advice when necessary, and following up any non-attendances. The national evaluators reported that 'trackers' had been employed in 64 per cent of cases (Moore *et al.* 2004). Practitioners per-ceived the flexibility of tracking to be particularly valuable. Trackers could use incentives and/or sanctions, and/or seek to establish a degree of trust, depending on which tactic seemed most appropriate at any given time. A fur-ther perceived benefit was the ability of those staff designated as trackers to develop positive relationships with the young people. In this respect, there is a clear overlap between 'tracking' and the role of mentoring. Similarly to the Intensive Treatment initiatives of the 1980s, ISSP trackers can be used to assist individuals to gain understanding of their offending, and to encourage them to develop a more constructive lifestyle (Errington 1985).

Police involvement in ISSPs can add a degree of robustness and credibility to the programme. The police can provide the charging data necessary to identify eligible young people, share information and intelligence gathered within the community about individuals, and ensure that breach action against a young person results in a swift return to court. With regard to ISSP surveillance, police involvement can serve to let young people know that their behaviour is being monitored by other agencies, and may help to reas-sure the community that the young people are being effectively monitored.

In the Youth Justice Board/Association of Chief Police Officers *Guide to Good Practice* (2003), it is suggested that the police response to ISSPs has 'gen-erally been good, both strategically and operationally ... there have been some excellent examples of operational information sharing, but the good practice is not uniform and there are too many police officers on the ground who have not heard of ISSP'. The report identifies certain 'next steps' that might be taken to improve police involvement and co-operation in ISSPs, including the following:

- intra-force communication;
- training about ISSPs within forces;
- protocols between police and ISSP team;
- police input to ISSP staffing;
- the role of Yot police officers.

The ISSP national evaluation found that many practitioners saw the presence of a police officer within the ISSP team as vital for sharing intelligence, and important in terms of ease of interaction between rank-and-file officers and the ISSP (Moore *et al.* 2004). Where police officers formed an integral part of the ISSP team, the routine access to police ICT (information and communi-cations technology) and intelligence systems, and their contribution to risk assessment and programme planning, were greatly welcomed by ISSP staff. Moreover, such police integration into the ISSP team greatly enhanced up-to-date knowledge about the activities or whereabouts of the young people on the programme, and lent an immediacy of intelligence under which action could be initiated. In terms of street policing, it was felt that the officers should have a clear understanding of ISSPs and a commitment to informally monitoring young people on the programme.

Practitioners viewed the combination of the tag and trackers as a particularly stringent and effective form of surveillance. Furthermore, use of the tag appeared to be most effective and more acceptable to young people where its use was linked with the human form of surveillance.

Notably, the national evaluation found that many of those who were breached on an ISSP were allowed to continue with their programme. Continuation remained popular with sentencers where young people breached a second and even third time. However, use of this option gradually declined, with custody the most common outcome of a third breach (Moore *et al.* 2004).

When sentencers were asked about the appropriateness of a custodial sentence for breach of an ISSP, their responses indicated a need for some discretion in this area (Moore *et al.* 2004). It was also noted that, in certain instances, breach could be a useful tactic to try to ensure future compliance. Nevertheless, there was an overriding desire to maintain the credibility of the ISSP as a tough, rigorous programme. Detailed reports of a young person's progress on an ISSP up to the date of the court hearing are thus invaluable in helping sentencers to make an informed decision. Where a young person has generally been complying, the information may encourage magistrates to allow the order to continue.

> It depends upon the nature of the breach, if there's been reoffending at the same time, their compliance up to the court date, and what the Yot is saying about the young person. It could well be that they're looking for us to rap them on the knuckles. In that sense, it's a reinforcing message. This is where the liaison between the court and the Yot is crucial. But if it was a really serious breach with added factors then custody could be appropriate. (*Sentencer*) (Moore *et al.* 2004)

The national evaluators reported that of those cases who completed the ISSP successfully, 35 per cent had been breached at some stage. Certainly, breaching can have a positive impact on young people's commitment. McIvor (1992) found that in relation to enforcement, a consistent but rigorous approach that is clearly conveyed with fairness and regularity encourages increased compliance. It also serves to increase the 'legitimacy' of the supervisor, thereby encouraging greater commitment by the young person (Rex 1999). Equally, inconsistency in applying sanctions is likely to result in resentment, lack of commitment and, ultimately, limited compliance.

The principles of effective practice and ISSP

Risk classification

Given that ISSP is intended as an alternative to custody, it is clear that an assessment of risk should indicate a seriousness of offending that would normally warrant a custodial sentence. The Audit Commission review (2004) suggests that young people who would otherwise have received community sentences may be being drawn into ISSP. This implication was supported by site visits, which suggested that some young people were receiving DTOs who did not reach the eligibility threshold for an ISSP.

The principle of risk classification might also be usefully applied to decisions related to breach. The Audit Commission reported that the numbers breached and sent to custody was high (2004). The national evaluation of ISSP put the actual figure at 31 per cent, although it should be noted that the quality of the data could not allow the reseachers to determine whether this figure was any higher than it might have been if ISSP had not existed (Moore *et al.* 2004; Gray *et al.* 2005).

It remains the case though, that the response to breach ought to be proportionate to the level of breach if the principle of risk classification is to be achieved, with custody considered as a last resort (Audit Commission 2004). This might apply especially to those on ISSPs as part of a DTO, who are at higher risk of returning to custody if they breach the conditions of the programme.

Intervention modality

It is argued that ISSPs are truly multidimensional, adhering to the principle of 'intervention modality'. This identifies multi-modal programmes geared to the variety of problems presented by young people who offend as the most consistently effective (Utting and Vennard 2000). The programmes also reflect the research evidence from North America, which indicates that intensive programmes need to have a treatment component (e.g. counselling, supervised activities) to have an impact on rates of further offending (Gendreau *et al.* 2000).

Other possible ideas include developing joint policies, inviting key providers to participate on ISSP steering groups, or providing regular feedback on the outcomes of cases. In many cases, young people on ISSPs are not linked into mainstream services. For example, the national evaluation showed that only 19 per cent of those of statutory school age were attending mainstream school, while over a quarter had no main source of educational provision. Of those no longer of statutory school age, 56 per cent were unemployed (Gray *et al.* 2005). However, ISSP teams were shown to have an important role in urging external agencies into action, and many have succeeded in providing opportunities for young people in order to address their problems (Moore *et al.* 2004).

The ISSP framework has implications for inter-agency working. The need for intensive programmes to establish relationships with a range of departments or organisations and to provide good-quality contact, rather than simply more contact, has been highlighted by previous evaluations (Altschuler 1998; Goodstein and Sontheimer 1997; Lobley *et al.* 2001; Key 2001).

The ISSP national evaluation found (through observations and through interviews with young people, parents and staff) that the quality of the relationship between the young person and their supervising officer could have a very strong impact on outcomes (Moore *et al.* 2004). In some instances, key workers were seen to have more authority than parents who had got to 'the end of their tether'. Through daily contact, officers were able to obtain valuable information to challenge behaviour and maintain compliance. Indeed, young people often disclosed very personal information, such as previous sexual abuse, self-harm, health problems or family issues. Schemes with assertive and experienced staff have tended to deliver the programme more efficiently and consistently than others. Practitioners thus may have an important role in modelling to young people and their families the types of behaviour that ISSPs try to encourage and promote – for example, good timekeeping, sticking to the planned work, respect for those around you and honouring commitments.

Evidence from the national evaluation (Moore *et al.* 2004) suggested that because of the short lead-in, difficulties were sometimes reported in producing a balanced and/or individually tailored timetable for bail ISSP cases. However, as bail cases take up a large proportion of a scheme's caseload, being ready to plan, access and deliver ISSPs at short notice forms a regular and important part of a practitioner's role.

Community based

The design of ISSP as an intervention focuses on the concept of community base; providing interventions designed to tackle offending behaviour in the community as an alternative to removing young people to a custodial establishment. There are some tensions in this, particularly with respect to the response of the community. For this reason, community reassurance is a key objective of the ISSP, but the ability to reassure the public is hindered by lack of awareness of the programme. This suggests that opportunities to bring the ISSP into the public realm in a positive light should be actively sought and capitalised upon.

Many teams have demonstrated potentially promising practice in this area (Youth Justice Board 2003c). Liaison with the police and community consultative groups can provide opportunities to explain to the public what action is being taken to address the problems created by young people who persistently offend. Other methods for communicating information about the ISSP include:

- neighbourhood watch groups;
- leaflets circulated to community groups;
- inviting the press to activities.

Programmes in the community near the young person's home environment appear to have yielded the most positive outcomes. Workers may be able to assist young people to reintegrate into their local community by encouraging them to find a local support network (by linking them to local agencies or voluntary projects) and use facilities such as local gyms, libraries and other resources. This may provide young people with opportunities to meet their personal and social needs.

Programme integrity

Previous evaluations of intensive programmes have highlighted the need for a well-trained, supported and cohesive staff team (Goodstein and Sontheimer 1997; Lobley *et al.* 2001; Key 2001). The intensity of an ISSP can be demanding on workers both physically and emotionally. Staff, therefore, need to be committed and supported in their roles by senior practitioners, managers and the organisation as a whole.

Evaluation findings indicated that those teams with a broad, influential steering group were more able to secure service-level agreements with outside agencies and monitor their performance. Such groups typically benefited from representation at a decision-making level (Yot managers, borough commanders, senior court clerks, representatives from external agencies, Electronic Monitoring contractor managers, ISSP managers) and from having a clear purpose. This suggests that in the absence of an effective group, it may be advisable for ISSP managers or practitioners to meet service providers on a one-to-one basis.

Effective programmes have been shown to be those whose stated aims are embedded into the methodology employed. This implies that ISSP staff should have sound theoretical and practical understanding of the basis of the programme, be adequately trained, and be prepared to review and monitor their work with a supervisor. Communicating what an ISSP means and involves to young people and their parents or carers may also contribute to the success of a programme.

Criminogenic need

As ISSPs now target 'serious' as well as 'persistent' offending, there is a potential need to cater for those who have committed serious sexual offences or acts of violence. More generally, young people with serious and persistent offending behaviour have differing criminogenic risk factors, which need to be taken into account in developing their individual programmes. However, as shown by Figure 11.1, the ISSP national evaluation found that the offending behaviour of many of those referred on to the programme was both persistent and serious (Moore *et al.* 2004).

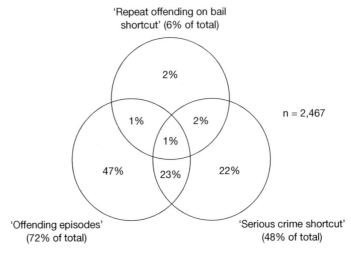

'Repeat offending on bail shortcut' (6% of total)

2%

n = 2,467

1%   2%

1%

47%   23%   22%

'Offending episodes' (72% of total)

'Serious crime shortcut' (48% of total)

2% met none of the criteria

Figure 11.1 Overlapping eligibility criteria
Source: Moore *et al* (2006: 92)

Further information on the profile of young people referred to ISSP is detailed earlier in the chapter. In determining criminogenic need practitioners need to take account of such complex profiles and determmime priority action for tackling offending behaviour.

Responsivity

In terms of engagement, teaching and motivation, the principle of responsivity implies that ISSP supervision should use methods which take account of how young people learn best. For example, young people may wish to contribute to the content of their timetable and state their preferred subjects to study. Or it may be more convenient to deliver some activities at weekends and in the evenings. Similarly, supervision should also aim to be culturally sensitive to young people's religion, language and environment. Thorough assessments and regular consultation with young people will help workers to provide 'responsive' supervision.

The national evaluation found that the young people on ISSPs had greater mental health problems than the wider population (Moore *et al.* 2004). This finding is similar to previous research findings. For approximately half of the young people on ISSPs, their daily functioning was assessed as being significantly affected by their problems.

This can make both their progression and time on an ISSP much more difficult, but should not exclude them from being considered for the programme. In some cases, ISSPs have been given to young people with severe mental health problems who would otherwise have received custody because 'there was nothing else that could be done with them' (Moore *et al.* 2004).

Dosage

A high 'dosage' is conceived as central to the design and implementation of ISSP. Some fundamental issues with the recording of delivery and compliance were identified by the ISSP evaluation (Moore *et al.* 2004). See Chapter 1, 'Dosage', p. 25.

During the ISSP national evaluation, many practitioners noted that the transition between the differing intensity phases created tensions for young people, some of whom admitted to feeling 'at a loose end'. Practitioners often supported cases for longer hours during the shift, and favoured a tapering off of hours over the months towards completion of the programme. In reality, the distinction between the intensive and less-intensive periods did not seem to be as marked as might have been expected, given the pre-existing legislation (Moore *et al.* 2004).

There are no set minimum or maximum hours per supervision module, aside from the emphasis on ETE provision. The overall requirement is for a minimum of 25 hours' supervision per week in the first intensive period of the ISSP. Although this number of hours may appear to be significantly greater than for other community programmes, the national evaluation stressed that the majority of ISSP staff who were consulted felt that levels of supervision were 'about right'. Many workers emphasised the value of the rigorous nature of ISSPs and, when asked to comment on the most effective aspects of the programme, highlighted the intensity of supervision. Interestingly, a significant proportion of young people also indicated in their exit interviews that they welcomed the high and consistent levels of contact with ISSP staff. As identified in the national evaluation, the issues around recording of hours delivered make it difficult to establish the amount of actual contact with young people (Moore *et al.* 2004).

A recent study of young people in ISSP identified that only 19 per cent of young people of statutory school age out of a sample of 1,640 were attending mainstream school (Youth Justice Board 2006c). This may be seen as an area for concern, given the problems and poor outcomes associated with segregated education provision. See Chapter 3, pp 72–3.

The challenges for practice

ISSPs in practice: challenges and opportunities

ISSPs may be considered as offering new opportunities, not least because of the resources available and the amount of time and attention that can be given to individual young people. Actual outcomes depend very much on the practice in the individual ISSP teams. As Bateman (2001) argues, 'the success of the national project will be determined by local implementation: questions of practice are here to the fore'.

Research on protective factors that may help young people to desist from offending has identified the significance of new opportunities and turning points (Communities that Care 2001).

One challenge for practitioners and service providers may be to help young people to see the ISSP as a chance for a positive turning point. This might require a range of professional skills and knowledge, for example in relation to areas such as conducting assessments, working within the legal frameworks of youth justice and children's rights, practising 'motivational interviewing', establishing and maintaining appropriate boundaries in relationships with young people, and delivering programmes. The national evaluation found that ISSP managers viewed the quality of the relationship between young person and ISSP worker as crucial. A productive relationship, it was thought, could have a catalytic effect on the young person's attitudes and behaviour.

Lack of access to necessary services may affect the assessment of suitability for an ISSP. For example:

> While drug users who have chaotic lifestyles should not automatically be assessed as unsuitable, resources must be in place to support them adequately throughout the entire programme. (*ISSP case manager*) (Moore *et al*. 2004)

In practice, schemes appear to differ in their approach to assessing suitability. Some focus on ensuring that only those with the highest risk of custody or the most entrenched problems are referred on to an ISSP. Others feel that it is important to give eligible young people at least one chance on an ISSP. Practitioners have also highlighted the need to avoid 'cherry-picking' those young people with the least pronounced problems, who are most likely to succeed, or in cases where another community order would be sufficient.

The Youth Justice Board has emphasised, however, that schemes should not use the extended power to run an excessively long period of high intensity, as this could lead to overreliance on the programme. The goal is to manage the transition to sustainable, community-based provision.

Evidence from the national evaluation also highlighted two further problems encountered by teams in sourcing educational provision. The first concerns young people of school age who are 'unofficially excluded' from school or have not attended for a long time. Yots could find themselves conflicting with schools over this issue, particularly if they wish to see funds reallocated to alternative provision for this group of young people. Resolving the issue is likely to require the involvement of the Yot education worker and the LEA.

The second problem is that ETE provision can sometimes be limited to one or two providers that the Yot is unhappy about using. Rather than accessing mainstream provision, Yots have explored providing their own on-site ETE using home tutors or part-time teachers for under-16s (Moore *et al.* 2004). Prospective outcomes both in terms of educational progression and offending do seem far more limited in such segregated settings (see ETE Chapter 3 pp 72–3). For those over 16, some Yots have worked with Connexions or directly with training providers for work experience.

The National Audit Office has recently reported that Yots find it difficult to arrange accommodation for young people who offend, often because of a lack of housing provision for 16- and 17-year-olds, and the policy of some providers not to make arrangements until a young person is physically homeless (National Audit Office 2004). Similarly, the national evaluation found that accommodation was a fairly complicated area. ISSP managers explained that accommodation needs could be 'immediate', and finding swift solutions for this client group could be difficult (Moore *et al.* 2004).

Maintaining good lines of communication with all relevant service providers may be regarded as a challenge for ISSP teams, given the intensity of the intervention and the requirements attached to the programme. Evidence showed that young people sometimes did not understand what was involved in an ISSP. During interviews, young people often referred to their programme as 'the tag' (Moore *et al.* 2004). Similarly, many were unaware of the timescales or requirements of their order. Indeed, staff commented that some young people did not find it easy to grasp the complexity of the programme.

Some breakdowns in communication between ISSP schemes and electronic monitoring contractors have also been detected (Moore *et al.* 2004). It is therefore regarded as important to maintain regular contact and communication. At a basic level, a contractor needs to know which young people are on ISSPs, and the necessary information will need to be shared regarding ISSP curfews (Youth Justice Board 2002c).

The combination of supervision and surveillance means that ISSPs, perhaps more than any other community intervention, have to manage the difficult balance between the demands of 'care and control' (Raynor 1993).

Summary

- The ISSP is intended as a multi-modal, highly rigorous intervention which targets young people aged 10–17 who offend, as an alternative to custody.

- ISSP is not currently a court order and no new legislative powers relate specifically to the programme, although the long-term intention is to establish the programme as a court order in its own right.

- One of the aims of the 12-month ISSP is to divert young people eligible for the programme from custody. It does not appear to have been effective in this aim and tensions have been identified between the objective of reducing the use of custody and a community penalty which is rigorously enforced by means of breaching.

- It may be that the increased levels of surveillance which form an integral part of the ISSP may serve to raise recorded reconviction rates.

- Some commentators have expressed concerns about the intrusive nature of the ISSP and that it may be used as a substitute for other, more lenient, community disposals rather than as an alternative to custody.

Notes

1 The Youth Justice Board has advised that schemes opt for the Supervision Order option as this enables a longer period of intensive provision; the CRO is to be absorbed into the generic community sentence for adults when the Criminal Justice Act 2003 is implemented.
2 With regard to the 12-month ISSP, the criteria for eligibility remain persistence or seriousness, and a custodial sentence being the only alternative. Schemes have been asked to profile those young people who were eligible for the six-month ISSP but were turned down by courts or the scheme, or who committed a breach and were sent to custody.

Further reading

Moore, R. Gray, R., Roberts, E., Merrington, C., Waters, S., Fernandez, I., Hayward, R. G. and Rogers, R. (2004) *ISSP: The Initial Report*. London: Youth Justice Board.

Moore, R. (2004) 'Intensive supervision and surveillance programmes for young offenders: the evidence base so far,' in R. Burnett and C. Roberts (eds) *What Works in Probation and Youth Justice: Developing Evidence-Based Practice*. Cullompton: Willan Publishing.

12

Custody and resettlement

This chapter mainly focuses on resettlement in its own right, although it begins with a brief consideration of custody as a response to young people who have offended. The issue of custody raises some important questions in relation to evidence-based and effective practice as reconviction rates for young people who have experienced a custodial intervention are high. With regard to resettlement, it explores some of the models that have been proposed, all of which stress the importance of continuity of care, smooth transitions between custodial and community-based interventions and maintenance of strong links between a young person and their communities while they are removed from them. It also highlights the consistent failure as shown by evaluation of achieving such continuity through the fracturing that continues to occur for young people when they enter and leave custodial establishments and/or are moved between them.

Custody

Custody occupies a particular and highly political place in the youth justice system and its attraction for the public may be little influenced by discussions of effectiveness. Judging effectiveness is also complicated by the range of outcomes that custody is expected to achieve: 'for those whose offending is serious or persistent, custody may, however, be the only way of protecting the public from further offending. It may be the best way of bringing home to the young person the seriousness of his or her behaviour and the best way of preventing the young person from continuing to offend. Placing a young person in a secure environment that provides discipline, structure, education and training, as well as programmes to tackle offending behaviour, may provide a vital opportunity for the young person to break out of a pattern of offending and regain control of his or her behaviour' (Home Office 1998, paragraph 9). This list of intended outcomes has a notable omission – punishment.

There are generally four justifications for the use of custody for young people: incapacitation, deterrence, rehabilitation and punishment. There is little convincing evidence to support all or any of these justifications. In relation to the American evidence Howell (2003: 134) concluded that: 'large, congregate, custodial juvenile corrections facilities are not effective in rehabilitating juvenile offenders ... Post release recidivism rates for correctional populations range from about 55 per cent to 90 per cent and prior placement in a juvenile correctional facility is one of the strongest predictors of returning. It is clear that housing juvenile offenders in large reformatories is not an effective way to prevent or reduce juvenile offending.'

Reconviction rates for young people from England and Wales leaving custody Home Office statistics indicate that 78 per cent of young people discharged from custody in the first quarter of 2004 reoffended within a year (cited by Fayle 2007). A Youth Justice Board study showed that 27 per cent had offended in the first month of release (ECOTEC 2001b). There is emerging evidence to suggest that higher reconviction rates are associated with younger children. A third of the children aged 12 to 14 leaving Medway STC in 1998/1999 were reported by their supervising officers to have committed criminal offences leading to rearrest within a month of release, and 67 per cent were said to have committed offences before the expiry of their sentence (Hagell et al. 2000).

Incapacitation is effective in the sense that it prevents the young person from committing crime in their communities while they are detained in custody. In relation to a dangerous individual there is certainly a high degree of effectiveness at least in the short term. Where the argument weakens is that to have an effect on offending of even a few per cent would necessitate locking up very large numbers of young people (Greenwood et al. 1994; Tarling 1993). Even at the level of the individual there may be intrinsic aspects of custody that increase risks of reoffending.

Deterrent effects appear to be weak at both general and individual levels given the relatively low chances of detection. Experience of custody might even lead some young people to regard it as a badge of honour (Hagell 2005). While punishment has a powerful resonance with the public and incarceration is seen as valuable in achieving this, studies suggest that such an approach is likely not only to be ineffective but may be counter-productive (Lipsey 1995; Goldson and Peters 2000).

Rehabilitation in the sense of improved behaviour and attitudes may occur within a custodial institution but there is limited evidence of their continuation upon release into the community (Hagell et al. 2000; Hobbs and Hook 2001; ECOTEC 2001a).

The secure estate for young people comprises three different types of institution – YOIs, STCs and LASCHs and their relative effectiveness may vary. There has been some systematic comparison work carried out for institutions providing custody for young people who offend. One such study compared the reconviction outcomes for young people who had committed grave crimes and who were accommodated in YOIs compared to LASCHs. The main differences between the approaches of the two types of institution were that the LASCHs ensured stronger ties with the families (39 per cent received family visits at least three times a month compared with 1 per cent of those in YOIs), more contact with the external community (over two thirds of those in the LASCHs had weekly trips away from the institution compared to 1 per cent of those in YOI) and a wider range and higher volume of education and training. The emphasis on education was highlighted by the fact that a much higher proportion attained educational qualifications in the LASCHs.

Reconviction rates were significantly higher after two years for those leaving YOIs (53 per cent) compared to those leaving the LASCHs (40 per cent); there was also a much higher incidence of reconviction for violent offences for those in YOIs. While these young people form a small minority of even the custodial population, let alone the wider population of young people who offend, these findings do suggest that an approach that maintains ties with family, community and education and training can have a positive effect on later outcomes (Ditchfield and Catan 1992).

Removing young people by force or circumstance from their immediate communities appears to have a significant negative impact on young people's education, training and employment prospects. Custody means that the most delinquent and damaged peer groups live together. Institutional life may lessen the resilience of a young person by weakening or preventing the growth of those protective factors that enable some young people to surmount adversities that defeat others. The stifling of autonomy in custodial institutions could have such an effect.

Custody appears to have three innate weaknesses that weaken protective factors and increase risks. First, it curtails decision-making and planning skills in those who require them the most. Second, learning is provided in such an abnormal environment that the subsequent application of this learning in the community is extremely limited. This has long been recognised. The Reverend J. Turner, who established the Philanthropic Society, in his evidence to the parliamentary committee in 1850 asserted that 'the best prisoner makes the worst free boy ... because he has been so accustomed to depend upon the mere mechanical arrangements about him, that he finds self-action almost impossible' (Carpenter 1968: 339). Finally, by removing young people who have only a tenuous attachment to formal education (even if only a PRU with part-time provision), further dislocation is caused for a young person, their parents/carers and the relevant professionals.

While custody cannot be deemed effective and is probably in many cases ineffective in promoting desistance from offending, this does not mean that its negative aspects cannot to an extent be ameliorated by practitioners. The evidence suggests that placements in smaller establishments, maintaining links with significant adults in the community, full-time high-quality education and training that links to their reintegration in the community, assistance with resisting drugs and an overall pro-social ethos may in some cases limit the negative effects (Ditchfield and Catan 1992; Hazel *et al.* 2002).

What is unclear is whether it is custody itself that impacts so negatively with regard to recidivism and other outcomes for individual young people or whether it is the fractured structures and systems that characterise the operation of custodial regimes that are to blame. Stephenson (2007) has identified a number of significant institutional issues relating to the operation of secure facilities themselves and weaknesses of multi-agency working, including:

- weak case management and supervision structures;
- the lack of integration between separate planning systems and the wider sentence planning process coupled with the poor transmission of key information relating to need and progress made by young people between custodial and community providers;
- difficulties in establishing stable learning groups within custodial establishments due to population churn resulting from a large number of short sentences and the transfer of young people between establishments;
- the high turnover rate of staff working in custodial establishments;
- lack of continuity between custodial-based services and those provided (if at all) in the community;
- overcrowding in large secure establishments has also been shown to have a deleterious effect on recidivism. The impact of large numbers of young people in confined spaces coupled with low staffing levels is likely to result in an overemphasis on regime security and the greater use of punitive sanctions, overriding the effective delivery of services (Howell 2003). The net result of this is to make regimes more akin to boot camps, shown in research to have no impact on recidivism (Lipsey *et al.* 2000; ECOTEC 2001a; Howell 2003).

The evidence base for resettlement

'Resettlement' is the term currently used within youth justice to describe the process relating to young people who have been held in custody and who will be returning to the community. Nearly three quarters of young people in custody at any one time are those on DTOs, where half their sentence is served in a YOI, STC or LASCH, and the other half is served in the community. The remainder of the sentenced population are serving sentences for 'grave crimes' under Section 90 or 91 of the Powers of Criminal Courts (Sentencing) Act 2000.

At any one time, about 3,100 young people are held in the juvenile secure estate and around 175 of these are young women. About 16 per cent of this total population are on remand, with the remainder serving sentences.

In any one year an annual throughput of approximately 6,500 young people sentenced to a DTO enter (and leave) the juvenile secure estate. And while approximately 1,900 young people are serving the custodial part of a DTO at any one time, the same number of young people is serving the second part of their sentence in the community. This makes a total of nearly 4,000 young people requiring supervision at any point in time.

The majority of young people serving DTOs are aged 16 or 17. Around 78 per cent are above the statutory school-leaving age. The majority are white (around 80 per cent). Certain ethnic groups though are overrepresented in the custodial population, in particular young black men (8 per cent compared with 2 per cent of the population nationally) and those of dual heritage (5 per cent compared with 1.2 per cent of the population) (ECOTEC 2001b).

What the available research tells us about the profile of these young people indicates that they are highly likely to:

- have received little or no education or training for some time prior to their admission to custody. The *Review of the Pre- and Post-custodial Education and Training Experiences of Young People* (ECOTEC 2001b) showed that between a quarter and a third of young people had no education or training available to them immediately prior to release;

- have low levels of literacy and numeracy: nearly half of young people in custody have literacy and numeracy levels below those expected nationally of an 11-year-old; over a quarter have literacy and numeracy levels at or below what is expected nationally of a 7-year-old (ECOTEC 2001b);

- have some kind of special educational need. Figures from *Asset* suggest this might be around 35 per cent, although this is likely to be an underestimate given the numbers of young people who have not been accessing any formal education prior to custody;

- experience some kind of mental health difficulty. The Office for National Statistics (1997) reported that two fifths of sentenced young men and two thirds of sentenced young women had symptoms of anxiety, depression, fatigue and/or concentration problems, compared with one tenth of young people in the population generally; between 46 per cent and 81 per cent had mental health problems; and 10 per cent exhibited signs of psychotic illness;

- experience issues related to substance misuse. A Youth Justice Board commissioned study of the substance use of young people subject to custodial sentences in the juvenile secure estate (2004h) showed that by the age of 15, 76 per cent had become regular smokers (nearly 3.5 times the national average according to the Department of Health), 74 per cent had drunk alcohol more than once a week, 72 per cent had used cannabis on a daily basis in the 12 months before their arrest, 26 per cent had used ecstasy more than a few times a week, and 10 per cent had used heroin on a daily basis;

- come from chaotic and disrupted family backgrounds. Various studies have found that: two out of five young women and one in four young men report having suffered violence at home; one in three young women and one in 20 young men report sexual abuse; 17 per cent are on the child protection register; 41 per cent have been in the care of the local authority at some point in their lives, with a significant proportion of these still being looked after at the point of sentence (Hazel *et al.* 2002).

Definitions of resettlement

Resettlement is a relatively new term for processes that have historically been referred to as 'aftercare' (also used widely in the USA, though lately superseded by 're-entry') and 'throughcare' (current until the late 1990s). 'Throughcare' refers to a single rehabilitative process, which starts with sentence planning and continues into the community: the 'seamless approach' as envisaged in the 1991 Criminal Justice Act (Raynor 2004b). 'Aftercare' implies that the process is only relevant once a young person has been released into the community (Gies 2003).

The term 'resettlement' was introduced by the Home Office in 1998 as an alternative to the use of 'throughcare'. The change in terminology was justified on the basis that throughcare was a term 'unlikely to be properly understood outside of prison and probation worlds', and that 'public and sentencer confidence would be enhanced if the focus was on the ultimate goals of "throughcare" – high-quality sentence planning and successful resettlement in the community' (Home Office, 1998). In this sense, resettlement refers to the outcomes of a throughcare process.

Raynor (2004b) points out that some possible concepts of resettlement may be contradictory. For example, does resettlement mean:

- restoration to a condition and social environment roughly corresponding to that existing before imprisonment (in which case, is this the correct term when so many young people who enter custody have been living in conditions that could hardly be described as 'settled')?

- attempted establishment of a basic adequate standard of living and opportunity, which may not have been experienced before?

- re-establishment of social contacts, links or relationships with family/carers and/or peers?

- establishment of new links and connections with pro-social influences and resources?

- action to identify and address defined needs?

In addition, resettlement as defined in national policy terms may be largely an adult concept, which makes generalisation to the juvenile context difficult. The state has additional responsibilities for young people (particularly those below statutory school-leaving age) in terms of providing education, and for those young people who are looked after. This also means that the support provided for young people in custody carries similar obligations to those that exist in the care system. The sentencing framework is also different for juveniles.

In some respects, resettlement can also be seen as an umbrella term for a range of interventions and approaches, which are subsumed within other areas of practice, such as mental health, substance misuse and education, training and employment. Constructing effective resettlement programmes for young people therefore requires practitioners to consider the range of other areas of practice in developing interventions based on the best evidence of promising approaches.

Dimensions and models of resettlement

Raynor (2004b) defines the difficulties for people experiencing custody for relatively short periods of time as falling into two categories:

1 Access to opportunities and resources;

2 Individuals' attitudes, beliefs and habitual responses.

These categories are not distinct and they may interact to reinforce each other in complex ways. For example, practical or situational difficulties in accessing services (for example education, training, accommodation or substance misuse services) may lead to negative emotions such as anger or depression, and difficulties in seeing ways of dealing with the problem other than by offending (Zambe and Quinsey 1997, cited by Raynor 2004b).

It could also be argued that assumptions about young people's offending lie along a continuum of responsibility on the part of the young person, with young people assuming they are victims of circumstance at one end of the continuum, and exercising choice about how they respond to circumstances at the other (Raynor 2004b).

Raynor also defines the relevant methods or approaches that are likely to be most appropriate at either end of the spectrum in terms of intervention. Advice, support, sympathy, advocacy and referral are linked to those with no confidence in their capacity to initiate change and cognitive challenge, and motivational and pro-social input for those with high levels of self-efficacy. A combination of these methods leads to effective programme design for resettlement. The implication is that services address not only the difficulties relating to the situations that young people experience, but also young people's personal resources, strategies and motivations for responding to these difficulties.

This view is borne out by research related to youth transitions more generally. Coles (2000) suggests that the development of a youth transition model should include balancing 'the two sides of the careers equation'. On one side, this equation has young people's behaviour and the decisions they make. On the other side, it has the decisions made by those in social and statutory institutions and agencies which impact on young people's lives. This equation is linked to the concept of providing young people with more control over decision-making. One of the key challenges with regard to custody is its capacity to remove the need for independent decision-making by young people.

A core principle underpinning most resettlement models is the dimension of continuity ('continuity of care' in the USA). The whole DTO structure and the Youth Justice Board's *Framework for Action for Youth Resettlement* (2005g) are based on the principle that a seamless approach to resettlement is likely to yield better outcomes. It should be noted, however, that there is no real evidence for these models that can be shown from research or evaluation of specific resettlement programmes.

The concept of continuity is deceptively simple and appears very hard to achieve in reality. This is because the context of resettlement necessarily implies time spent in two different places, with one (custody) often providing a fundamentally different social environment, level of control and range of services and programmes to that experienced in the community. The difficulty is compounded by the lack of continuity when young people are moved between custodial establishments.

Much of the work relating to aftercare in the USA has focused on developing a model based on the broad principles of effective practice emphasising the importance of:

- assessment and planning from the earliest stages;

- custodial programmes that focus on developing skills that will have application in the community;

- community programmes that build on the work done in the custodial phase;

- an overarching case management system providing direct supervision and brokering access to relevant services.

The Intensive Aftercare Programme (IAP) model is theory-driven, risk- and needs assessment-based and empirically grounded (Altschuler and Armstrong 1994a, 1994b; Altschuler *et al.* 1999; Gies 2003). It proposes an intensive, fully integrated mix of support for young people at 'high risk' of reoffending, with an overarching case management process incorporating:

- substantial control over young people once they are released to the community;

- enhanced service delivery that focuses on recognised risk and protective factors.

The principles for programme design underpinning the IAP model are based on the best evidence of emerging effectiveness in terms of preventing offending:

- preparing young people for progressively increased responsibility and freedom in the community;
- facilitating involvement and interaction between young people and their communities;
- working with young people and targeted community support systems (families, peers, schools, colleges, employers) on the qualities needed by all for constructive interactions that advance young people's integration into the community;
- developing new resources, support services and opportunities as required;
- monitoring and testing young people's capacity to receive (and the community's capacity to provide) services and support.

> The intent is to have community-based aftercare services parallel those that are first initiated in the institution, and institutional services geared to achieve essentially the same purposes as those that will be achieved in the community (Altschuler *et al.* 1999)

Clearly, there are similarities here with the principles applied to interventions for young people at serious risk of offending or reoffending in England and Wales. The DTO as a framework for resettlement, for example, emphasises the significance of a supported transition through consistent case management by a Yot practitioner from the pre-sentence stage through to the end of the sentence.

Based on continuity of care and some features of the IAP model, Rees and Conalty (2004) have defined a four-phase approach, which reflects the DTO framework. In this approach, a comprehensive resettlement process begins at the pre-sentence stage, continues through the defined custodial and community phases of the sentence, and carries on beyond the end of the sentence. The four-phase model emphasises the point that there is no real end to resettlement, and that being genuinely 'settled' is a longer-term process than relatively short sentences allow for. This approach also emphasises the importance of the intensity and quality of case management by the Yot supervising officer in ensuring continuity across the phases.

Current resettlement models are underpinned by three straightforward principles:

1 All plans for resettlement should be based on a rigorous assessment of individual risk and need.

2 Planning for resettlement should begin at the earliest opportunity (pre-sentence).

3 Seamless provision of services (education, health, etc.) across the custodial and community phases should be supported by the timely transmission of information to ensure that continuity of approach, content and materials is maintained.

The research and resettlement

One difficulty in defining what is effective in relation to resettlement is that there is little in the way of specific programme evaluation (Howell 2003). Attempts at evaluating the models proposed above have been undermined by a range of issues largely relating to maintaining programme integrity. What little research exists focuses solely on custodial interventions, is based on outcomes for adults rather than young people, or is methodologically flawed (Altschuler and Armstrong 2002; Howell 2003).

Research which focuses only on custodial interventions often overemphasises the positive change in young people's attitudes within institutions without considering the impact on recidivism in the community (Hobbs and Hook Consulting 2001). Furthermore, research looking at resettlement processes is often bedevilled by issues relating to research methodology (small sample sizes and poorly matched control groups, for example) and/or focuses on programmes that are poorly designed or not implemented faithfully according to their principles:

> Flawed implementation is a substantial limitation, because, from an evidence-based and research-driven perspective, it is only when continuity of care is reflected in practice ... that it becomes possible to determine whether and in what ways continuity of care contributes to success. (Altschuler and Armstrong 2002)

For example, recent interim evaluation of the IAP programme in the USA has shown less than promising results in relation to recidivism (Weibush 2001, cited by Howell 2003). But the significance of this finding is called into question because sample sizes were small and the control group at one of the sites received some aspects of the intervention which should have been received only by the treatment group.

One aftercare programme in the US has produced positive short-term effects (Josi and Sechrest 1999, cited by Howell 2003). The Lifeskills '95 programme was designed to reinforce progress made while helping young people to confront the fears of the communities to which they were returning. The programme was based on six principles:

1 Improving the social skills necessary for successful reintegration;

2 Reducing criminal activity, in terms of both amount and severity;

3 Reducing the need for, or dependence on, drugs and alcohol;

4 Improving lifestyle choices (e.g. social, and education, training and employment);

5 Reducing the need for participation in delinquent peer groups and gangs as a support mechanism;

6 Reducing the rate of short-term reconvictions.

Researchers found that individuals assigned to the control group were twice as likely as those in the experimental group to have been arrested, to be unemployed, to find it difficult to gain and maintain employment, and to have abused drugs and alcohol frequently after release.

It should be noted that much of the available evaluation and research specifically related to juveniles comes from the US. The extent to which this can be applied to young people in England and Wales, where the social and legal context is different, should be considered. Research conducted in this country, largely driven by the Youth Justice Board, has focused on implementation of the DTO (Hagell *et al.* 2000; Hazel *et al.* 2002; ECOTEC 2001a and 2001b; Youth Justice Board, 2002b, 2003e, 2003f, 2004f, 2004g, 2005f). Whether concentrating on education, training and employment or on substance misuse, this research describes a system that is fractured and beleaguered by difficulties in inter-agency co-operation, leading to a breakdown of continuity between community and custodial-based services.

In many respects, more is known about what does not appear to be effective in this country with regard to resettlement than about what is effective. Examples include the poor transmission of information between establishments and from custody to the community, and the associated failure to provide continuity of approaches, materials and courses across key transition points.

Given the paucity of positive evidence of effectiveness in relation to resettlement from custody, the most helpful approach for devising programmes is likely to be through extracting principles and guidelines for effective interventions as revealed by meta-analysis (Howell 2003; McGuire 1995).

Lipsey and Wilson (1998) conducted a systematic review of the evidence for effective intervention with young people whose offending behaviour was deemed to be serious. They reviewed around 200 studies relating mostly to young men aged between 14 and 17, and looked at the evidence in relation to non-institutionalised and institutionalised young people. A summary of their findings on the most and least effective types of treatment is given in Table 12.1.

Table 12.1 Summary of the most and least effective types of treatment regarding recidivism rates

Types of treatment used with non-institutionalised* young people	Types of treatment used with institutionalised** young people
Positive effects, consistent evidence	
Individual counselling	Interpersonal skills
Interpersonal skills	Teaching in family homes
Positive effects, less consistent evidence	
Multiple services	Behavioural programmes
Restitution, probation/parole	Community residential
	Multiple services
Mixed but generally positive effects, inconsistent evidence	
Employment related	Individual counselling
Academic programmes	Guided group counselling
Advocacy/casework	Group counselling
Family counselling	
Group counselling	
Weak or no effects, inconsistent evidence	
Reduced caseload, probation/parole	Employment related
	Drug abstinence
	Wilderness/challenge
Weak or no effects, consistent evidence	
Wilderness/challenge	Milieu therapy
Early release, probation/parole	
Deterrence programmes	
Vocational programmes	

*'Non-institutionalised young people' refers to young people under the authority of the juvenile justice system at the time of treatment, supervised through probation.
**'Institutionalised young people' refers to those in custody at the time of treatment. Of the studies focusing on institutionalised young people, 74 related to juvenile justice institutions and the other nine to residential facilities under private or mental health administration.

Lipsey and Wilson (1998) went on to draw separate conclusions about the effectiveness of interventions with both groups of young people. With regard to institutionalised young people, effectiveness was increased if interventions were of longer duration, if the level of monitoring was high, or if the programme was well established. The duration factor was also important for non-institutionalised young people, but interventions were more effective with fewer contact hours.

Lipsey and Wilson also found that for non-institutionalised young people the programme's characteristics were less important than offence-related characteristics, especially previous offences. The opposite effect was the case for institutionalised young people, with programme type and length being particularly important. For the institutionalised young people, offence-related characteristics appeared insignificant.

While there is still a gap between research and practice in relation to promising approaches in resettlement, it should be possible, by applying the principles of effective practice, to improve the outcomes for young people who are subject to custodial sentences.

The principles of effective practice and resettlement

Risk classification

Young people with experience of custody are likely to be the most at risk of reoffending. This is because they are often the most detached from education, training and employment, and are more likely to misuse drugs and alcohol and have mental health issues, which are all known risk factors.

Enhanced risk might be where:

- a young person is returning to changed, less stable or no accommodation; one study has shown that 30 per cent of young people had a different place of accommodation on release than they had before entering custody (ECOTEC 2001b);

- a school has taken the young person off its roll and there is no mainstream, full-time equivalent placement arranged immediately on return to the community;

- the young person is pessimistic about his/her chances of not reoffending.

The last of these may be a particular issue for young people suffering from depression or other mental health issues, which may have been exacerbated by the experience of custody.

It is also likely that risk factors may change over the course of a sentence. For example, a young person's participation in a substance misuse programme in custody may have reduced the risk this represented at the start of the sentence. If no support is available to continue this work or help the young person to transfer positive learning to their community setting, the risk factor remains. Indeed, the risk may be increased in some cases as a result of disappointment or a sense of frustration on the part of the young person when that support is removed abruptly or without warning.

The pre-sentence stage can supply important information about what young people need in an appropriate intervention to reduce the risk of reoffending. Pre-sentence reports should specify the elements of a programme's design that reflect the young person's risk factors, without necessarily assuming that custody will be the outcome of sentencing. This can also provide a useful starting point for practitioners in secure establishments in terms of:

- providing custody-based interventions that emulate as far as possible what happens in the community relevant to individual young people;
- ensuring that young people develop the specific skills they will need in order to gain access, participate and make progress when they return to their communities.

Criminogenic need

In working with young people who have multiple barriers to effective participation, and are high-risk in relation to offending behaviour, there may be a danger of developing programmes that try to tackle all their difficulties, regardless of how salient they are to the risk of reoffending. This may lead to a confused programme of support that is unfocused and lacks a clear sense of priority.

This may be a particular issue in relation to short sentences where decisions have to be made about what can be done within the time available, focusing on those risks that are most salient and susceptible to being changed. This should not though be a justification for not providing the appropriate volume of learning and skills for young people, particularly those on short sentences. Detachment from the learning process has been identified as one of the most significant risk factors for offending behaviour (Communities that Care 2001). This suggests that the immediate provision of appropriate education, training and employment should always remain a priority.

The Yot supervising officer (as the case manager) also has a duty to ensure that referrals are made to appropriate agencies and follow-up action is monitored if young people have needs that are not currently being met, but are not necessarily criminogenic in nature.

Providing relevant assessments is important for planning and delivering appropriate interventions. Young people experiencing custody are often subjected to multiple and often repeat assessments as they move between custody and community and between different custodial establishments. This would suggest that all assessment information should travel with young people when they make such transitions.

Also significant are the records of action taken in starting the resettlement process, and progress made to date. If continuity of care is to be achieved, these records would seem to be key in terms of a young person's progression over the course of his/her sentence, and as a tool for disseminating information to the various agencies and service providers who work with young people in the community. These include Connexions/Careers Wales, drug action teams, LEAs, schools, colleges, training providers, accommodation services, leaving care teams, social services and health services.

Community based

Current evidence suggests that programmes in the community have more effective outcomes than those in custody or other segregated settings. The reason for this is probably that the learning is more likely to occur in a context that is meaningful to the young person and can be readily transferred to his/her everyday experiences. The implication for practice is that approaches which emulate certain features of community orders may make for a more successful custodial experience in terms of changing behaviours (Tolbert 2002).

One of the practical implications of the community-based principle might be that secure establishments and Yots should look for opportunities to provide Release on Temporary Licence (RoTL). Visits to arrange housing can be particularly useful in preparing for release. Similarly, home visits to the actual or potential host education institution have proved effective in securing immediate placements post-custody and smoothing the transition to the community.

Benefits may also be accrued from RoTL in terms of fostering greater independence and graduated autonomy. For example, the use of town visits local to the establishment to practise life skills such as shopping, engaging in leisure activities, and using community facilities, could help to reinforce skills and minimise the shock of returning to relative freedom in the community.

In addition to RoTL, wider use of video-conferencing could serve to bring young people closer to their communities. Yots and secure establishments can, for example, use video-conferencing to hold case meetings at a distance involving the Yot supervising manager, other key agency representatives from the community base and parents/carers.

While the family circumstances of young people subject to custodial sentences may be difficult in many ways, parents/carers (and other family members and significant others) also provide a bridge to the community. Parental involvement in planning and review meetings, from pre-sentence through to the end of the sentence, may provide an important forum for understanding what the young person is trying to achieve. It could indicate to parents/carers what kind of support they might provide in order to facilitate positive change.

A number of young people in custody will be parents themselves. Maintaining links between young parents and their children might also be considered, both to help the young people in custody to maintain ties, where this is appropriate, and for the sake of their children.

Intervention modality

It is likely that programmes for working with young people at risk of offending are most promising when skills-based, and when they emphasise problem-solving within a cognitive-behavioural framework. In relation to resettlement, this would indicate that whatever methods are used reflect community-based situations. Those that focus solely on behaviours that enable young people to cope within a secure environment are unlikely to have relevance when a young person returns to his/her community.

Young people who end up in custody are likely to have complex, multiple needs that place them at risk of further offending. Programmes to meet those needs will usually comprise a range of different and often complex interventions: education and training, offence-related work, health care, and work with parents/carers, families and peer groups, for example.

The implication of this would seem to be that resettlement programmes need to comprise a degree of direct input by youth justice practitioners and, particularly in the community phase of the sentence, services brokered from a range of providers and other agencies. As with any complex multi-modal intervention, the intensity and quality of consistent case management (the responsibility of the Yot supervising officer) would seem to be key to ensuring continuity of care.

It is important not to prolong a young person's connection with the Yot unnecessarily. However, support is likely to be needed beyond the end of the statutory sentence. Connexions in England and Careers Wales might have a role to play in this respect.

While the networks required are inevitably complex, it would seem important that these are drawn up and understood between staff in custody, Yots and other agencies/service providers.

It is possible that there may be a level of resistance from some service providers and employers to engaging with young people returning from custody. It may therefore be important for the Yot supervising officer to establish good relationships with existing service providers and develop new ones with those prepared to work with this group of young people. Practitioners may need to beware of relying entirely on those service providers and agencies that work exclusively with groups on the margins. This may simply result in replicating the deviant and delinquent peer groups that place young people at further risk.

Although service provision is fundamentally important, so is preparation of the young person's immediate community, parents/carers and peers. Everyone involved with the young person has the potential to encourage and reinforce pro-social behaviour. Research on risk factors shows that family, peers and social networks may not be in a position to provide this support without specific input to improve the situation and strengthen their capacity to provide support.

Responsivity

While there does not appear to be sufficient evidence to support the notion that all young people at risk of offending/reoffending are 'active' learners, the focus instead could be on helping young people develop a range of strategies for managing their lives, particularly important when considering the structure of the DTO. This implies that work done while in custody might focus less on giving young people practical 'things to do' and more on helping them develop a broader range of strategies for managing tasks and solving problems.

Young people who have had negative experiences of the education system may have developed a range of inappropriate responses to certain situations in which they are asked to undertake new challenges and take risks. In addition, the custodial context is likely to create more situations in which young people feel exposed in front of their peers. They may also have developed a range of strategies for avoiding tasks, and/or a number of useful strategies that have only been employed in the exercise of antisocial behaviours. Young people are unlikely to see the transferability of these strategies to more pro-social activities, such as work, learning and community life generally.

In relation to resettlement, it is likely to be important then that the learning strategies young people develop while in custody are those that will help them to function more effectively in the community. If new strategies learned in the context of a secure setting only have meaning in relation to surviving in a custodial environment, they may not easily survive transfer to the community (Stephenson 2000). To this end, information on learning strategies should be passed between key agencies and service providers so that these strategies can be enhanced and developed further in the new context. Integration of the individual learning plan with the sentence plan may be critical in this respect. It could also be important in terms of ensuring that all those who deliver programmes (including health, offence-related and other programmes) understand the implications for the work they carry out with young people.

Dosage

It appears that the most promising programmes for young people who are most at risk of offending provide larger amounts of meaningful contact over longer periods (Lipsey and Wilson 1998). This suggests that frequent, high-quality interaction between practitioners and young people, both in custody and in the community, is more likely to ensure successful resettlement.

The dosage is specified in terms of educational programmes: 30 hours per week in custody and 25 hours per week in the community. However, this intensity of provision relies on planning being started very quickly on entry to custody, both for the custodial-based component and in arranging provision to be available immediately on release.

It should be noted that levels of effectiveness relate to what provision is *received* by a young person, not just what is *arranged*. The evaluation of Youth Justice Board funded ETE interventions showed a direct correlation between attendance and lower offending rates (Youth Justice Board 2003g). Evidence from schools shows that a same-day response to absence has proved effective in preventing further non-attendance (DfEE 1995). While most of the evidence relates to education and training, it has implications for attendance and punctuality in any element of a resettlement programme, for example offence-related and substance misuse work. A prompt response to non-attendance or poor punctuality implies the need for:

- clearly defined procedures for monitoring attendance and punctuality in all programme elements and across all phases of the sentence;

- tight, supportive supervision, particularly in the community phase of the sentence;

- clear lines of communication among relevant staff members;

- the support of parents/carers in encouraging regular attendance and punctuality;

- discussion about attendance and punctuality at all review meetings.

Close monitoring of young people once they return to their communities is likely to be a critical factor in the success of programmes, for example monitoring their attendance at school/college and ensuring that they are attending appointments.

Evidence shows that overreliance on surveillance in the absence of other programme components is likely to be ineffective (Raynor 2004a). In addition, technology (such as tagging) used in the surveillance of young people in the community may reduce the amount of active involvement of Yot supervising officers and other practitioners with young people and their parents/carers which, in turn, may compromise the outcomes of the intervention with regard to repeat offending (Altschuler and Armstrong 1994b).

Programme integrity

Critiques of recent and past intervention programmes for young people at risk of offending have repeatedly commented on the uneven and poor quality of implementation, the ambiguity or absence of a theoretical rationale and conceptual base, and flawed evaluations. This is an even greater problem when programmes are complex, and the more components they comprise, as is inevitably the case with resettlement programmes.

The lack of a clear rationale makes it likely that a programme will become a disconnected set of activities, with problems such as:

- services provided, sanctions and incentives used, and community resources and social networks tapped, are determined in an *ad hoc* and fragmented fashion;

- individual staff pursue their own direction and inclinations;

- target-group criteria, referrals and selection are not matched to the most appropriate programme or person;

- a lack of coherence and continuity between programme components, features and processes;

- young people's major difficulties or needs are not met, leaving gaps in service or wasted opportunities.

When case-managing complex resettlement programmes, therefore, the challenge for Yot supervising officers is to ensure that all stakeholders are clear about the programme's overall rationale and their role/responsibility within it, and that they are implementing the programme in ways which are faithful to the overall design. The full range of stakeholders includes the young people themselves, their parents/carers, teachers, health workers and Connexions/Careers Wales advisers.

As recidivism rates for young people who have experienced custody are so high, it is vital for managers and strategic partnerships to monitor and evaluate the elements of programme design that contribute to positive outcomes at the four stages of implementation:

1 Pre-sentence;

2 Custody under sentence;

3 Community under sentence;

4 Community post-sentence.

Evaluation of a resettlement programme requires objective data collection and analysis of the type of young people, the nature and amount of intervention and supervision, and how the programme is implemented and with what input. Specifically, this entails systems for collecting data on outcomes for young people reintegrating from custody, and for documenting the processes involved in providing the resettlement programme, within three broad areas:

1 The extent to which programme elements, services and activities provided, and the population served, reflect the philosophy and principles of effective practice;

2 The quality and nature of implementation, including:
   - staffing policies, patterns, roles and responsibilities;
   - management structure and lines of authority;
   - incorporation of services into programme components, features and processes;

- the number and type of young people being resettled;
- the services they receive, and from whom;
- the length of services and their results;

3 The problems, obstacles and difficulties encountered, for example:
   - funding and community resources;
   - co-operation from secure establishments, magistrates and other public and private agencies;
   - community relations.

The challenges for practice

A conceptual difficulty for staff working in the youth justice system, particularly in the juvenile secure estate, is that custody appears to weaken protective factors and increase risk factors in relation to offending behaviour (Stephenson 2007). In this respect, preventing young people from entering custody in the first place may be the most effective in terms of preventing further offending.

Furthermore, the experience of custody means that young people are forced to live, learn and socialise entirely with a peer group whose common characteristic is their offending behaviour, which is another well-attested risk factor (Communities that Care 2001).

For some young people, incarceration may be another stage in what Fleisher (1995, cited in Howell 2003) calls the 'street life cycle', where custody represents a safe haven from the chaos of young people's lives and the pull toward antisocial behaviours exerted by their communities. Custody may provide not only a safe haven for some young people, but also a highly structured environment where there is limited choice and which is governed by strict rules and relatively simplistic systems of reward and sanction, again in contrast to their experiences in their communities.

But custody also has an immediate labelling effect, branding a young person in the eyes of the public, professionals and employers as not only an 'offender', but a 'dangerous' one at that. Ironically, this in itself is likely to present a further barrier to maximising mainstream opportunities (school, college, employment, housing) in addition to any other barriers experienced by the young person prior to custody.

These difficulties may be further compounded by institutional issues relating to the operation of secure facilities and the failure of multi-agency working, including the following:

● weak case-management and supervision structures. Support from the Yot supervising officer appears to drop off while the young person is in custody, and planning for release happens too late and too slowly;

- lack of integration between separate planning systems and the wider sentence planning process, coupled with poor transmission of key information (on young people's needs and progress made) between custodial establishment and the community;

- difficulties in establishing stable learning groups within secure establishments because of population turnover resulting from a large number of short sentences and the transfer of young people between establishments;

- the high turnover rate of staff working in secure establishments;

- lack of continuity between custodial-based services and those provided (if at all) in the community;

- community-based services shutting down for some young people while they are in custody, making seamless reintegration when they return to their communities that much harder.

The geographical distance between young people in secure establishments and their home communities is another significant barrier to resettlement. As there are relatively few secure establishments for juveniles, this means that young people are often placed far from home, which reduces the capacity for contact with family members and carers. Research from social care indicates that where looked-after young people lack positive family support, they are more likely to have poor post-care outcomes and experience greater difficulty in making and sustaining relationships with others (Biehal *et al.* 1995, cited in DoH 2003). The same is also likely to be the case for young people who are removed very suddenly from their communities and then return fairly abruptly with little interim support or contact.

Geographical distance also appears to exacerbate difficulties of communication between Yots and secure establishments. Practitioners continue to highlight this issue as a barrier to effective case management and co-operative working to ensure seamless resettlement from custody (Youth Justice Board 2004g).

It is generally argued that programmes delivered in the community are more likely to be effective. The legitimacy of this argument may need testing by further research, particularly if programme integrity is so threatened by the organisational and structural weaknesses of custodial care identified above. Sanctions such as the loss of liberty provide only the context for service delivery; it is the intervention within that setting that may have the capacity to initiate change in young people.

In many respects, resettlement from custody resembles the experience of young people leaving care. The evidence suggests that looked-after young people make better educational progress, for instance, if they have had relatively stable care careers and pro-active support from carers, social workers and teachers (Biehal *et al.* 1995, cited in DoH 2003). There appears to be a tendency for support from these sources to fall away soon after a young person leaves care. This experience seems to mirror that of most young people subject to DTOs, where the level of support provided when they leave custody diminishes considerably and very suddenly.

In addition, the complete withdrawal of support at the end of the sentence when the statutory component has been fulfilled may be too sudden and too soon to enable young people to sustain any positive progress. The post-sentence support needs of young people should be considered carefully; the involvement of agencies such as Connexions/Young People's Partnerships (Wales) is key to this.

Young people's perceptions

The full participation of young people and their parents/carers is seen as vital for effective resettlement. It is also generally accepted that the process of resettlement should be 'seamless', with continuity of approaches and services between custody and the community across all specific elements of a programme. This concept of 'seamlessness' may not accord with young people's perceptions. The contrast between custody and their community lives is inevitably very stark and the capacity of young people to perceive seamlessness therefore may be very limited in this context.

The concept of a 'resettlement programme' may also have limited currency in young people's eyes. It may require the knowledge and skill of relevant professionals (particularly the case manager based in the home Yot) and other supportive adults or peers to help young people to make the links between different areas of service delivery.

The timeliness and speed at which things need to happen to facilitate seamlessness, particularly in arranging accommodation or suitable ETE for example, can be a further challenge, especially where young people are on short sentences. Even very short time lapses during which nothing is arranged or available can have a profound impact on increasing the likelihood of reoffending. What might seem like a short space of time to a professional could feel like a long time in a young person's life.

The challenge for managers and practitioners is, therefore, to use evidence of any promising approaches to develop interventions for preventing reoffending that:

● start at the pre-court stage and continue beyond the official end of the sentence;

● minimise the negative impact of custody;

● reduce the organisational and systemic barriers to providing timely, consistent and coherent interventions across secure and community settings.

Summary

- Custody is associated with high levels of reconviction and other poor outcomes, although the evidence is unclear as to whether this is to do with custody itself or how custody is currently configured, with its emphasis on punishment and the smooth operation of the regime as opposed to focusing more on rehabilitation and meeting the individual needs of young people.

- Resettlement is a relatively new term which is hard to define. Further, it implies young people were 'settled' prior to entry to custody which is far from the case for many.

- It is difficult to establish what is effective in relation to resettlement as there is little in the way of specific programme evaluation, and what little research does exist focuses solely on custodial interventions, is based on outcomes for adults rather than young people, or is methodologically flawed.

- A core principle underpinning most resettlement models is the dimension of continuity: the DTO as a framework for resettlement emphasises the significance of a supported transition through consistent case-management by a Yot practitioner from pre-sentence stage through to the end of the sentence.

Further reading

Hagell, A., Hazel, N. and Shaw, K. (2000) *Evaluation of Medway Secure Training Centre* Occasional Paper. London: Home Office.

Hazel, N., Magell, A., Liddle, M., Archer, D., Grimshaw, R. and King, J. (2002) *Assessment of the DTO and its Impact on the Secure Estate across England and Wales.* London: Policy Research Bureau.

Stewart, G. and Tutt, N. (1987) *Children in Custody.* Aldershot: Avebury.

UNIVERSITY OF WINCHESTER
LIBRARY

Conclusion

In reviewing the evidence about the effectiveness of interventions with young people who offend, what is striking is how little rather than how much is known. The causes of persistent and serious offending remain opaque and there is heavy reliance on risk and prediction studies derived from associated factors. Their findings need to be treated with caution as many children experiencing early risk factors do not go on to have an offending career while many become involved in persistent offending who would not have been predicted to do so. The unpredictable experiences of young adults and their involvement or not with particular agencies may be equally important in influencing offending careers.

Applying the broad-brush findings of meta-analysis to an individual young person is very challenging and has to be filtered through professional judgement. Inevitably any intervention will only work with some young people in some circumstances and then only some of the time. The idea that interventions can be neatly formulated and applied so that they provide an entirely predictable, controllable, outcome is unsustainable when faced with the complex, ambiguous and uncertain circumstances in which many young people involved in offending find themselves. Equally, hiding behind nebulous notions of 'best' or 'good' practice does little to develop effectiveness. The premise here is that the body of research evidence, such as it is, should be used to derive pragmatic inferences for practice.

If evidence-based practice is to be taken seriously by practitioners and other key decision makers in the youth justice system there needs to be openness about its limitations. The basic contexts associated with offending; such as poverty and childhood abuse, may be very difficult to ameliorate. Devising interventions that are of an intensity, duration and sophistication that match the multiple challenges facing some young people such as detachment from education and employment, homelessness, substance misuse, and poor mental health is often beyond the resources available to a Yot let alone an individual practitioner.

While evidence-based practice is about cultural change there is little evidence that unified cultures exist within or between Yots. This is despite the array of targets, national standards, guidance, inspection, youth justice plans and data returns designed to create consistency of implementation and outcomes. Extending a common evidence-based culture to key decision makers such as police, prosecutors and sentencers may be harder still. One of the key challenges in youth justice is the management of expectations and particularly the management of disappointment. Where interventions based on research evidence have been proposed and accepted by the court, subsequent reoffending can not only bring the validity of the intervention and indirectly the evidence into question but also accelerate the use of custody as it creates the perception that 'nothing works'.

Effectiveness is unlikely to be enhanced if the provision of evidence-based practice is perceived to be clumsily prescriptive and to be about stifling debate and creativity. Improvements in practice and innovative interventions will be more likely to occur through the critical analysis of what exists in conjunction with rigorous research evidence. Developing a youth justice workforce that comprises managers and practitioners who analyse critically and reflect upon the rationale for their actions through drawing upon research evidence is surely key to improving effectiveness. Arguably some of the skills involved in research should also be common to youth justice practitioners. Both are concerned with developing understanding and testing out the predictions of their theories or assumptions. It cannot be denied that youth justice policy is highly political and expresses certain values, both openly and covertly. The evidence-based practice movement cannot pretend that it is somehow apolitical and offers a completely objective way forward. Recognition of the wider political pressures is an important part of working in youth justice but these are beyond the scope of individuals to influence. Irrespective of the particular policy environment therefore, a culture within youth justice that can draw upon and also add to the research base in order to improve day-to-day practice is surely worth striving to achieve.

References

Adey, P., Fairbrother, R. and William, D. (1999) A *Review of Research on Learning Strategies and Learning Styles*. King's College: London School of Education.

Altschuler, D. (1998) 'Intermediate sanctions and community treatment for serious and violent juvenile offenders', in R. Loeber and D. Farrington (eds), *Serious and Violent Juvenile Offenders: Risk Factors and Successful Interventions*. Thousand Oaks, CA: Sage.

Altschuler, D. and Armstrong, T. (1994a) *Intensive Aftercare for High-risk Juveniles: A Community Care Model. Program Summary*. Washington, DC: Office of Juvenile Justice and Delinquency Prevention, US DoG.

Altschuler, D. and Armstrong, T. (1994b) *Intensive Aftercare for High-risk Juveniles: Policies and Procedures. Program Summary*. Washington, DC: Office of Juvenile Justice and Delinquency Prevention, US DoG.

Altschuler, D. and Armstrong, T. (2002) 'Juvenile corrections and continuity of care in a community context – the evidence and promising directions', *Federal Patrol: A Journal of Correctional Philosophy and Practice*, Special Issue, 'What Works' in Corrections, Sept. 2002.

Altschuler, D., Armstrong, T. and Layton MacKenzie, D. (1999) *Reintegration, Supervised Release and Intensive Aftercare*. Juvenile Justice Bulletin July 1999. Washington, DC, USA: Office of Juvenile Justice and Delinquency Prevention.

Andrews, D. (1995) 'The psychology of criminal conduct and effective treatment', in J. McGuire (ed.), *What Works: Reducing Re-offending: Guidelines from Research and Practice*. Chichester: John Wiley and Sons.

Andrews, D. and Bonta, J. (1994) *The Psychology of Criminal Conduct*. Cincinnati, OH: Anderson Publishing.

Andrews, D., Zinger, I., Hoge, R., Bonta, J., Gendreau, P. and Cullen, F. (1990) 'Does correctional treatment work? A clinically relevant and psychologically informed meta-analysis', *Criminology*, 28: 369–404.

Annison, J. (2005) 'Risk and protection', in T. Bateman and J. Pitts (eds), *The RHP Companion to Youth Justice*. Lyme Regis: Russell House Publishing Ltd.

Arnull, E. *et al.* (2005) *Persistent Young Offenders. A Retrospective Study*. London: Youth Justice Board.

Audit Commission (1996) *Misspent Youth: Young People and Crime*. London: Audit Commission.

Audit Commission (1999a) *Children in Mind – Child and Adolescent Mental Health Services*. London: Audit Commission.

Audit Commission (1999b) *Missing Out: LEA Management of School Attendance and Inclusion*. London: Audit Commission.

Audit Commission (2004) *Youth Justice 2004. A Review of the Referred Youth Justice System*. London: Audit Commission.

Baker, K., Jones, S., Roberts, C. and Merrington, S. (2002) *The Evaluation of the Validity and Reliability of the Youth Justice Board's Assessment for Young Offenders: Findings from the First Two Years of the Use of ASSET*. Oxford: Centre for Criminological Research, University of Oxford.

Baker, K., Jones, S., Merrington, S. and Roberts, C. (2005) *Further Development of Asset*. London: Youth Justice Board.

Bandura, A. (1995) *Self-efficacy in Changing Societies*. Cambridge: Cambridge University Press.

Barlow, J. (1997) *Systematic Review of the Effectiveness of Parent-Training Programmes in Improving Behaviour Problems in Children aged 3–10 years*. Oxford: Health Services Research Unit, Department of Public Health.

Barn, R. (2001) *Black Youth on the Margins*. London: York Publishing Services for the Joseph Rowntree Foundation.

Batchelor, S. and McNeill, F. (2005) 'The young person-worker relationship', in T. Bateman and J . Pitts (eds), *The RHP Companion to Youth Justice*. Lyme Regis: Russell House Publishing Ltd.

Bateman, T. (2001) 'Custodial sentencing of children: prospects for reversing the tide', *Youth Justice*, 1 (1): 28–39

Bateman, T. and Pitts, J. (eds) (2005) *The RHP Companion to Youth Justice*. Dorset: Russell House Publishing.

Beaumont, B. and Mistry, T. (1996) 'Doing a good job under duress', *Probation Journal*, 43 (4): 200–4.

Bennett, T. (1998) 'Crime prevention', in M. Tonry (ed.), *The Handbook of Crime and Punishment*. New York: Oxford University Press.

Berridge, D., Brodie, I., Pitts, J., Porteous, D. and Tarling, R. (2001) *The Independent Effects of Permanent Exclusion from School on the Offending Careers of Young People*. London: Home Office.

Bonta, J. (1996) 'Risk-needs assessment and treatment', in A. Harland (ed.), *Choosing Correctional Options that Work*. Thousand Oaks, CA: Sage.

Bonta, J., Rooney, J. and Wallace-Capretta, S. (1999) *Electronic Monitoring in Canada*. Canada: Public Works and Government Services.

Bonta, J., Wallace-Capretta, S. and Rooney, J. (2000) 'A quasi-experimental evaluation of an intensive rehabilitation supervision program', *Criminal Justice and Behaviour*, 27: 312–29.

Borduin, C., Heiblum, N., Jones, M. and Grabe, S. (2000) 'Community-based treatments of serious anti-social behavior in adolescents', in W. E. Martin and J. L. Swartz-Kulstad (eds), *Person-environment Psychology and Mental Health: Assessment and Intervention*. Hillsdale, NJ: Erlbaum.

Boswell, G. (1996) *Young and Dangerous: The Backgrounds and Careers of Section 53 Offenders*. Aldershot: Avebury.

Boswell, G., Davies, M. and Wright, A. (1993) *Contemporary Probation Practice*. Avebury: Ashgate Publishing.

Bottoms, A. (1995) *Intensive Community Supervision for Young Offenders: Outcomes, Process and Cost*. Cambridge: Institute of Criminology.

Bottoms, A. (2005) 'Methodology matters', *Safer Society*, 25: 10–12.

Bowles, R., Pradiptyo, R. and Garcia Reyes, M. (2006) *Estimating the Impact of the Safer Schools Partnerships Programme*. York: University of York.

Box, L. (2001) 'Supporting black and minority ethnic teenagers and their parents', in J. Coleman and D. Roker (eds), *Supporting Parents of Teenagers, A Handbook for Professionals*. London: Jessica Kingsley Publishers.

Braithwaite, J. (2002) *Restorative Justice and Responsive Regulation*. Oxford: Oxford University Press.

Bramley, G. and Pawson, H. (2002) 'Low demand for housing: incidence, causes and UK national policy implications', *Urban Studies*, Vol. 39, No. 3, pp. 393–422.

Bridges, A. (1998) *Increasing the Employability of Offenders: An Inquiry into Probation Service Effectiveness*. Oxford: Probation Studies Unit Report No. 5.

Brooks, G. (2002) *What works for children with literacy difficulties? The effectiveness of intervention schemes*. Research Report RR380. London: Department for Education and Skills.

Budd, T., Sharp, C., Weir, G., Wilson, D. and Owen, N. (2005) *Young People and Crime: Findings from the 2004 Offending Crime and Justice Survey*. Home Office Statistical Bulletin 20/05. Home Office, RDS, London.

Burgess, A. (2002) *Fathers and Families*. London: Parent Education and Support Forum.

Burnett, R. and Appleton, C. (2002) *Teaming Up to Reduce Youth Crime: A Study of the Oxfordshire Yot*. Oxford: Centre for Criminological Research.

Burnett, R. and Appleton, C. (2004) *Joined-up Youth Justice: Tackling Youth Crime in Partnership*. Lyme Regis: Russell House Publishing Ltd.

Butt, J. and Box, L. (1998) *Family Centred: A Study of the Use of Family Centres by Black Families*. London: Race Equality Unit.

Bynner, J. (2001) 'Childhood risks and protective factors in social exclusion', *Children and Society*, 15: 285–301.

CRG Research (2005) *Positive Activities for Young People National Evaluation*, End of Year 2 Report. London: DfES.

Cabinet Office (1999) *Modernising Government*. London: The Stationery Office.

Carpenter, M. (1968) *Reformatory Schools for the Children of the Perishing and Dangerous Classes, and for Juvenile Offenders*. London: Woburn Press.

Catalano, R. and Hawkins, J. (1996) 'The social development model: a theory of antisocial behaviour', in J. Hawkins (ed.), *Delinquency and Crime: Current Theories*. Cambridge: Cambridge University Press.

Chapman, T. (2000) *Time to Grow*. Lyme Regis: Russell House Publishing.

Chapman, T. and Hough, M. (1998) *Evidence Based Practice: A Guide to Effective Practice*. London: HM Inspectorate of Probation/Home Office.

Chitty, C. (2005) 'The impact of corrections on re-offending: conclusions and the way forward', in G. Harper and C. Chitty (eds), *The Impact of Corrections on Re-offending: A Review of 'What Works'*, Home Office Research Study 291. London: Home Office Research, Development and Statistics Directorate.

Cicchetti, D. and Rogosch, F. (1997) 'The role of self-organisation in the promotion of resilience in maltreated children', *Development and Psychopathology* 9: 797–815.

Clutterbuck, D. and Ragins, B. (2002) *Mentoring and Diversity: An International Perspective*. Boston: Reed Publishing.

Coffey, D. and Gemignani, M. (1994) *Effective Practices in Juvenile Correctional Education: A Study of the Literature and Research 1980–1992*. USA: Office of Juvenile Justice and Delinquency.

Coffield, F., Mosely, D., Hall, E. and Ecclestone, K. (2004) *Learning Styles for Post-16 Learners: What Do We Know?* London: Learning and Skills Research Centre.

Coleman, J. and Roker, D. (2001) 'Setting the scene: parenting and public policy', in J. Coleman and D. Roker (eds), *Supporting Parents of Teenagers, A Handbook for Professionals*. London: Jessica Kingsley Publishers.

Coles, B. (2000) *Joined-up Youth Research, Policy and Practice: A New Agenda for Change?* Leicester: Youth Work Press.

Communities that Care (2001) *Risk and Protective Factors for Youth Crime – Prevalence, Salience and Reduction*. Report for the Youth Justice Board for England and Wales. London: Youth Justice Board.

Corbett, R. and Petersilia, J. (1994) 'Intensive rehabilitation supervision: the next generation in community corrections?' *Federal Probation*, 58: 72–8.

Cottle, C., Lee, R. and Heilbrun, K. (2001) 'The prediction of criminal recidivism in juveniles', *Criminal Justice and Behaviour*, 28(3): 367–94.

Crawford, A. and Newburn, T. (2002) 'Recent developments in restorative justice for young people in England and Wales: community participation and representation', *British Journal of Criminology*, (42): 476–95.

Crawford, A. and Newburn, T. (2003) *Youth Offending and Restorative Justice: Implementing Reform in Youth Justice*. Cullompton: Willan Publishing.

Curry, D., Knight, V., Owens-Rawle, D., Patel, S., Semenchuk, M. and Williams, B. (2004) *Restorative Justice in the Juvenile Secure Estate*. London: Youth Justice Board.

Cusick, J. (2001) *Working with Fathers*. Brighton: Trust for the Study of Adolescence.

Daly, K. (2003) 'Making variation a virtue: evaluating the potential and limits of restorative justice', in E. Weitekamp and H. J. Kerner (eds), *Restorative Justice in Context*. Cullompton: Willan Publishing.

Davies, K., Lewis, J., Byatt, J., Purvis, E. and Cole, B. (2004) *An Evaluation of the Literacy Requirements of General Offending Behaviour Programmes*, Home Office Findings 233. London: Home Office.

Department for Education and Employment (1994) *The Education of Children with Emotional and Behavioural Difficulties*. Circular 9/94. London: DfEE.

Department for Education and Employment (1995) *More Willingly to School?: An Independent Evaluation of the DfEE's Truancy and Disaffected Pupils (TDP) GEST Programme*. London: DfEE.

Department for Education and Employment (1999) *Social Inclusion: Pupil Support Truancy and School Exclusion*. Circular 10/99. London: DfEE.

Department for Education and Employment (2000) *Connexions: The Best Start in Life for Every Young Person*. London: DfEE.

Department for Education and Skills (2004a) *Every Child Matters: Change for Children*. London: DfES.

Department for Education and Skills (2004b) *14–19 Curriculum and Qualifications Reform: Final Report of the Working Group on 14–19 Reform*. London: DfES.

Department for Education and Skills/Department of Health (2000) *Guidance on the Education of Children and Young People in Public Care*. London: DfES.

Department of Health (2003) 'Leaving Care', Research Briefing No. 6. London: DoH.

Desforges, C. and Abouchaar, A. (2003) *The Impact of Parental Involvement, Parental Support and Family Education on Pupil Achievement and Adjustment: A Literature Review*, DfES Research Report No. 433. London: Queen's Printer.

Diamond, C., Floyd, A. and Misch, P. (2004) *Key Elements of Effective Practice – Mental Health Source Document*. London: Youth Justice Board.

Dignan, J. (2000) *Youth Justice Pilots Evaluation: Interim Report on Reparative Work and Youth Offending Teams*. London: Home Office.

Dignan, J. (2002) 'Reparation orders', in B. Williams (ed.), *Reparation and Victim-Focused Social Work*. London: Jessica Kingsley.

Dillon, L., Chivite-Matthews, N., Grewal, I., Brown, R., Webster, S., Weddell, E., Brown, G. and Smith, N. (2007) *Risk, Protective Factors and Resilience to Drug Use: Identifying Resilient Young People and Learning from their Experiences*. Home Office Online Report 04/07. London: Home Office RDS.

Ditchfield, J. and Catan, L. (1992) *Juveniles Sentenced for Serious Offences: A Comparison of Regimes in Youth Offender Institutions and Local Authority Community Homes*. London: Home Office.

Dodge, K. and Schwartz, D. (1997) 'Social information processing mechanisms in aggressive behaviour', in D. M. Stoff, *Handbook of Antisocial Behaviour*. New York: Wiley.

Downes, D. and Morgan, R. (2002) 'The skeletons in the cupboard: the politics of law and order at the turn of the millennium', in M. Maguire, R. Morgan and R. Reiner (eds), *The Oxford Handbook of Criminology*. Oxford: Oxford University Press.

Drugscope and DPAS (2001) *Assessing Local Need: Planning Services for Young People*. Drug Prevention Advisory Service.

Dubois, D. L., Holloway, B. E., Valentine, J. C. and Cooper, H. (2002) 'Effectiveness on mentoring programs: a meta-analytic review', *American Journal of Community Psychology*, 30.

Eadie, T. and Canton, R. (2002) 'Practising in a context of ambivalence: the challenge for youth justice workers', *Youth Justice*, 2 (1).

ECOTEC (2001a) *An Audit of Education and Training Provision within the Youth Justice System*. London: Youth Justice Board.

ECOTEC (2001b) *Review of the Pre- and Post-custodial Education and Training Experiences of Young People*. London: Youth Justice Board.

Elliot, L., Orr, L., Watson, L. and Jackson, A. (2001) *Drug Treatment Services for Young People: A Systematic Review of Effectiveness and Legal Framework*. Edinburgh: Scottish Executive Effective Interventions Unit.

Elliott, A., Lindfield, S. and Cusick, J. (2002) *Parents' Views*. Brighton: Trust for the Study of Adolescence.

Emler, N. (2001) *Self-esteem: The Costs and Causes of Low Self-worth*. York: York Publishing Services.

Errington, J. (1985) 'In defence of tracking', *Social Work Today*, 21 January: 3.

Farrington, D. (1991) 'Childhood aggression and adult violence', in D. Pepler and K. Rubin (eds), *The Development and Treatment of Childhood Aggression*. Hillsdale, New Jersey: Lawrence Erlbaum.

Farrington, D. (1992) 'Explaining the beginning, progress and ending of antisocial behaviour from birth to adulthood', in J. McCord (ed.), *Facts, Frameworks and Forecasts: Advances in Criminological Theory*, Vol. 3. New Brunswick, New Jersey: Transaction.

Farrington, D. (1996) *Understanding and Preventing Youth Crime*. York: Joseph Rowntree Foundation.

Farrington, D. (1997) 'Human development and criminal careers', in M. Maguire, R. Morgan and R. Reiner (eds), *The Oxford Handbook of Criminology* (2nd edn). Oxford: Oxford University Press.

Farrington, D. (2000) 'Psychosocial Predictors of Adult Anti-social Personality and Adult Convictions', *Behavioural Science and the Law*, 18, 605–22.

Farrington, D. (2002) 'Developmental criminology and risk-focused prevention', in M. Maguire, R. Morgan and R. Reiner (eds), *The Oxford Handbook of Criminology* (3rd edn). Oxford: Oxford University Press.

Farrington, D., Ditchfield, J., Hancock, G., Howard, P., Jolliffe, D., Livingston, M. and Painter, K. (2002) *Evaluation of Two Intensive Regimes for Young Offenders*, Home Office Research Study 239. London: Home Office.

Fayle, J. (2007) *Locked in Battle*, *The Guardian* 14/02/07.

Feilzer, M. and Hood, R. (2004) *Differences or Discrimination? Minority Ethnic People in the Youth Justice System*. London: Youth Justice Board.

Feilzer, M., Appleton, C., Roberts, C. and Hoyle, C. (2004) *Cognitive Behaviour Projects: The National Evaluation of the Youth Justice Board's Cognitive Behaviour Projects*. London: Youth Justice Board.

Feinstein, L. and Sabates, R. (2005) *Education and Youth Crime: Effects of Introducing the Education Maintenance Allowance Programme*. DfES Research Brief no. RCB01–05.

Fergusson, D., Lynskey, M. and Horwood, J. (1996) 'Factors associated with continuity and changes in disruptive behaviour patterns between childhood and adolescence', *Journal of Abnormal Child Psychology*, 24: 533–54.

Flood-Page, C., Campbell, S., Harrington, V. and Miller, J. (2000) *Youth Crime: Findings from the 1998/99 Youth Lifestyles Survey*. Home Office Research Study 209. London: Home Office.

Fonagy, P., Target, M., Cottrell, D. and Phillips, J. (2002) *What Works for Whom? A Critical Review of Treatments for Children and Adolescents*. New York and London: The Guilford Press.

Forehand, R. and Kotchick, B. (2002) 'Behavioral parent training: current challenges and potential solutions', *Journal of Child and Family Studies*, 11: 377–84.

Forrest, S., Myhill, A. and Tilley, N. (2005) *Practical Lessons for Involving the Community in Crime and Disorder Problem-solving*. Home Office Development and Practice Report 43. London: Home Office RDS.

Fredericks, J., Blumenfeld, P. and Paris, A. (2004) 'School engagement: potential of the concept, state of the evidence', *Review of Educational Research*, Spring 2004, 74(1): 59–109.

Frisher, M., Crome, I., Macleod, J., Bloor, R. and Hickman, N. (2007) *Protective Factors for Illicit Drug Use among Young People: A Literature Review*. Home Office Online Report 05/07. London: Home Office RDS.

Fullwood, C. and Powell, H. (2004) 'Towards effective practice in the Youth Justice System', in R. Burnett and C. Roberts (eds), *What Works in Probation and Youth Justice: Developing Evidence-based Practice*. Cullompton: Willan Publishing.

Galloway, D. (1985) *Schools and Persistent Absentees*. Oxford: Pergamon.

Gay, B. and Stephenson, J. (1998) 'The mentoring dilemma: guidance and/or direction?', *Mentoring and Tutoring*, 6(1): 43–54.

Gelsthorpe, L. and Sharpe, G. (2006) 'Gender, youth crime and justice', in B. Goldson and J. Muncie (eds), *Youth Crime and Justice*. London: Sage Publications.

Gemignani, R. (1994) *Juvenile Correctional Education: A Time for Change*. Washington, DC: Office of Juvenile Justice and Delinquency Prevention.

Gendreau, P., Goggin, C. and Fulton, B. (2000) 'Intensive supervision in probation and parole settings', in C. Hollin (ed.), *Handbook of Offender Assessment and Treatment*. Chichester: Wiley.

Ghate, D. and Hazel, N. (2002) *Parenting in Poor Environments: Stress, Support and Coping*. London: Jessica Kingsley Publishers.

Ghate, D. and Ramella, M. (2002) *Positive Parenting: The National Evaluation of the Youth Justice Board's Parenting Programme*. London: Youth Justice Board.

Gies, S. (2003) *Aftercare Services*, Juvenile Justice Bulletin. Washington, DC: Office of Juvenile Justice and Delinquency Prevention, US DoJ.

Goldson, B. (2000) 'Wither diversion? Interventionism and the new youth justice', in B. Goldson (ed.), *The New Youth Justice*. Lyme Regis: Russell House Publishing.

Goldson, B. (2005) 'Beyond formalism: towards 'informal' approaches to youth crime and youth justice', in T. Bateman and J. Pitts. (eds) *The RHP Companion to Youth Justice*. Lyme Regis: Russell House Publishing.

Goldson, B. and Muncie, J. (eds) (2006) *Youth Crime and Justice*. London: Sage Publications.

Goldson, B. and Peters, E. (2000) *Tough Justice: Responding to Children in Trouble*. London: The Children's Society.

Goodstein, L. and Sontheimer, H. (1997) 'The implementation of an intensive aftercare program for serious juvenile offenders', *Criminal Justice and Behaviour*, 24: 352–59.

Gottfredson, D. (2001) *Schools and Delinquency*. Cambridge: Cambridge University Press.

Goulden C. and Sondhi, A. (2001) *At the Margins: Drug Use by Vulnerable Young People in the 1998/99 Youth Lifestyles Survey*. Home Office Research Study 228. London.

Graham, J. and Bowling, B. (1995) *Young People and Crime*. Home Office Research Study 145. London: Home Office.

Gray, J. A. M. (2000) 'Evidence-based Public Health' in L. Trinder and S. Reynolds (eds) *Evidence-Based Practice: A Critical Appraisal*. Oxford: Blackwell Science.

Gray, P. (2005a) 'Community interventions' in T. Bateman and J. Pitts (eds), *The RHP Companion to Youth Justice*. Lyme Regis: Russell House Publishing.

Gray, P. (2005b) 'The politics of risk and young offenders' experience of social exclusion and restorative justice', *British Journal of Criminology*, (45): 938–57.

Gray, E., Taylor, E., Roberts, C., Merrington, S., Fernandez, R. and Moore, R. (2005) *Intensive Supervision and Surveillance Programme. The Final Report*. London: Youth Justice Board.

Gray, P., Mosely, J. and Browning, S. (2003) *An Evaluation of the Plymouth Restorative Justice Programme*. Plymouth: University of Plymouth.

Greenwood, P., Rydell, P., Abrahamse, A., Caulkins, J., Model, K. and Kelin, S. (1994) *Three Strikes and You're Out: Estimated Benefits and Costs of California's New Mandatory Sentencing Laws*. Santa Monica, CA: RAND.

Griffin, P. (1999) 'Juvenile probation in the schools', *NCJJ in Focus*, 1(1): 1–10.

Grimshaw, R. and Berridge, D. (1994) *Educating Disruptive Children: Placement and Progress in Residential Special Schools for Pupils with Emotional and Behavioural Difficulties*. London: National Children's Bureau.

Grisso, T. and Schwartz, R. (eds) (2000) *Youth on Trial: A Developmental Perspective on Juvenile Justice*. London: University of Chicago Press.

Grossman, J. B. and Rhodes, J. E. (2002) 'The test of time: predictors and effects of duration in youth mentoring relationships', *American Journal of Community Psychology*, 30.

Grossman, J. B. and Tierney, J. P. (1998) 'Does mentoring work? An impact study of the Big Brothers/Big Sisters program', *Evaluation Review*, 22.

HM Inspectorate of Prisons (2006) *Annual Report of HM Chief Inspector of Prisons for England and Wales 2004–2005*. London: The Stationery Office.

HM Inspectorate of Probation (2002) *Annual Report 2001–2002*. London: Home Office.

HM Inspectorate of Probation (2004) *Joint Inspection of Youth Offending Teams First Phase: Annual Report*. London: Home Office.

HM Inspectorate of Probation (2006) *Joint Inspection of Youth Offending Teams Annual Report 2005/2006*. London: HM Inspectorate of Probation.

Hagell, A. (2002) *The Mental Health of Young Offenders*. London: Mental Health Foundation.

Hagell, A. (2005) 'The use of custody for children and young people', in T. Bateman and J. Pitts (eds) *The RHP Companion to Youth Justice*. Lyme Regis: Russell House Publishing Ltd.

Hagell A. and Newburn, T. (1994) *Persistent Young Offenders*. London: Policy Studies Institute.

Hagell, A., Hazel, N. and Shaw, K. (2000) *Evaluation of Medway Secure Training Centre, Occasional Paper*. London: Home Office.

Hazel, N., Hagell, A., Liddele, M., Archer, D., Grimshaw, R. and King, J. (2002) *Assessment of the DTO and its Impact on the Secure Estate across England and Wales*. London: Policy Research Bureau.

Haines, K. and Drakeford, M. (1998) *Young People and Youth Justice*. Basingstoke: Macmillan Press.

Haines, K. and O'Mahony, D. (2006) 'Restorative approaches, young people and youth justice', in B. Goldstein and J. Muncie (eds) *Youth Crime and Justice*. London: Sage.

Hammersley, R., Marsland, L. and Reid, M. (2003) *Substance Use by Young Offenders: The Impact of the Normalisation of Drug Use in the Early Years of the 21st Century*. London: Home Office Study 261.

Harper, G. and Chitty, C. (2005) *The Impact of Corrections on Re-offending: A Review of 'What Works'*. Home Office Research Study 291. London: Home Office Research, Development and Statistics Directorate.

Harper, R. and Hardy, S. (2000) 'An evaluation of motivational interviewing as a method of intervention with clients in a probation setting', *British Journal of Social Work*, 30: 393–400.

Harrington, D. and Bailey, S. (2005) *Mental Health Needs and Effectiveness of Provision for Young Offenders in Custody and in the Community*. London: Youth Justice Board.

Hayward, G., Hodgson, A., Johnson, J., Oancea, A., Pring, R., Spours, K., Wilde, S. and Wright, S. (2005) *The Nuffield Review of 14–19 Education and Training Annual Report 2004–05*. Oxford: University of Oxford Department of Educational Studies.

Hazel, N. *et al.* (2002) *Assessment of the DTO and its Impact on the Secure Estate across England and Wales*. London: Policy Research Bureau.

Hazel, N., Hagell, A., Liddle, M., Archer, D., Grimshaw, R. and King, J. (2002) *Detention and Training: Assessment of the Detention and Training Order and its Impact on the Secure Estate Across England and Wales*. London: Youth Justice Board.

Health Advisory Service (2001) *The Substance of Young Needs, Review 2001*. London: HMSO.

Hendrick, H. (2006) 'Histories of youth crime and justice', in B. Goldson and J. Muncie (eds), *Youth Crime and Justice* London: Sage Publications.

Henricson, C., Coleman, J. and Roker, D. (2000) 'Parenting in the youth justice context', *The Howard Journal*, Vol. 39, No. 4, pp. 325–8.

Henricson, C. (2003) *Government and Parenting: Is There a Case for a Policy Review and a Parents' Code?* York: Joseph Rowntree Foundation.

Henry, B., Caspi, A., Moffitt, T. and Silva, P. (1996) 'Temperamental and familial predictors of violent and non-violent criminal convictions: age 3 to age 18', *Developmental Psychology*, 32: 614–23.

Hoaken, P. and Stewart, S. (2003) 'Drugs of abuse and the elicitation of human aggressive behavior', *Addictive Behaviours* 28, 1533–54.

Hobbs and Hook Consulting (2001) *Research into Effective Practice with Young People in Secure Facilities*. Youth Justice Board (Research Note No. 3).

Hodges, H. (1982) 'Madison prep – alternatives through learning styles', in Keefe, W. (ed.), *Student Learning Styles and Brain Behaviour Progress, Instrumentation, Research.* Reston VA: National Association of Secondary School Principals (28: 31).

Hollin, C. (1995) 'The meaning and implications of programme integrity', in J. McGuire (ed.), *What Works: Reducing Re-offending: Guidelines from Research and Practice.* Chichester: John Wiley and Sons.

Hollin, C., McGuire, J., Palmer, E., Bilby, C., Hatcher, R. and Holmes, A. (2002) *Introducing Pathfinder Programmes into the Probation Service: An Interim Report.* Home Office Research Study 247. London: Home Office.

Holloway, K., Bennett, T. and Farrington, D. (2005) *The Effectiveness of Criminal Justice and Treatment Programmes in Reducing Drug-Related Crime: A Systematic Review.* Home Office Online Report, 26/05. London: Home Office.

Home Office (1998) *Joining Forces to Protect the Public: Prisons-Probation.* London: Home Office.

Home Office (2004a) *Juvenile Reconviction: Results from 2001 and 2002 Cohorts.* London: Home Office.

Home Office (2004b) *The Role of Education in Enhancing Life Chances and Preventing Offending.* Home Office Development and Practice Report 19. London: Home Office.

Home Office (2007) *Identifying and Exploring Young People's Experiences of Risk, Protective Factors and Resilience to Drug Use.* Home Office Development and Practice Report: 47. London, Home Office RDS.

Home Office and Youth Justice Board (2002) *Final Warning Scheme: Guidance for the Police and Youth Offending Teams.* London: Home Office.

Home Office Research, Development and Statistics Directorate (2002) *The Road to Ruin? Sequences of Initiation into Drug Use and Offending by Young People in Britain.* Home Office Research Study 253. London: The Stationery Office.

Hope, T. (1996) 'Communities, crime and inequality in England and Wales', in T. Bennett (ed.), *Preventing Crime and Disorder. Targeting Strategies and Responsibilities* (Cropwood Series). Cambridge: Institute of Criminology.

Hope, T. (2001) 'Crime, victimisation and inequality in risk society', in R. Matthews and J. Pitts (eds), *Crime Prevention, Disorder and Community Safety.* London: Routledge.

Hough, M., Jacobson, J. and Millie, A. (2003) *The Decision to Imprison: Sentencing and the Prison Population.* London: Prison Reform Trust.

Howell, J.C., Krisberg, B., Hawkins, J. D. and Wilson, J.J. (1995) *A Sourcebook: Serious, Violent & Chronic Juvenile Offenders.* London: Sage.

Howell, E. and Montuschi, O. (2002) *Groupwork with Parents of Adolescents.* London: Parenting Education and Support Forum.

Howell, J. (2003) *Preventing and Reducing Juvenile Delinquency: A Comprehensive Framework.* London: Sage Publications.

Hoyle, C., Young, R. and Hill, R. (2002) *Proceed with Caution – An Evaluation of the Thames Valley Initiative in Restorative Cautioning.* York: York Publishing Services.

Hughes, J. (2005) *Doing the Arts Justice: A Review of Research Literature, Practice and Theory.* Canterbury: The Unit for the Arts and Offenders, Centre for Applied Theatre Research.

Hughes, N. and Fielding, A. (2006) *Targeting Preventative Services for Children: Experiences from the Children's Fund.* Research Report RR 777. London: DfES.

Hurry, J. (2003) *Youth Justice Board Intervention Programme: Education, Training and Employment.* Central Evaluators' Final Report. London: Youth Justice Board.

Hurry, J., Brazier, L. and Moriarty, V. (2006) 'Improving the literacy and numeracy skills of young people who offend: can it be done and what are the consequences?', *Numeracy and Literacy Studies*.

Hurry, J., Brazier, L., Snapes, K. and Wilson, A. (2005) *Improving the Literacy and Numeracy of Disaffected Young People in Custody and in the Community: Summary Interim Report of the First Eighteen Months of Study*. London: National Research and Development Centre.

Hustler, D., Callaghan, J., Cockett, M. and McNeill, J. (1998) *Choices for Life: An Evaluation of Rathbone CI's Work with Disaffected and Excluded School Pupils*. Manchester Metropolitan University: Didsbury Educational Research Centre.

INCLUDE (2000) *Approaches to Effective Practice for Yots: Engaging Young Offenders in Education, Training and Employment*. London: Youth Justice Board.

Jekielek, S. M., Moore, K. A., Hair, E. C. and Scarpura, H. J. (2002) *Mentoring: A Promising Strategy for Youth Development*, Child Trends Research Brief. Washington, DC: Child Trends.

Jermyn, H. (2004) *The Art of Inclusion*. Research Report 35. London: Arts Council.

Jessor, R. and Jessor, S. (1977) *Problem Behaviour and Psycho-Social Development: A Longitudinal Study of Youth*. New York: Academic Press.

John, P. (1996) 'Damaged goods? An interpretation of excluded pupils' perceptions of schooling', in E. Blyth and J. Milner (eds), *Exclusion from School: Inter-Professional Issues for Policy and Practice*. London: Routledge.

Jones, D. (2002) 'Questioning New Labour's Youth Justice Strategy: a review article', *Youth Justice*, 1(3): 14–26.

Keeling, P., Kibblewhite, K. and Smith, Z. (2004) 'Evidence-based practice in young people's substance misuse services', in D. White (ed.), *Social Work and Evidence-based Practice*. London: Jessica Kingsley.

Kendall, S., Kinder, K., Halsey, K., Fletcher-Morgan, C., White, R. and Brown, C. (2002) *An Evaluation of Alternative Education Initiatives*. London: DfES.

Key, J. (2001) 'The Rotherham experience of intensive supervision: a message from a seasoned practitioner', *Youth Justice Matters* 1: 10–12.

Kinder, K., Halsey, K., Kendall, S., Atkinson, M., Moor, H., Wilkin, A., White, R. and Rigby, B. (2000) *Working Out Well, Effective Provision for Excluded Pupils*. Slough: NFER.

Krueger, R., Caspi, A., Moffitt, T. and White, J. (1996) 'Delay of gratification, psychopathology, and personality: is low self-control specific to externalising problems?' *Journal of Personality*, 64: 107–29.

Kumpfer, K. (1993) *Strengthening America's Families: Promising Parenting and Family Strengthening Strategies for Delinquency Prevention*. Washington, DC: Office of Juvenile Justice and Delinquency Prevention, US Department of Justice.

Kumpfer, K. and Alvarado, R. (1998) 'Effective family strengthening interventions', *Juvenile Justice Bulletin*, Nov. 1998. Office of Juvenile Justice Delinquency Prevention, Office of Justice Programmes, US Department of Justice.

Lader, D., Singleton, N. and Meltzer, H. (1997) *Psychiatric Morbidity among Young Offenders in England and Wales*. London: Office for National Statistics.

Latimer, J., Dowden, C. and Muise, D. (2001) *The Effectiveness of Restorative Justice Practices: A Meta-Analysis*. Ottawa: Department of Justice Canada.

Lindfield, S. (2001) *Human Rights Act and Parenting Orders, Key Points for Parenting Practitioners*. Brighton: Trust for the Study of Adolescence.

Lindfield, S. and Cusick, J. (2001) 'Working with parents in the youth justice context', in J. Coleman and D. Roker (eds), *Supporting Parents of Teenagers, A Handbook for Professionals*. London: Jessica Kingsley Publishers.

Lipsey, M. (1995) 'What do we learn from 400 research studies on the effectiveness of treatment with juvenile delinquents?', in J. McGuire (ed.), *What Works: Reducing Offending*. Chichester: Wiley.

Lipsey, M. and Wilson, D. (1998) 'Effective intervention for serious juvenile offenders: a synthesis of research', in R. Loeber and D. Farrington (eds), *Serious and Violent Juvenile Offenders: Risk Factors and Successful Interventions* Thousand Oaks, CA: Sage.

Lipsey, M., Wilson, D. and Cothern, L. (2000) *Effective Intervention for Serious Juvenile Offenders*. Washington, DC: Office of Juvenile Justice and Delinquency Prevention.

Little, M., Kogan, J., Bullock, R. and Van Der Laan, P. (2004) 'ISSP: an experiment in multi-systemic responses to persistent young offenders known to children's services', *British Journal of Criminology*, 44: 225–40.

Lloyd, C. (1998) 'Risk factors for problem drug use: identifying vulnerable groups', *Drugs: Education, Prevention and Policy*, 5 (3), 217–32.

Lloyd, E. (1999) *Parenting Matters: What Works in Parenting Education*. Barnardo's: Essex.

Lloyd, T. (2001) *What Works With Fathers?* London: Working With Men.

Lobley, D., Smith, D. and Stern, C. (2001) *Freagarrach: An Evaluation of a Project for Persistent Juvenile Offenders, Crime and Criminal Research Findings No. 53*. Edinburgh: The Stationery Office.

Loeber, R. and Le Blanc, M. (1990) 'Toward a developmental criminology', in M. Tonry and N. Morris (eds), *Crime and Justice*, Vol. 12. Chicago: University of Chicago Press.

Loeber, R. and Stouthamer-Loeber, M. (1986) 'Family factors as correlates and predictors of antisocial conduct problems and delinquency', in N. Morris and M. Tonry (eds), *Crime and Justice*, Vol. 7. Chicago: University of Chicago Press.

Loeber, R., Kammen, W. B. and Manghon, B. (1993) 'Development pathways in disruptive child behaviour', *Development and Psychopathology*, 5: 103–33.

Lord Chief Justice (2001) *Prison Reform Trust Annual Lecture*.

Loxley, C., Curtin, L. and Brown, R. (2002) *Summer Splash Schemes 2000: Findings from Six Case Studies*. London: Home Office, Research, Development and Statistics Directorate.

Luthar, S. S. (2003) (ed) *Resilience and Vulnerability: Adaptation in the Context of Childhood Adversities*. Cambridge: Cambridge University Press.

Maguin, E. and Loeber, R. (1996) 'Academic performance and delinquency', in M. Tonry (ed.), *Crime and Justice: A Review of Research*, Vol. 20. Chicago: University of Chicago Press.

Marshall, T. (1999) *Restorative Justice: An Overview*. London: HMSO.

Marshall, T. and Merry, S. (1990) *Crime and Accountability. Victim Offender Mediation in Practice*. London: HMSO.

Martinson, R. (1974) 'What works? Questions and answers about prison reform', *The Public Interest*, 35.

Masters, G. (2005) 'Restorative justice and youth justice', in T. Bateman and J. Pitts (eds), *The RHP Companion to Youth Justice*. Lyme Regis: Russell House Publishing.

Matrix Research and Consultancy and ICPR (2007) *Evaluation of Drug Interventions Programme Pilots for Children and Young People: Arrest, Referral, Drug Testing and Drug Treatment and Testing Requirements*. Home Office Online Report 07/07. London: Home Office RDS.

Maxwell, G. and Morris, A. (1993) *Family, Victims and Culture: Youth Justice in New Zealand*. New Zealand: Department of Social Welfare.

May, C. (1999) *Explaining Reconviction Following a Community Sentence: The Role of Social Factors* (HORS 192). London: Home Office.

McCold, P. and Wachtel, T. (2002) 'Restorative justice theory validation', in Weitekamp, E. and Kerner, H. J. (eds), *Restorative Justice: Theoretical Foundations*. Cullompton: Willan Publishing.

McGarrell, E., Olivares, K., Crawford, K. and Kroovand, N. (2000) *Returning Justice to the Community: The Indianapolis Juvenile Restorative Justice Experiment*. Indianapolis: Hudson Institute.

McGuire, J. (1995) *What Works: Reducing Re-offending: Guidelines from Research and Practice*. Chichester: J Wiley and Sons.

McGuire, J. (2000) *Cognitive Behavioural Approaches: An Introduction to Theory and Research*. London: HM Inspectorate of Probation.

McGuire, J. and Priestley, P. (1995) 'Reviewing "what works": past, present and future', in J. McGuire (1995) *What Works: Reducing Re-offending: Guidelines from Research and Practice*. Chichester: J. Wiley and Sons.

McGuire, J., Kinderman, K. and Hughes, C. (2002) *Offending Behaviour Programmes*. London: Youth Justice Board.

McIntosh, S. (2003) *The Early Post-school Experiences of the Unqualified/Low Qualified: Using the Labour Force Survey to Map the 14–16 Year Old Low-achievers*. London: Centre for Economic Performance.

McIvor, G. (1990) *Sanctions for Serious or Persistent Offenders: A Review of the Literature*. Stirling: Social Work Research Centre, University of Stirling.

McIvor, G. (1992) *Sentenced to Serve: The Operation and Impact of Community Services by Offenders*. Aldershot: Avebury.

McMahon, G., Hall, A., Hayward, G., Hudson, C., Roberts, C., Fernandez, R. and Burnett, R. (2004) *Basic Skills Programmes in the Probation Service: Evaluation of the Basic Skills Pathfinder*. London: Home Office.

McNeill, F. and Batchelor, S. (2002) 'Chaos, containment and change: responding to persistent offending by young people', *Youth Justice*, 2: 1.

Meltzer, H., Gatward, R., Goodman, R. and Ford, T. (2000) *Mental Health of Children and Adolescents in Great Britain* (2nd edn). London: Office for National Statistics.

Mental Health Foundation (1999) *Bright Futures – Promoting Children and Young People's Mental Health*. London: Mental Health Foundation.

Merrington, S. (1998) *A Guide to Setting Up and Evaluating Programmes for Young Offenders*. Winchester: Waterside Press.

Miers, D., Maguire, M., Goldie, S., Sharpe, K., Hale, C., Netten, A., Uglow, S., Doolin, K., Hallam, A., Enterkin, J. and Newburn, T. (2001) *An Exploratory Evaluation of Restorative Justice Schemes*, Crime Reduction Research Series 9. London: Home Office.

Mihalic, S., Irwin, K., Elliott, D., Fagan, A. and Hansen, D. (2001) *Blueprints for Violence Prevention*. Washington, DC: Office of Juvenile Justice and Delinquency Prevention.

Miller, W. and Rollnick, S. (1991) *Motivational Interviewing: Preparing People to Change Addictive Behaviours*. New York: Guilford Press.

Mischkowitz, R. (1994) 'Desistance from a delinquent way of life?', in E. Weitekamp and H. J. Kerner (eds), *Cross-National Longitudinal Research on Human Development and Criminal Behaviour*. London: Kluwer.

Moffitt, T. (1993) 'Adolescence-limited and life-course persistent antisocial behaviour: a developmental taxonomy', *Psychological Review*, 100: 674–701.

Monaghan, G. (2005) 'Children's human rights and youth justice', in T. Bateman and J. Pitts (eds), *The RHP Companion to Youth Justice.* Lyme Regis: Russell House Publishing.

Moon, J. (1999) *Reflection in Learning and Professional Development: Theory and Practice.* London: Kogan Page.

Moore, D. and Arthur, J. (1989) 'Juvenile delinquency', in T. Ollendick and M. Hersen, *Handbook of Child Psychopathology.* New York: Plenum.

Moore, K. J., Sprengelmeyer, P. G. and Chamberlain, P. (2001) 'Community-based treatment for adjudicated delinquents: the Oregon Social Learning Center's "Monitor" Multidimensional Treatment Foster Care program', *Residential Treatment for Children and Youth,* 18.

Moore, R. (2004) 'Intensive supervision and surveillance programmes for young offenders: the evidence base so far', in R. Burnett and C. Roberts (eds), *What Works in Probation and Youth Justice: Developing Evidence-Based Practice.* Cullompton: Willan Publishing.

Moore, R., Gray, R., Roberts, E., Merrington, C., Waters, S., Fernandez, I., Hayward, R. G. and Rogers, R. (2004) *ISSP: The Initial Report.* London: Youth Justice Board.

Moore, T., Gray, E., Roberts, C., Taylor, E., Merrington, S. (2006) *Managing Persistent and Serious Offenders in the Community: intensive community programmes in theory and practice.* Cullompton: Willan Publishing.

Moran, P., Ghate, D. and van der Merwe, A. (2004) *What Works in Parenting Support? A Review of the International Evidence.* Research Report 574. London: DfES.

Morgan Harris Burrows (2003) *Evaluation of the Youth Inclusion Programme.* London: Youth Justice Board.

Morgan, R. (2006) 'Enabling compliance: more than enforcement', *Youth Justice Board News,* No. 32.

MORI (2004) *MORI Youth Survey 2004.* London: Youth Justice Board.

Morris, A. (2002) 'Critiquing the critics: a brief response to the critics of restorative justice', *British Journal of Criminology,* (42): 596–615.

Morrow, V. (1999) 'Conceptualising social capital in relation to the well-being of children and young people: a critical review', *The Sociological Review,* 47(4): 745–65.

Mortimer, E. (2001) *Electronic Monitoring of Released Prisoners: An Evaluation of the Home Detention Curfew Scheme.* Home Office Research Findings 139. London: Home Office.

Mortimore, P., Davies, J., Varlaam, A. and West, A. (1983) *Behaviour Problems in Schools: An Evaluation of Support Centres.* London: Croom Helm.

Muncie, J. (2000) 'Pragmatic realism? Search for criminology in the new youth justice', in B. Goldson (ed.), *The New Youth Justice.* Lyme Regis: Russell House Publishing.

Muncie, J. (2001) 'A new deal for youth? Early intervention and correctionalism', in G. Hughes, E. Mcloughlin and J. Muncie (eds), *Crime Prevention and Community Safety: New Directions.* London: Sage.

Muncie, J. (2002) 'Policy transfers and "what works": some reflections on the comparative youth justice', *Youth Justice,* 3: 1.

Muncie, J. (2004) *Youth and Crime.* London: Sage Publications.

Munn, P., Lloyd, G. and Cullen, M. (2000) *Alternatives to Exclusion from School.* London: Paul Chapman Publishing.

Myner, J., Santman, J., Cappelletty, G. and Perlmutter, B. (1998) 'Variables related to recidivism among juvenile offenders', *International Journal of Offender Therapy and Comparative Criminology,* 42 (1): 65–80.

NHS Health and Social Care Information Centre (2006) *Statistics on Young People and Drug Misuse: England, 2006.* London: NHS.

Nacro (2000) *Proportionality in the Youth Justice System.* Nacro Youth Crime Briefing. London: Nacro.

Nacro (2006) *Effective Practice with Children and Young People Who Offend – Part 1,* Youth Crime Briefing September 2006. London: Nacro.

Narain, B. (2001) *Parenting Orders and the Human Rights Act 1998.* London: Aire Centre/Brighton Trust for the Study of Adolescence.

National Assembly for Wales (2000) *Child and Adolescent Mental Health Services for Wales: Everybody's Business.* Consultation Strategy Document. Cardiff: National Assembly for Wales.

National Association of Probation Officers (2002) *Accredited Programmes Policy.* London: NAPO.

National Audit Office (2004) *Youth Offending: The Delivery of Community and Custodial Sentences.* London: National Audit Office.

National Probation Service (2003) *Closure of Sherborne House – Letter of 14 January 2003 to London Youth Offending Team Managers.* London: National Probation Service.

National Treatment Agency (2005) *Young People's Substance Misuse Treatment Services – Essential Elements.* London: NTA.

Nellis, M. and Lilly, R. (2001) 'Accepting the tag: probation officers and home detention curfew', *Vista: Perspectives on Probation* 6(1): 68–80.

Newburn, T., Crawford, A., Earle, R., Goldie, S., Hale, C., Hallam, A., Masters, G., Netten, A., Saunders, R., Sharpe, K. and Uglow, S. (2001) *The Introduction of Referral Orders into the Youth Justice System: 2nd Interim Report.* London: Home Office.

Newburn, T., Crawford, A., Earle, R., Goldie, S., Hale, C., Hallam, A., Masters, G., Netten, A., Saunders, R., Sharpe, K. and Uglow, S. (2002) *The Introduction of Referral Orders into the Youth Justice System: Final Report.* Home Office Research Study 242. London: Home Office.

Newburn, T., Shiner, M., Groben, S. and Young T. (2005) *Dealing with Disaffection: Young People, Mentoring and Social Inclusion.* Cullompton: Willan Publishing.

Newman, T. (2004) *What Works in Building Resilience?* Ilford: Barnardo's.

Office for Criminal Justice Reform (2005) *Code of Practice for Victims.* London: Office for Criminal Justice Reform.

Office for National Statistics (1997) *Psychiatric Morbidity among Young Offenders in England and Wales.* London: Office for National Statistics.

Office for National Statistics (2004) 'Suicide rates: by sex and age', *Social Trends,* 34.

Ofsted (1995) *Pupil Referral Units: The First Twelve Inspections.* London: The Stationery Office.

Ofsted (2003) *Annual Report of Her Majesty's Chief Inspector of Schools: Standards and Quality in Education 2001/2002.* London: The Stationery Office.

Ofsted (2004) *Out of School.* London: The Stationery Office.

Olweus, D. (1991) 'Bully/victim problems among schoolchildren: basic facts and effects of a school-based intervention programme', in D. Pepler and K. Rubin (eds), *The Development and Treatment of Childhood Aggression.* Hillsdale, New Jersey: Lawrence Erlbaum.

Olweus, D. (1993) *Bullying at School: What We Know and What We Can Do.* Oxford: Blackwell.

Parker, H,, Aldridge, J. and Measham, F. (1998) *Illegal Leisure: the Normalisation of Adolescent Drug Use.* London: Routledge.

Parrish, J. M., Charlop, M. H. and Fenton, L. R. (1986) 'Use of a stated waiting list contingency and a reward opportunity to increase appointment keeping in an outpatient pediatric psychology clinic', *Journal of Pediatric Psychology,* 11: 81–89.

Parsons, C. and Howlett, K. (2000) *Investigating the Reintegration of Permanently Excluded Young People in England*. Ely: INCLUDE.

Pawson, R. (1997) 'Evaluation methodology: back to basics', in G. Mair (ed.), *Evaluating the Effectiveness of Community Penalties*. Aldershot: Avebury.

Pawson, R. (2000) 'The evaluator's tale', in D. Wilson and A. Reuss (eds), *Prison(er) Education: Stories of Change and Transformation*. Winchester: Waterside Press.

Pawson, R. (2006) *Evidence-based Policy*. London: Sage Publications.

Pawson, R. and Tilley, N. (1997) *Realistic Evaluation*. London: Sage Publications.

Pearson, G. (1983) *Hooligan: A History of Respectable Fears*. Basingstoke: Macmillan.

Peile, E. (2004) 'Reflections from medical practice: balancing evidence-based practice with practice-based evidence', in G. Thomas and R. Pring (eds), *Evidence-Based Practice in Education*. Maidenhead: Open University Press.

Peplow, M. (2002) 'Full of goodness', *New Scientist*, 176 (2369): 38–41.

Petersilia, J. and Turner, S. (1992) 'An evaluation of intensive probation in California', *Journal of Criminal Law and Criminology*, 83: 610–58.

Pickburn, C., Lindfield, S. and Coleman, J. (2005) 'Working with parents', in T. Bateman and J. Pitts (eds), *The RHP Companion to Youth Justice*. Lyme Regis: Russell House Publishing.

Piper, H. and Piper, J. (2000) 'Disaffected young people as the problem, mentoring as the solution, education and work as the goal', *Journal of Education and Work*, 13(1): 77–94.

Pitcher, J., Bateman, T., Johnston, V. and Cadman, S. (2004) *Provision of Health, Education and Substance Misuse Services*. London: Youth Justice Board.

Pitts, J. (2001a) 'Korrectional karaoke: New Labour and the zombification of youth justice', *Youth Justice*, 1: 2, 3–16.

Pitts, J. (2001b) *The New Politics of Youth Crime: Discipline or Solidarity?* Basingstoke: Palgrave.

Pitts, J. (2001c) 'The new correctionalism: young people, youth justice and new labour', in R. Matthews and J. Pitts (eds.), *Crime, Disorder and Community Safety*. London: Routledge.

Pitts, J. (2002) 'The end of an era', in J. Muncie, G. Hughes and E. McLaughlin (eds), *Youth Justice: Critical Readings*. London: Sage.

Polanyi, M. (1969) 'The logic of tacit inference', in M. Grene (ed.), *Knowing and Being: Essays by Michael Polanyi*. London: Routledge and Kegan Paul.

Porporino, D. and Robinson, F. (1992) *Can Educating Adult Offenders Counteract Recidivism?* Ottowa: Research and Statistics Branch of the Correctional Service of Canada.

Powell, H. (2004) *The National Evaluation of the Youth Justice Board's Crime Prevention Projects*. London: Youth Justice Board.

Pring, R. (2004) 'Conclusion: evidence-based policy and practice', in G. Thomas and R. Pring (eds), *Evidence-based Practice in Education*. Maidenhead: Open University Press.

Quinton, D., Pickles, A., Maughan, B. and Rutter, M. (1993) 'Partners, peers and pathways: assortative pairing and continuities in conduct disorder', *Development and Psychopathology*, 5: 763–83.

R (on the application of U) v. Metropolitan Police Commissioner and R (on the application of R) v. Durham Constabulary (2002), reported in *Justice of the Peace*, 166, December.

Rand, A. (1987) 'Transitional life events and desistance from delinquency and crime', in M. E. Wolfgang, T. P. Thornberry and R. Figlio (eds), *From Boy to Man, From Delinquency to Crime*. Chicago: University of Chicago Press.

Raynor, P. (1993) *Social Work, Justice and Control*. London: Whiting and Birch.

Raynor, P. (2002) 'What works: have we moved on?', in D. Ward, J. Scott and M. Lacey (eds), *Probation: Working for Justice*. Oxford: Oxford University Press.

Raynor, P. (2004a) 'Opportunity, motivation and change: some findings from research on resettlement,' in R. Burnett and C. Roberts (eds), *What Works in Probation and Youth Justice: Developing Evidence-based Practice*. Cullompton: Willan Publishing.

Raynor, P. (2004b) 'Seven ways to misunderstand evidence-based probation', in D. Smith (ed.), *Social Work and Evidence-based Practice*. London: Jessica Kingsley Publishers.

Read, T. and Tilley, N. (2000) *Not Rocket Science? Problem-solving and Crime Reduction*. Crime Reduction Research Services Paper 6. London: Home Office RDS.

Rees, C. and Conalty, J. (2004) *Taping the Seams in the Resettlement Process: Successfully Reintegrating Young Ex-offenders into Employment, Education and Training Opportunities*. London: Rainer.

Respect Task Force (2006) *Respect Action Plan*. London: Home Office.

Rex, S. (1999) 'Desistance from offending: experiences of probation', *Howard Journal*, 38(4): 366–83.

Reynolds, S. (2000) 'The anatomy of evidence-based practice: principles and methods', in L. Trinder with R. Reynolds (eds), *Evidence-Based Practice: A Critical Appraisal*. Oxford: Blackwell Science Ltd.

Richardson, H. and Roker, D. (2002) *An Evaluation of the YMCA England 'Dads and Lads' Initiative*. Report submitted to YMCA, England.

Riggs, P., Baker, S., Mikulich, S.,Young, S. and Crowley, T. (1995) 'Depression in Substance-Dependent Delinquents'. *Journal of American Academy of Child and Adolescent Psychiatry*, 34, 764–71.

Roberts, C. (2004) 'Offending behaviour programmes: emerging evidence and implications for practice', in R. Burnett and C. Roberts (eds), *What Works in Probations and Youth Justice: Developing Evidence-based Practice*. Cullompton: Willan Publishing.

Roche D (2001) 'The Evolving Definition of Restorative Justice.' *Contemporary Justice Review* 4, no. 3–4, pp. 341–54.

Roker, D. and Coleman, J. (1998) 'Parenting Teenagers Programmes: A UK Perspective', *Children and Society* 12: 359–72.

Runyan, D., Hunter, W., Socolar, R., Amaya-Jackson, L., English, D., Landsverk, J. Dubowitz, H., Browne, D., Bangdiwala, S. and Mathew, R. (1998) 'Children who prosper in unfavourable environments: the relationship to social capital', *Pediatrics*, 101 (1, Pt.1): 12–18.

Rutter, M. (1997) *Heterogeneity of Antisocial Behaviour: Causes, Continuities, and Consequences*. Lincoln, Nebraska: University of Nebraska Press.

Rutter, M., Giller, H. and Hagell, A. (1998) *Antisocial Behaviour by Young People*. Cambridge: Cambridge University Press.

Sackett, D., Richardson, W., Rosenberg, W. and Haynes, R. (1997) *Evidence-based Medicine: How to Practice and Teach EBM*. New York: Churchill Livingstone.

Safer Custody Group (2003) *Draft Guidance on Managing Prisoners Who Self-harm*. London: HM Prison Service.

Sampson, R. and Laub, J. (1993) *Crime in the Making: Pathways and Turning Points through Life*. Cambridge, Mass: Harvard University Press.

Sanders, M., Markie-Dadds, C. and Turner, K. (2003) *Theoretical, Scientific and Clinical Foundations of the Triple P-Positive Parenting Program: A Population Approach to the Promotion of Parenting Competence*. Queensland: Parenting and Family Support Centre, Queensland University.

Sarno, C., Hearnden, I., Hedderman, C. and Hough, M. (2000) *Working Their Way Out of Offending: An Evaluation of Two Probation Employment Schemes* (HORS 218). London: Home Office.

Saylor, W. and Gaes, G. (1997) 'PREP: Training inmates through industrial work participation and vocational and apprenticeship instruction', *Corrections Management Quarterly,* 1(2).

Schon, D. (1983) *The Reflective Practitioner: How Professionals Think in Action.* New York: Basic Books.

Shea, G. F. (1992) *Mentoring: A Guide to the Basics.* London: Kogan Page.

Sherman, L. and Strang, H. (2007) *Restorative Justice: The Evidence.* London: The Smith Institute.

Sherman, L., Strang, H. and Woods, D. (2000) *Recidivism Patterns in the Canberra Re-integrative Shaming Experiments (RISE).* Canberra, Australia: Centre for Restorative Justice, Australian National University.

Sherman, L. W., Gottfredson, D., MacKenzie, D., Eck, J., Reuter, P. and Bushway, S. (1997) *What Works, What Doesn't and What's Promising.* Washington, DC: University of Maryland.

Shiner, M., Young, T., Newburn, T. and Groben, S. (2004) *Mentoring Disaffected Young People: An Evaluation of Mentoring Plus.* York: Joseph Rowntree Foundation.

Simourd, L. and Andrews, D. (1994) 'Correlates of delinquency: a look at the gender differences', *Forum on Corrections Research,* 6: 26–31.

Smith, C. (1996) *Developing Parenting Programmes.* London: National Children's Bureau.

Smith, D. (ed.) (2005) *Social Work and Evidence-based Practice.* London: Jessica Kingsley Publishers.

Smith, R. (2003) *Youth Justice: Ideas, Policy, Practice.* Cullompton: Willan.

Smith, R. (2006) 'Actuarialism and early intervention in contemporary youth justice', in B. Goldson and J. Muncie (eds), *Youth Crime and Justice.* London: Sage Publications.

Social Exclusion Task Force (2006) *Reaching Out: An Action Plan on Social Exclusion.* London: Cabinet Office.

Social Exclusion Unit (1998) *Bringing Britain Together: A National Strategy for Neighbourhood Renewal.* London: Cabinet Office.

Social Exclusion Unit (2001) *Preventing Social Exclusion.* London: Social Exclusion Unit.

Social Exclusion Unit (2002) *Reducing Re-offending by Ex-Prisoners.* London: Cabinet Office.

St James-Roberts, I. and Singh, C. (2001) *Can Mentors Help Primary School Children with Behaviour Problems?* Home Office Research Study 233. London: Home Office Research and Statistics Directorate.

Staudt, M. (2003) 'Mental health services utilization by maltreated children: research findings and recommendations', *Child Maltreatment: Journal of the American Professional Society on the Abuse of Children,* 8: 195–203.

Steedman, H. and Stoney, S. (2004) *Disengagement 14–16: Context and Evidence Centre for Economic Performance.* Discussion Paper No. 654.

Stephenson, M. (1996) 'Cities in Schools: a new approach for excluded children and young people', in E. Blyth and J. Milner (eds), *Exclusion from School.* London: Routledge.

Stephenson, M. (2000) 'Inclusive learning', in B. Lucas and T. Greany (eds), *Schools in the Learning Age.* London: Campaign for Learning.

Stephenson, M. (2007) *Young People and Offending: Education, Youth Justice and Social Inclusion*. Cullompton: Willan Publishing.

Steurer, S., Smith, L. and Tracy, R. (2001) *Three State Recidivism Study*. Lanham, MD: Correctional Education Association.

Strang, H. (2001) 'Justice for victims of young offenders: the centrality of emotional harm and restoration', in A. Morris and G. Maxwell (eds), *Restorative Justice for Juveniles – Conferencing, Mediation and Circles*. Oxford: Hart Publishing.

Strang, H. (2002) *Repair or Revenge: Victims and Restorative Justice*. Oxford: Clarendon Press.

Street, C. (2000) *Whose Crisis?: Meeting the Needs of Children and Young People with Serious Mental Health Problems*. London: Young Minds.

Sutton, C., Utting, D. and Farrington, D. (2004) *Support from the Start*. Research Report 524. London: DfES.

Tarling, R. (1993) *Analysing Offending*. London: HMSO.

Tarling, R., Davison, J. and Clarke, A. (2004) *Mentoring Projects: The National Evaluation of the Youth Justice Board's Mentoring Projects*. London: Youth Justice Board.

Thomas, G. (2004) 'Introduction: evidence and practice', in G. Thomas and R. Pring (eds), *Evidence-based Practice in Education*. Maidenhead: Open University Press.

Thornberry, T. (1996) 'Empirical support for interactional theory: a review of the literature', in J. Hawkins, *Delinquency and Crime: Current Theories*. Cambridge: Cambridge University Press.

Tierney, J. P., Grossman, J. B. and Resch, N. L. (1995) *Making a Difference. An Impact Study of Big Brothers/Big Sisters*. Philadelphia, PA: Public/Private Ventures.

Tilley, N. (2006) 'Knowing and doing: guidance and good practice in crime prevention', *Crime Prevention Studies*, Vol. 20: 217–52.

Tilley, N., Smith, J., Finer, S., Erol, R., Charles, C. and Dobby, J. (2004) *Problem-solving Street Crime: Practical Lessons from the Street Crime Initiative*. London: Home Office RDS.

Tolbert, M. (2002) *State Correctional Education Programs: State Policy Update*. Washington, DC: National Institute for Literacy.

Tonry, M. (1998) 'Intermediate sanctions', in M. Tonry (ed.), *The Handbook of Crime and Punishment*. Oxford: OUP.

Topping, K. (1983) *Educational Systems for Disruptive Adolescents*. Beckenham: Croom Helm Ltd.

Torgerson, C., Brooks, G., Porthouse, J., Burton, M., Robinson, A., Wright, K. and Watt, I. (2004) *Adult Literacy and Numeracy Interventions and Outcomes: A Review of Controlled Trials*. London: National Research and Development Centre.

Trinder, L. (2000) 'Introduction: the context of evidence-based practice', in L. Trinder with S. Reynolds (eds), *Evidence-based Practice: A Critical Appraisal*. Oxford: Blackwell Science.

Trinder, L. and Reynolds, S. (eds) (2000) *Evidence-based Practice: A Critical Appraisal*. Oxford: Blackwell Science

Trotter, C. (1996) 'The impact of different supervision practices on community corrections', *Australian and New Zealand Journal of Criminology*, 28: 2.

Trotter, C. (2000) 'Social work education, pro-social orientation and effective probation practice', *Probation Journal*, 47: 4.

Truax, R. and Carkhuff, C. (1967) *Towards Effective Counselling and Psychotherapy*. Chicago: Aldine.

Umbreit, M. (1994) *Victim Meets Offender*. New York: Willow Tree Press.

Umbreit, M., Coates, R. and Vos, B. (2001) 'Victim impact of meeting with young offenders: two decades of victim–offender mediation practice and research', in A. Morris and G. Maxwell (eds), *Restorative Justice for Juveniles – Conferencing, Mediation and Circles*. Oxford: Hart Publishing.

Underdown, A. (1998) *Strategies for Effective Offender Supervision*. London: HM Inspectorate of Probation: Home Office.

Utting, D. (ed.) (1999) *A Guide to Promising Approaches*. London: Rosebery House/ Communities that Care.

Utting, D. and Vennard, J. (2000) *What Works with Young Offenders in the Community?* Essex: Barnardo's.

Walker, S. (2003) *Working Together for Healthy Young Minds – A Practitioner's Workbook*. Lyme Regis: Russell House Publishing.

Wallace, S.A., Crown, J.M., Berger, M. and Cox, A.D. (1997) 'Child and Adolescent Mental Health', in A. Stevens and J. Raftery (eds.) *Health Care Needs Assessment*, 2nd series, Oxford: Radcliffe Medical Press.

Walter, I. (2002) *Evaluation of the National Roll-out of Curfew Orders*. Home Office Online Report 15/02.

Walter, I., Sugg, D. and Moore, L. (2001) *A Year on the Tag: Interviews with Criminal Justice Practitioners and Electronic Monitoring Staff about Curfew Orders*. Home Office Research Findings 140. London: Home Office.

Weare, K. (2000) *Promoting Mental, Emotional and Social Health – A Whole-school Approach*. London and New York: Routledge.

Weissberg, R. and Caplan, M. (1998) *Promoting Social Competence and Preventing Antisocial Behavior in Young Urban Adolescents*. Philadelphia: Temple University, Center for Research in Human Development and Education, Laboratory for Student Success.

Wilcox, A. and Hoyle, C. (2002) *Final Report for the Youth Justice Board on the National Evaluation of Restorative Justice Projects*. Oxford: Centre for Criminological Research, University of Oxford.

Wilcox, A., Young, R. and Hoyle, C. (2004) *Two Year Re-sanctioning Study: A Comparison of Restorative and Traditional Cautions*. Home Office Online Report 32/04. London: Home Office.

Wilkin, A., Hall, M. and Kinder, K. (2003) *Learning Support Unit Strand Study*. Slough: NFER.

Williams, D. J. and Strean, W. B. (2002) 'The transtheoretical model and quality of life promotion: towards successful offender rehabilitation', *Probation Journal*, 49: 3.

Williams, J., Clemens, S., Oleinikova, K. and Tarvin, K. (2003) *The Skills for Life Survey: a National Needs and Impact Survey of Literacy, Numeracy and ICT Skills*. DfES Research Brief 490. DfES: London.

Wilson, H. (1980) 'Parental supervision: a neglected aspect of delinquency', *British Journal of Criminology*, 20: 203–35.

Wilson, T. and Kelling, G. (1982) 'Broken windows: the police and neighbourhood safety', *Atlantic Monthly*, March: 29–38.

Witton, J. (2001) *Cannabis and the Gateway Hypothesis*. A review paper prepared for DrugScope's submission to the Home Affairs Select Committee.

Worrall, A. and Walton, D. (2000) 'Prolific offender projects, and the reduction of volume property crime: targeted policing and case management', *VISTA* 7: 34–7.

YoungMinds (1999) *Spotlight Briefing Paper No. 1*, March.

Youth Justice Board (2000a) *Intensive Supervision and Surveillance Programmes,* unpublished.

Youth Justice Board (2000b) *Research into Effective Practice with Young People in Secure Facilities.* London: Youth Justice Board.

Youth Justice Board (2002a) *Building on Success: Youth Justice Board Review 2001/2002.* London: Youth Justice Board.

Youth Justice Board (2002b) *Evaluation of the PLUS Programme.* London: Youth Justice Board.

Youth Justice Board (2002c) *ISSP Electronic Monitoring Protocol.* London: Youth Justice Board.

Youth Justice Board (2002d) *Key Elements of Effective Practice – Offending Behaviour Programmes.* Source Document. London: Youth Justice Board.

Youth Justice Board (2002e) *National Specification for Learning and Skills for Young People on a Detention and Training Order.* London: Youth Justice Board.

Youth Justice Board (2002f) *The Final Warning Scheme – Guidance for Youth Offending Teams.* London: Youth Justice Board.

Youth Justice Board (2003a) *Corporate and Business Plan 2003/04 to 2005/06.* London: Youth Justice Board.

Youth Justice Board (2003b) *Evaluation of the Youth Inclusion Programme.* London: Youth Justice Board.

Youth Justice Board (2003c) 'ISSP goes live across England and Wales', *Youth Justice News.* 20: 1.

Youth Justice Board (2003d) *Key Elements of Effective Practice – Intensive Supervision and Surveillance Programmes.* London: Youth Justice Board.

Youth Justice Board (2003e) *Progress Report on the Implementation of the Youth Justice Board's National Specification for Learning and Skills in the Juvenile Prison Estate 2002–03.* London: Youth Justice Board.

Youth Justice Board (2003f) *Restorative Justice in the Juvenile Secure Estate.* London: Youth Justice Board.

Youth Justice Board (2003g) *Youth Justice Board Intervention Programme: Education, Training and Employment – Central Evaluator's Final Report.* London: Youth Justice Board.

Youth Justice Board (2004a) *Effective Practice In-Service Training (Youth Justice): Substance Misuse.* London: Youth Justice Board.

Youth Justice Board (2004b) *Keeping Young People Engaged Project: Interim Evaluation of Good Practice in Developing Re-engagement Capability for Education, Training and Employment – Year 1.* London: Youth Justice Board.

Youth Justice Board (2004c) *Key Elements of Effective Practice – Resettlement.* Source Document. London: Youth Justice Board.

Youth Justice Board (2004d) *National Standards for Youth Justice.* London: Youth Justice Board.

Youth Justice Board (2004e) *Progress Report on the Implementation of the Youth Justice Board's National Specification for Learning and Skills in the Juvenile Prison Estate 2003–04.* London: Youth Justice Board.

Youth Justice Board (2004f) *Research and Evaluation to Determine the Most Effective Means of Ensuring that Young People in the Youth Justice System are Fully Engaged in Education, Training or Employment.* London: Youth Justice Board.

Youth Justice Board (2004g) *Substance Misuse and the Juvenile Secure Estate.* London: Youth Justice Board.

Youth Justice Board (2004h) *The Galahad Report*. London: Youth Justice Board.

Youth Justice Board (unpublished) (2005a) *Diversity in Learning: Establishing the Cognitive Styles and Learning Strategies of Young People in the Youth Justice System*. London: Youth Justice Board.

Youth Justice Board (2005b) *Keeping Young People Engaged Year 2: Final Report September 2004–August 2005*. London: Youth Justice Board.

Youth Justice Board (2005c) *Managing Risk in the Community*. London: Youth Justice Board.

Youth Justice Board (2005d) *Monitoring and Evaluating the Safer School Partnerships Programme*. London: Youth Justice Board.

Youth Justice Board (2005e) *Youth Justice Annual Statistics 2003/04*. London: Youth Justice Board.

Youth Justice Board (2005f) *Progress Review on the implementation of the Youth Justice Board's National Specification for Learning and Skills 2004–2005*. London: Youth Justice Board.

Youth Justice Board (2005g) *Youth Resettlement: A framework for Action*. London: Youth Justice Board.

Youth Justice Board (2006a) *Anti-social Behaviour Orders*. London: Youth Justice Board.

Youth Justice Board (2006b) *Annual Report and Accounts 2005/06*. London: Youth Justice Board.

Youth Justice Board (2006c) *Barriers to Engagement in Education, Training and Employment for Young People in the Youth Justice System*. London: Youth Justice Board.

Youth Justice Board (2006d) *Mental Health Screening Tool*. London: Youth Justice Board.

Youth Justice Board / Association of Chief Police Officers (2003) *Guide to Good Practice*. London: Youth Justice Board and Association of Chief Police Officers.

Youth Justice Trust (2004a) *On the Case: A Survey of Over 1,000 Children and Young People Under Supervision by Youth Offending Teams in Greater Manchester and West Yorkshire*. Manchester: Youth Justice Trust.

Youth Justice Trust (2004b) *The Learning Alliance National E2E Offender Pilot: Final Evaluation Report*. Manchester: Youth Justice Trust.

Index

UNIVERSITY OF WINCHESTER
LIBRARY